AN ILLUSTRATED PRACTICAL GUIDE TO

ATTRACTING & FEEDING
BACKYARD BIRDS

AN ILLUSTRATED PRACTICAL GUIDE TO

ATTRACTING & FEEDING BACKYARD BIRDS

THE COMPLETE BOOK OF BIRD FEEDERS, BIRD TABLES BIRDBATHS, NEST BOXES, AND GARDEN BIRD-WATCHING

25 step-by-step projects for birdhouses • Expert advice on feeding • A directory of wild bird species • 760 photographs and illustrations

Contributing editor: JEN GREEN

LORENZ BOOKS

This edition is published by Lorenz Books
an imprint of Anness Publishing Ltd
Hermes House
88–89 Blackfriars Road
London SE1 8HA
tel. 020 7401 2077; fax 020 7633 9499

www.lorenzbooks.com
www.annesspublishing.com

If you like the images in this book
and would like to investigate using
them for publishing, promotions, or
advertising, please visit our website
www.practicalpictures.com for
more information.

North American agent/distributor:
National Book Network;
tel. (301) 459–3366; fax (301) 429–5746;
www.nbnbooks.com
UK agent: The Manning Partnership Ltd.;
tel. 01225 478444; fax 01225 478440;
sales@manning-partnership.co.uk
UK distributor: Grantham Book Services Ltd.;
tel. 01476 541080; fax 01476 541061;
orders@gbs.tbs-ltd.co.uk
Australian agent/distributor:
Pan Macmillan Australia;
tel. 1300 135 113; fax 1300 135 103;
customer.service@macmillan.com.au
New Zealand agent/distributor:
David Bateman Ltd.; tel. (09) 415 7664;
fax (09) 415 8892

Publisher: Joanna Lorenz
Senior Editor: Dr Felicity Forster
Text: Dr Jen Green, David Alderton,
  Christine and Michael Lavelle, Mary
  Maguire, Deena Beverley, Andrew
  Newton-Cox, and Stephanie Donaldson
Photography: Peter Anderson, Michelle
  Garrett, David Parmiter, Robert Pickett,
  and Peter Williams

Illustrations: Peter Barrett, Studio Galante,
  Lucinda Ganderton, Stuart Jackson-
  Carter, Martin Knowelden, Liz Pepperell,
  and Tim Thackeray
Maps: Anthony Duke
Jacket Design: Adelle Morris
Designer: Nigel Partridge
Production Controller: Steve Lang

ETHICAL TRADING POLICY
Because of our ongoing ecological
investment program, you, as our
customer, can have the pleasure and
reassurance of knowing that a tree is
being cultivated on your behalf to naturally
replace the materials used to make
the book you are holding. For further
information about this program, go to
www.annesspublishing.com/trees.

PUBLISHER'S NOTE
Although the advice and information in this
book are believed to be accurate and true
at the time of going to press, neither the
authors nor the publisher can accept any
legal responsibility or liability for any errors
or omissions that may be made.

Front cover: Red-headed woodpecker
(T. Kitchin and V. Hurst/NHPA/Photoshot);
American goldfinch (AllCanadaPhotos/
Photoshot); blue jay (Stephen Krasemann/
NHPA/Photoshot). Page 1: White-breasted
nuthatch. Page 3: Tree swallow; yellow
warbler; eastern bluebird.

CONTENTS

INTRODUCTION

Birds have been a source of fascination and inspiration to people all over the world for many years. Attracting birds to your backyard and observing the variety of species that visit can develop into an absorbing pastime—and one that offers an unparalleled insight into the natural world.

Birds have influenced human cultures across the world, featuring in customs, religious festivals, and also in many common sayings. For example, hummingbirds feature in many stories from mythology, while the return of songbirds, such as bluebirds (*Sialia* species), from their wintering grounds is eagerly awaited as a sign that spring is on the way.

Whether your garden or backyard is in the countryside, a town, or a city, it can play an important part in the conservation of wildlife, and especially birds. As farming becomes more intensive, and more and

Below: *Goldfinches are among the most common visitors to American backyards. These small birds use their acrobatic abilities to balance on bird feeders.*

more of the countryside is swallowed up by new housing and industrial developments, the natural habitats of many birds are being reduced or lost altogether. Backyards are now more essential for the survival of birds than ever. A little planning will ensure that your backyard is a haven for birds.

HELPING BIRDS

The average backyard is regularly visited by 15–20 species of birds, with occasional visits from 10 less common species. By simply erecting a bird table and nest box, you will not only be offering nature a helping hand, but also provide yourself with hours of interest and entertainment. Your helpful backyard friends will return the favor by controlling pests, such as aphids, slugs, and snails, that threaten your flower beds and vegetable plot.

ABOUT THIS BOOK

This book is a celebration of backyard birds and sets out to reveal the diversity in both their form and lifestyles. The opening section describes the main features of birds and explores how they live. The second section offers detailed advice on how your backyard can be planted or adapted to attract birds. It demonstrates how, with a little thought, you can greatly increase the number and variety of birds that visit your yard. It offers tips on what to feed birds and when, and how to garden with birds in mind. There are planting ideas to help you achieve an ideal home for feathered friends.

Birdhouses are a charming addition to any yard. They help to ornament and personalize it, and give an even greater satisfaction if you have made them yourself. The third section of this book offers a wide range of projects that will encourage birds. The projects given here range from simple decorated nest boxes to elaborate houses. There are creative ideas for feeders and birdbaths, with something to suit every backyard and every level of practical expertise. There are also tips on maintaining birdhouses, where and when to site them, and how to keep visiting birds safe from predators. All the projects in this book represent practical as well as attractive solutions for providing food, drink, and shelter for birds. The fourth and final main section provides an extensive illustrated guide to the bird species that are likely to be seen in backyards in North America.

Creating a haven for birds is a thoroughly satisfying activity. It is pure joy when you see a bird starting to build its new home in a box that you have made. The whole experience is rewarding, from the anticipation you feel while waiting for the eggs to be laid, and the pleasure experienced watching parent birds carrying food to the nest, to the excitement watching for the fledglings to emerge and finally take wing.

Right: *Once you know how to attract birds to your backyard, you will be rewarded with sights such as this woodpecker.*

HOW BIRDS LIVE

Birds display many diverse characteristics, but have several key features in common. The most obvious of these is the presence of feathers. The need for birds' bodies to be lightweight so that they can fly with minimum effort has led to evolutionary changes in their anatomy, and the basic skeletal structure of all birds is remarkably similar, irrespective of size. The other feature unique to birds is that all species reproduce by means of calcareous eggs. However, their actual breeding habits are diverse. There is even greater diversity in the feeding habits of birds, as reflected by differences in bill structure and also in digestive tracts.

Left: *The male Virginian cardinal is a spectacular scarlet color. It defends its territory aggressively against other males in the area.*

Above: *Birds such as this catbird have distinctive calls and songs that enable them to recognize others of their species.*

Above: *A stout, conical bill, such as that of this rose-breasted grosbeak, is useful for cracking tough-shelled seeds.*

Above: *Colorful plumage, such as that of the male mountain bluebird, is used to attract mates in the nesting season.*

PARTS OF A BIRD

The bird's skeleton has evolved to be light yet robust, both characteristics that help with flight. To this end, certain bones, particularly in the skull, have become fused, while others are absent, along with the teeth. The result is that birds' bodies are very light compared to those of other vertebrates.

In order to be able to fly, a bird needs a lightweight body so that it can become airborne with minimal difficulty. It is not just teeth that are missing from the bird's skull, but the associated heavy jaw muscles as well. These have been replaced by a light, horn-covered bill that is adapted in shape to the bird's feeding habits. Some of the limb bones, such as the humerus of the shoulder, are hollow, which also cuts down on weight. At the rear of the body, the bones in the vertebral column have become fused, which gives greater stability as well as support for the tail feathers.

AVIAN SKELETON

In birds, the greatest degree of specialization is evident in the limbs. The location of the legs is critical to enable a bird to maintain its balance. The legs are found close to the midline, set slightly back near the bird's center of gravity. The limbs are powerful, helping to provide lift at takeoff and absorb the impact of landing. Strong legs also let most birds hop over the ground with relative ease.

There are some differences in the skeleton between various groups of birds. For example, the neckbones of hornbills are slightly different to those of other birds.

FEET AND TOES

Birds' feet vary in length. The feet of wading birds are noticeably extended, which helps them to distribute their weight more evenly when moving over soft mud or floating vegetation. The four toes may be arranged either in a typical 3:1 perching grip, with three toes gripping the front of the perch and one behind, or in a 2:2 configuration, known as zygodactyl, which provides a surer grip. The zygodactyl grip is seen in a few groups of birds, notably woodpeckers and also parrots. Having two toes pointing in either direction gives the woodpecker a firm hold as it scales vertical tree trunks. The same arrangement helps some species of parrots to use their feet like hands for holding food.

Birds generally have claws at the ends of their toes, which have developed into sharp talons in the case of birds of prey, helping them to catch their quarry even in flight. Many birds also use their claws for preening, and they can also provide balance for birds that run or climb.

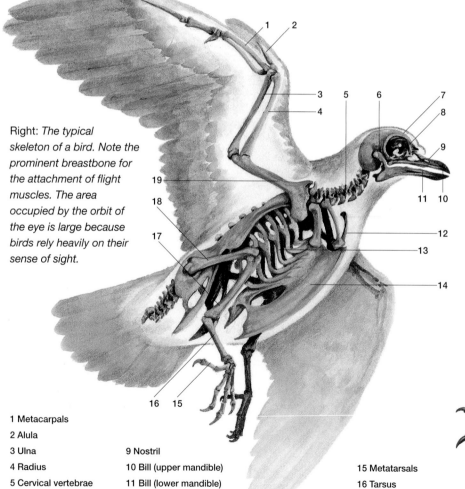

Right: *The typical skeleton of a bird. Note the prominent breastbone for the attachment of flight muscles. The area occupied by the orbit of the eye is large because birds rely heavily on their sense of sight.*

1 Metacarpals
2 Alula
3 Ulna
4 Radius
5 Cervical vertebrae
6 Ear
7 Cranium
8 Eye socket
9 Nostril
10 Bill (upper mandible)
11 Bill (lower mandible)
12 Clavicle (wishbone)
13 Ribs
14 Sternum (breastbone)
15 Metatarsals
16 Tarsus
17 Tibia and Fibula
18 Femur
19 Humerus

Parrot

Above: *Parrots use their feet for holding food, in a similar way to human hands.*

Bird of prey

Above: *In birds of prey, the claws have become talons for grasping victims.*

Wader

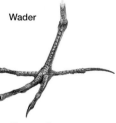

Above: *Long toes make it easier for waders to walk over muddy ground or water plants.*

Duck

Above: *The webbed feet of ducks provide propulsion in water.*

BILLS

The bills of birds vary widely in shape and size, and reflect their feeding habits. The design of the bill also has an impact on the amount of force that it can generate. The bills of finches, such as American goldfinches, are strong enough to crack tough seeds. A bird's bill has many purposes, being used not only for feeding but also for preening, building nests, and, where necessary, defense.

Above: *The narrow bill of waders, such as this curlew* (Numenius arquata), *enables the bird to probe for food in sand or mud.*

Above: *Woodpeckers, such as this pileated woodpecker, have straight, sharp bills ideal for chiseling under bark in search of insects.*

Above: *The American goldfinch* (Carduelis tristis) *has a short, stout, cone-shaped beak suited to cracking seeds.*

WINGS

A bird's wing is built around just three digits, which correspond to human fingers. The three digits of birds provide a robust structure. The power of the wings is further enhanced by the fusion of the wrist bones and the carpals to create the single bone known as the carpometacarpus, which runs along the rear of the wing.

At the front of the chest, the clavicles are joined together to form what in

Above: *Birds of prey, such as the bald eagle* (Haliaeetus leucocephalus), *rely on a sharp bill with a hooked tip to tear their prey apart.*

Above: *The broad bill of the mallard* (Anas platyrhynchos) *allows it to filter plant food from the water.*

Above: *Hummingbirds have long, slender bills that they use to probe tubular-shaped flowers to gain nectar.*

chickens is called the wishbone. The large, keel-shaped breastbone, or sternum, runs along the underside of the body. It is bound by the ribs to the backbone to provide stability, especially during flight. In addition, the major flight muscles are located in the lower body when the bird is airborne.

DARWIN'S FINCHES

In the 1830s, a voyage to the remote Galapagos Islands off South America helped the British naturalist Charles Darwin to formulate his theory of evolution. The finches of the Galapagos Islands are all believed to be descended from a single ancestor, but they have evolved in different ways. The changes are most obvious in their bill shapes. For example, some species have stout, crushing beaks for cracking seeds, while others have long, slender beaks to probe for insects. These adaptations have arisen to take full advantage of the range of edible items available on the islands, where food is generally scarce.

Below: *The finches of the Galapagos Islands typify Charles Darwin's theory of evolution. Some species have stout bills for crushing seeds, while those with pointed bills eat insects. Others have bills specialized for eating cactus, buds, and fruit. The woodpecker finch* (Camarhynchus pallidus, *bottom*) *uses a cactus spine to remove grubs hiding in tree bark.*

Seed eater

Insect eater

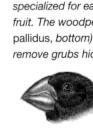

Cactus eater

Bud and fruit eater

Grub eater

FEATHERS

The presence of feathers is one of the main distinguishing characteristics that set birds apart from all other animals on the planet. The number of feathers on a bird's body varies considerably—a swan may have as many as 25,000 feathers, for instance, while a tiny hummingbird has just 1,000 in all.

Aside from the bill, legs, and feet, the entire body of the bird is covered in feathers. The plumage does not grow randomly over the bird's body, but develops along lines of so-called feather tracts, or pterylae. These are separated by bald areas known as apteria. The apteria are not conspicuous under normal circumstances, because the contour feathers overlap to cover the entire surface of the body. Plumage may also sometimes extend

down over the legs and feet as well, in the case of birds from cold climates, providing the extra insulation that is needed there.

Feathers are made of a tough protein called keratin, which is also found in our hair and nails. There are three main types of feathers on a bird's body: the body, or contour, feathers; the strong, elongated flight feathers on the wings; and the warm, wispy down feathers next to the bird's skin.

A diet deficient in sulfur-containing amino acids, which are the basic building blocks of protein, will result in poor feathering, creating "nutritional barring" across the flight and tail feathers. Abnormal plumage coloration can also have nutritional causes in some cases. These changes are usually reversible if more favorable environmental conditions precede the next molt.

FUNCTION OF FEATHERS
Plumage has a number of functions, not just relating to flight. It provides a barrier that retains warm air close to the bird's body and helps to maintain body temperature, which is higher in birds than mammals—typically between 106 and 110°F (41 and 43.5°C). The down feathering that lies close to the skin and the overlying contour plumage are vital for maintaining body warmth. Most species of bird have a small volume relative to their surface area, which can leave them vulnerable to hypothermia.

A special oil produced by the preen gland, located at the bottom of the tail, waterproofs the plumage. This oil, which is spread over the feathers as the bird preens itself, prevents water from penetrating the feathers, which would cause the bird to become so waterlogged that it could no longer fly.

Below: *The American robin, a member of the thrush family, has a characteristic red breast. The sexes look similar, although the female's coloring is paler.*

Left: *A bird's flight feathers are longer and more rigid than the contour feathers that cover the body, or the fluffy down feathers that lie next to the skin. The primary, or longest, flight feathers, which generate most thrust, are located along the outer rear wing edges. The tail feathers are often similar in shape to the flight feathers, with the longest in the center.*

1 Primaries
2 Secondaries
3 Axillaries
4 Rump
5 Lateral tail feathers
6 Central tail feathers
7 Breast
8 Cere
9 Auricular region (ear)
10 Nape
11 Back
12 Greater underwing coverts
13 Lesser underwing coverts

Above: *Like other birds, hummingbirds spend time each day preening. This helps to keep their feathers clean and tidy and also reduces parasites.*

The contour feathers that cover the body are also important for camouflage in many birds. Barring in particular breaks up the outline of the bird's body, helping to conceal it in its natural habitat.

The plumage has become modified in some cases, reflecting the individual lifestyle of the species concerned. Woodpeckers, for example, have tail feathers that are short and sharp at their tips, providing additional support for gripping onto the sides of trees. The woodpecker's stiff tail and feet with toes pointing forward and backward create a sturdy, tripodlike stance.

SOCIAL SIGNIFICANCE OF PLUMAGE

Plumage can also be important in social interactions between birds. Many species have differences in their feathering that separate males from females, and often juveniles can also be distinguished by their plumage. Although the rule does not apply in every case, cock birds are generally more brightly colored, which helps them to attract their mates, while the female's dull colors help to conceal her while she incubates the eggs on the nest. The

difference between the sexes in terms of their plumage can be very marked, for example in mallards *(Anas platyrhynchos)*. Cock birds of a number of species have feathers forming crests as well as magnificent tail plumes, which are seen most effectively in peacocks *(Pavo cristatus),* whose display is one of the most remarkable sights in the avian world.

Recent studies have confirmed that birds that appear relatively dull in color to our eyes, such as the starling *(Sturnus vulgaris),* with its blackish plumage, are seen literally in a different light by other birds. They can visualize the ultraviolet component of light, which is normally invisible to us, making these seemingly dull birds appear greener. Ultraviolet coloration may also be significant in helping birds to choose their mates.

MOLTING

Birds' feathering is maintained by preening, but it becomes frayed and worn over time. It is therefore replaced by new plumage during the process of molting, when the old feathers are shed. Many birds molt their feathers according to a given pattern, which varies according to species. In many cases the flight feathers are shed symmetrically, with the same number being lost from each wing at the same time. This helps the bird to remain balanced when flying.

Molting is most often an annual event. However, many young birds shed their nest feathers before they are a year old. Molting may also be triggered by the onset of the breeding season. Some birds become more strikingly colored at this time. Hormonal alterations in the body are important in triggering this process, with external factors, such as changing day length, also playing a part.

Right: *The feather shaft holds the feather in place in the skin. The barbs run off the shaft at regular intervals, much like the branches of a tree, and divide into smaller branches called barbules. These have tiny hooks attached to them that reinforce the structure of the flight feather, making it more rigid.*

IRIDESCENCE

Some birds are not brightly colored, but their plumage literally sparkles in the light, thanks to its structure, which creates an iridescent effect. One of the particular features of iridescence is that the color of the plumage alters, depending on the angle at which it is viewed, often appearing very dark or almost black from a side view. This phenomenon is particularly common in some groups of birds, notably members of the starling family (Sturnidae), which are described as having metallic feathers as a result.

In some cases, the iridescent feathering is localized, while in others it is widespread over most of the body. Green and blue iridescence is common, while reddish sheens are seen less often. Iridescence is especially seen in cock birds, helping them to attract their mates.

Below: *A starling* (Sturnus vulgaris) *displays its iridescent plumage.*

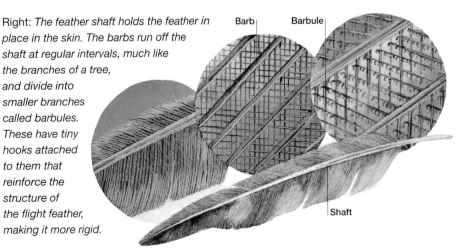

Barb

Barbule

Shaft

FLIGHT

Some birds seen in backyards spend much of their lives in the air, whereas others will only fly as a last resort if threatened. The mechanics of flight are similar in all birds, but flight patterns vary significantly, which can help you to identify the various groups in the air.

The structure of the bird's body has evolved to facilitate flight. It is important for a bird's body weight to be relatively light, because this lessens the muscular effort required to keep it airborne. The powerful flight muscles, which provide the necessary lift, can account for up to a third of the bird's total body weight. They are attached to the breastbone, or sternum, in the midline of the body, and run along the sides of the body from the clavicle along the breastbone to the top of the legs.

WEIGHT AND FLIGHT

There is an upper weight limit of just over 40 pounds (18kg), above which birds would not be able to take off successfully. Some larger birds, notably swans, need a run-up in order to gain sufficient momentum to lift off, particularly from water. Smaller birds can dart straight off a perch. Some of the heavier flying birds, such as pheasants, prefer to run rather than fly because of the effort involved in becoming airborne.

WING SHAPE AND BEAT

The shape of the wing is important for a bird's flying ability. Birds that remain airborne for much of their lives, such as swifts, have relatively long wings that let them glide with relatively little effort. The

Above: *The barn owl's feathers have fringed edges. This lets it fly without the slightest sound, and swoop down on its prey without being detected.*

swift's narrow wings make it fast and also maneuverable. Some larger predatory birds, such as kites and falcons, use rising columns of air called thermals, caused by warm air coming up from the ground, to provide uplift, and then circle around in them.

The number of wing beats varies dramatically between species. American hummingbirds are renowned for beating their wings more frequently than any other bird as they hover in front of flowers to harvest their nectar. Their wings move so fast—at over 200 beats per minute—that they produce a buzzing sound and appear

Above: *Hummingbirds, such as this rufous variety* (Selasphorus rufus), *have unparalleled aerial maneuverability, thanks to their rapid wing movements.*

as a blur to the eyes. At the other extreme, heavy birds, such as swans, fly with slow, deliberate wing beats.

LIGHTENING THE LOAD

The lightness of a bird's skeleton helps it to fly. There have been evolutionary changes in body organs, too, most noticeably in the urinary system. Unlike mammals, birds do not have a bladder that fills with urine. Instead, their urine is greatly concentrated, in the form of uric acid, and passes out of the body with their feces, appearing as a creamy white, semisolid component.

Below: *These illustrations show a typical takeoff sequence, as shown by a Harris's hawk* (Parabuteo unicinctus).

1 When resting, a bird typically has a relatively upright stance.

2 As it leans forward for takeoff, it raises its wings and starts to lift its legs.

3 Leaving its perch, the bird pushes off into the air and opens its wings.

Above: *Waterfowl, such as this mallard* (Anas platyrhynchos), *have relatively few difficulties becoming airborne from the surface of water, becase their plumage is designed to prevent waterlogging.*

FLIGHT PATTERNS

Different species of birds have various ways of flying, which can actually aid the bird-watcher in helping to identify them. For example, small birds, such as titmice (Paridae) and finches (Fringillidae), alternately flap their wings and fold them at their sides, adopting a streamlined shape, which helps to save energy. This produces a characteristic dipping flight, which aids recognition. Large birds, such as ducks and geese, generally maintain a straighter course at an even height.

In some cases, it is not just the individual flying skills of a bird that help it to stay airborne, but those of its fellows nearby. Birds flying in formation create a slipstream, which makes flying less effort for all the birds behind the leader. This is why birds often fly in formation, especially when covering long distances on migration.

THE AIRFOIL PRINCIPLE

Once in flight, the shape of the wing is crucial in keeping the bird airborne. Viewed in cross section from the side, a bird's wing resembles an airplane's wing, called an airfoil, and, in fact, airplanes use the same technique as birds to fly.

The wing is curved across the top, so the movement of air is faster over this part of the wing compared with the lower surface. This produces reduced air pressure on top of the wing, which provides lift and makes it easier for the bird to stay in the air.

The long flight feathers at the rear edge of the wings help to provide the thrust and lift for flight. The tail feathers, too, can help the bird remain airborne. The kestrel *(Falco tinnunculus),* for example, once it locates prey on the ground, spreads its tail feathers to help it remain aloft while it hovers to target its prey.

A bird's wings move in a regular figure-eight movement while it is in flight. During the downstroke, the flight feathers join together to push powerfully against the air. The primary flight feathers bend backward, which propels the bird forward. As the wing moves upward, the longer primary flight feathers move apart, which reduces air resistance. The secondary feathers farther along the wing provide some slight propulsion. After that the cycle repeats itself.

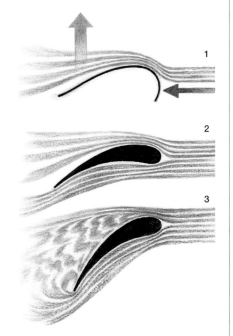

Above: *The way the air flows over a bird's wing varies according to the wing's position.*
1 When the wing is stretched out horizontally, an area of low pressure is created above the wing, causing lift.
2 As the wing is tilted downward, the flow of the air is disrupted, causing turbulence and loss of lift.
3 When the wing is angled downward, lift slows, which results in stalling. The bird's speed slows as a consequence. Splaying the tail feathers also increases drag and so slows the bird down, particularly prior to landing.

4 Powerful upward and downward sweeps of the wings propel the bird forward.

5 When coming in to land, a bird lowers its legs and slows its wing movements.

6 Braking is achieved by a vertical landing posture, with the tail feathers spread.

SENSES

The keen senses of birds are vital to their survival, in particular helping them to find food, escape from enemies, and find mates in the breeding season. Sight is the primary sense for most birds, but some species rely heavily on other senses to thrive in particular habitats.

All birds' senses are adapted to their environment, and the shape of their bodies can help to reflect which senses are most significant to them.

SIGHT
Most birds rely on their sense of sight to avoid danger, hunt for food, and locate familiar surroundings. The importance of

---

FIELD OF VISION
The positioning of a bird's eyes on its head affects its field of vision. The eyes of owls are positioned to face forward, producing an overlapping image of the area in front known as binocular vision. This lets the owl pinpoint its prey exactly, so that it can strike. In contrast, the eyes of birds that are likely to be preyed upon, such as woodcocks, are positioned on the sides of the head. This eye position gives a greatly reduced area of binocular vision, but it does give these birds practically all-round vision, enabling them to see danger from all sides.

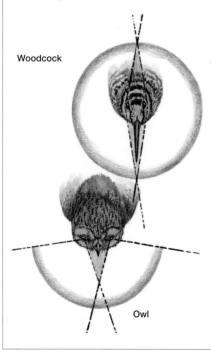

Woodcock

Owl

---

this sense is reflected by the size of their eyes, with those of starlings *(Sturnus vulgaris),* for example, making up 15 percent of the total head weight. The enlargement of the eyeballs and associated structures, notably the eye sockets in the skull, has altered the shape of the brain. In addition, the optic lobes in the brain, which are concerned with vision, are also enlarged, whereas the olfactory counterparts, responsible for smell, are poorly developed.

The structure of the eye also reveals much about a bird's habits. Birds of prey have large eyes in proportion to their head, and have correspondingly keen eyesight. Species that regularly hunt for prey underwater, such as kingfishers, can see well in the water. Some aquatic birds have a muscle in each eye that reduces the diameter of the lens and increases its thickness on entering water, so that their eyes can adjust easily to seeing underwater. In addition, some birds that dive underwater to catch prey have a lens that forms part of the nictitating membrane, or third eyelid, which is normally hidden from sight. Underwater, when this membrane covers the eye, its convex shape serves as a lens, helping the bird to see in these surroundings.

The positioning of the eyes on the head gives important clues to a bird's lifestyle. Most birds' eyes are set on the sides of their heads. Owls, by contrast, have flattened faces and forward-facing eyes that are critical to their hunting abilities. These features let owls target their prey.

There is a disadvantage to this arrangement. Owls' eyes do not give a rounded view of the world, so they must turn their heads to see about them. It is not just the positioning of owls' eyes that is unusual. They are also able to hunt effectively in almost complete darkness. This is made possible in two ways. First, their pupils are large, which maximizes the amount of light passing through to the retina behind the lens, where the image is formed. Second, the cells here consist

Above: *Sight is the main sense for most birds, including this common grackle. Having eyes on the side of the head gives this bird an all-round field of vision.*

mainly of rods rather than cones. While cones give good color vision, rods function to create images when background illumination is low.

The positioning of the eyes of game birds, such as American woodcocks *(Scolopax minor),* lets them see danger from almost any angle. It is even possible for them to see a predator sneaking up from behind. The only blind spot of these birds is just behind the head.

SMELL
The chemical senses (smell and taste) are relatively undeveloped in most birds, and backyard birds are no exception. Very few birds have a keen sense of smell, with kiwis of New Zealand and vultures (forming part of the order Falciformes) providing notable exceptions. Birds' nostrils are normally located above the bill, opening directly into the skull, but kiwis' nostrils are positioned right at the end of the long bill. They probably help these birds to locate earthworms in the soil. Vultures have very keen eyesight, which helps them to see dead animals on the ground from the air, but they also have a strong sense of smell, which helps them to home in on a carcass.

ECHOLOCATION

This technique helps species such as Mascarene swiftlets *(Collocalia francica)* navigate inside dark caves. These birds utter a stream of high-frequency clicks, which echo back off surfaces. The time lapse between clicks and echoes indicates the proximity of objects within range, which helps to prevent collisions.

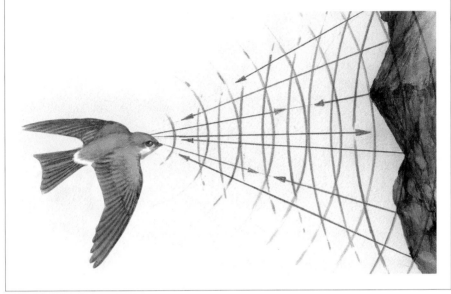

TASTE

The senses of smell and taste are linked, and most birds also have correspondingly few taste buds in their mouths. The number of taste buds varies, with differences between groups of birds. Some titmice may have as few as 24 taste buds. Pigeons possess around 50, while parrots have as many as 400. This compares to around 10,000 taste buds in our own mouths.

Below: *Birds have good color vision. It is this sense that encourages birds, such as this ruby-throated hummingbird* (Archilochus colubris), *to home in on purple flowers.*

Birds' taste buds are located all around the mouth, rather than just on the tongue, as in mammals. The close links between smell and taste can lead vultures, which feed only on fresh carcasses, to reject decomposing meat. They may start to eat it, but then spit it out once it is in their mouths, probably because of a combination of bad odor and taste.

HEARING

Birds generally do not have a highly developed sense of hearing. They lack any external ear flaps that would help to pinpoint sources of sound. The openings to their hearing system are located on the sides of the head, back from the eyes. These openings are usually hidden by the plumage, and so cannot be seen. Some owls have ear tufts, but these are usually unrelated to hearing.

However, hearing is of particular significance for nocturnal species, such as owls, which find their food in darkness. These birds are highly attuned to the high-pitched squeaks and rustling noises made by rodents. The broad shape of their skull has the additional advantage of spacing the ear openings more widely, which helps them to localize the source of the sounds with greater accuracy. Hearing is also important to birds during the breeding

season. They are able to pinpoint the calls of their own species within a chorus of birdsong, which helps to find mates. Later in the season, parent birds show particular sensitivity to sounds falling within the vocal range of their chicks, which helps them to locate their offspring easily in the critical early days after fledging.

TOUCH

The sense of touch is more developed in some birds than others. Species such as snipe (*Gallinago* species), which have long bills for seeking food, have sensitive nerve endings called Herbst corpuscles in their bills that pick up tiny vibrations caused by their prey. Vibrations that could suggest approaching danger can also register via other corpuscles located in the legs, so that the bird has a sensory awareness even when it is resting on a branch.

INTELLIGENCE

Birds have considerable intelligence, with species such as tits noted for their problem-solving abilities. Some groups of birds are more intelligent than others. Field studies of wild birds suggest that corvids (members of the crow family, such as jays and magpies) have very keen intellects. Jays are able to remember where they have cached food items, such as acorns. Both corvids and parrots do well in laboratory tests, including tests involving recognition, using tools, and basic counting.

Below: *Owls, such as this eastern screech owl* (Otus asio), *have forward-facing eyes specialized for hunting in dim light. Keen hearing also helps this nocturnal hunter to track prey, such as rodents.*

FINDING FOOD

The birds that visit your backyard feed on a wide range of foods, including seeds, berries, insects, and earthworms. A few hunt larger prey, including other backyard birds. The shape of a bird's body and especially its bill is suited to finding and dealing with its particular diet.

As small flying creatures, birds have a high-energy lifestyle. Finding an adequate supply of food is vital to daily survival, and is particularly essential in the breeding season. Birds' mating habits are timed so that abundant food is available during the period when parents must supply huge amounts of it to their hungry young.

Food not needed to fuel immediate activity is stored as fat, which is "burned" or consumed when food is scarce. The aim of every feeding bird is to gain maximum nutrition with the minimum of effort. For this reason, many birds switch between various foods as they become abundant at particular times of year.

MEAT EATERS

Animal foods, such as insects, spiders, mollusks, and earthworms, are high in energy and protein, but they also take considerable energy to capture and swallow. Backyard birds that are insect eaters aid gardeners in helping to control invertebrate pests. Species such as woodpeckers and kinglets hunt for bugs beneath the bark of trees. Other birds hunt among leaves or on the ground. Swifts,

Below: *Insects form much of the diet of tanagers, such as this summer tanager, but these birds also eat berries in fall.*

THE DIGESTIVE SYSTEM
Birds lack teeth, so their food must be small enough to be swallowed and digested easily. Birds have a storage organ known as the crop, located at the base of the neck. From here, food passes down into the proventriculus, where the digestive process starts, before entering the gizzard, which is equivalent to the mammalian stomach. Nutrients are then absorbed through the wall of the small intestine.

The digestive system of plant eaters differs in various respects from that of predatory species. For example, plants are a less nourishing food than meat, so plant eaters must possess longer digestive tracts than other birds to process the large quantities of food they consume in order to obtain enough nourishment. In addition, digesting plant matter poses certain difficulties. The gizzards of seed-eating species, such as finches, have especially thick muscular walls, which serve to grind up the seeds. These birds often swallow small stones and grit, which remain in their gizzards and help to break down the seeds.

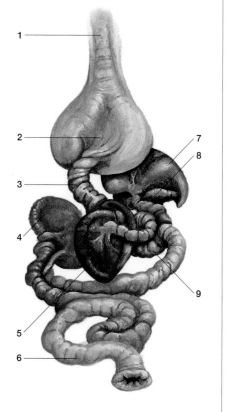

1 Esophagus	6 Large intestine
2 Crop	7 Liver
3 Proventriculus	8 Spleen
4 Pancreas	9 Small intestine
5 Gizzard	

swallows, and flycatchers hunt their food on the wing. Aerial hunters, such as flycatchers, prefer to feed on medium-size insects, which provide good nutrition for relatively little effort. Large insects, such as butterflies, are high in nourishment but take more energy to tackle, while large quantities of tiny insects, such as midges, must be eaten to provide a nourishing meal.

Juicy earthworms may satisfy most of the moisture requirements for American robins and some other thrushes, so these birds rarely need to drink. The same birds can die if they consume mollusks containing conventional pesticides, so be careful to use environmentally friendly pesticides if these species frequent your backyard.

PREDATORS AND SCAVENGERS

Some birds that visit backyards are active predators, seeking and killing prey, including smaller birds. Species such as American kestrels *(Falco sparverius)* and prairie falcons *(F. mexicanus)* will prey on small birds, such as sparrows and buntings. Another occasional backyard visitor, the peregrine falcon *(F. peregrinus)* is among the most agile of hunting birds. Many predatory birds are opportunistic feeders, hunting when food is plentiful but scavenging when it becomes scarce.

Corvids (members of the crow family), such as magpies and jays, are both hunters and scavengers. These birds are unpopular with bird lovers because of their habit of

Above: *American robins* (Turdus migratorius) *feed on earthworms and other invertebrates, and also berries.*

stealing the eggs and nestlings of songbirds. The same species will also alight on road kills and other casualties to find rich pickings.

PLANT EATERS

Many different types of birds are primarily plant eaters, whether feeding on flowers, fruit, nuts, seeds, or other plant matter. Plant eaters have to eat a large volume of food compared to meat-eating species, because of the low nutritional value of plants compared to that of prey, such as invertebrates. In the last century or so, many species have benefited from the

Below: *Towhees, such as the spotted towhee* (Pipilo maculatus), *feed mainly on seeds but may also eat insects in summer.*

spread of agriculture, which now provides them with large acreages of suitable crop plants to feed on. These birds' feeding habits bring them into conflict with farmers when they breed rapidly in response to a rapid expansion in their food supply.

FLOWER AND FRUIT EATERS

A number of birds rely on flowers as a source of food. Pollen is a valuable source of protein, while nectar provides sugars. Not surprisingly, flower feeders tend to be confined to mainly tropical areas, where flowers are in bloom throughout the year.

Hummingbirds (Trochilidae) use their narrow bills to probe flowers for nectar. Some hummingbirds have developed especially curved or elongated bills, which let them feed on particular flowers. These birds help to pollinate the plants on which they feed by transferring pollen from flower to flower as they feed. In Africa and Asia, sunbirds (Nectariniidae) fill a similar niche.

Exclusively frugivorous (fruit-eating) birds, such as fruit doves (*Ptilinopus* species), are found only in the tropics, where fruit is available throughout the year. Fruit and berry eaters help plants to reproduce. The seeds of the fruits they eat pass right through their digestive tracts unharmed, to be deposited far from the parent plant, which helps the plants to spread.

NUT AND SEED EATERS

Dry foods are a valuable resource for many types of birds, ranging from parrots to finches. However, cracking nuts' tough outer shells or husks can be a problem. Finches, such as grosbeaks, have evolved a strong bill for this purpose. The most

bizarre example of bill adaptation for eating seeds is seen in the crossbills (*Loxia* species) of northern coniferous forests. These birds have twisted upper and lower mandibles, which enable them to crack open the seeds inside larch cones, on which they feed.

OMNIVORES

These are birds that eat both plant and animal foods. Most of these species are opportunists, switching between foods as they come into season. Many feed mainly on plant foods, such as seeds or nuts, in fall and winter, and switch to insects to nourish themselves and their young in the breeding season.

ADAPTING TO THE SEASONS

Birds from temperate areas exist on a varied diet that is related to the seasons. Pine grosbeaks *(Pinicola enucleator),* for example, consume seeds, buds, fruit, berries, and also invertebrates at different times of year. Their bills, like those of most other members of the finch family, are stout and relatively conical, which helps them to crack seeds effectively.

Some birds store plant food when it is plentiful, to sustain them through the winter. Corvids, such as jays, collect nuts and acorns to feed on during winter. Some woodpeckers (*Melanerpes* species) drill holes in trees that they fill with acorns, creating an easily accessible pantry for the winter, when snow may cover the ground.

Below: *Red-bellied woodpeckers are omnivores, feeding on fruits, nuts, seeds, insects, and even songbird nestlings.*

SINGING, COURTSHIP AND PAIRING

Birdsong is a key element in pairing and breeding, serving to establish territory and attract mates. It is of particular interest to bird-watchers because it helps in species identification. Birds' breeding habits vary greatly. Some species pair up only fleetingly in the breeding season, while others pair for life.

In songbirds, the start of the breeding season generally coincides with the time of abundant food we know as spring. A number of factors trigger the onset of breeding. In temperate regions, as the days start to lengthen in spring, the increase in daylight is detected by the pineal gland in the bird's brain, which starts a complex series of hormonal changes in the body. Most birds form a bond with a single partner during the breeding season, which is often preceded by an elaborate display by the cock bird.

BIRDSONG

Many cock birds announce their presence by their song, which both attracts would-be mates and establishes a claim to a territory. Once pairing has occurred, the male may cease singing, but in some cases he starts to perform a duet with the hen, with each bird singing in turn.

Singing serves to keep members of the pair in touch with each other. In some species, the pair coordinate their songs so precisely that although the cock bird may sing the first few notes, then the hen, it

sounds as if the song is being sung by just one bird. Other birds may sing in unison. In a few species, it may even be possible for experts to tell the length of time that the pair have been together by the degree of harmony in their particular songs.

Above: *Like many other birds, northern cardinals* (Cardinalis cardinalis) *identify their mates by their song and color.*

Studies have revealed that young male birds will start warbling quietly, and then sing more loudly as they mature. Young songbirds know just the basics of their species' song by instinct. As they mature, they refine their singing by copying the songs of the adults around them. Finally, when their song pattern becomes fixed, it remains constant throughout the bird's life.

DIALECTS

It is obviously possible for even novice bird-watchers to identify different species by differences in their song patterns. However, there are sometimes marked variations between the songs of individuals of the same species that live in different places. Researchers have identified local dialects in various parts of a species' range, as in the case of white-crowned sparrows *(Zonotrichia leucophrys)* from different regions. In addition, as far as some songbirds are concerned, recent studies have shown that over the course of several generations, the pattern of songs produced by individuals can alter markedly.

Below: *In blue-winged warblers, as in many other species, the males sing to attract the females and warn away rival males.*

Below: *The wren's shrill song can be heard for hundreds of yards—a considerable distance for such a small bird.*

Above: *Ritualized feeding plays a role in the courtship behavior of pine siskins* (Carduelis pinus)*. During courtship the male offers the female food items, such as seeds, to prove he is a suitable partner. He also puts on an impressive display flight, circling the female's perch with rapidly fluttering wings, singing all the while.*

SONG PRODUCTION

Birds produce their sounds—even those species capable of mimicking human speech—without the benefit of a larynx and vocal cords like humans. The song is created in a voice organ called the syrinx, which is located in the bird's throat, at the bottom of the trachea, or windpipe.

The structure of the syrinx is very variable, being at its most highly developed in the case of songbirds, which possess as many as nine pairs of separate muscles to control the vocal output. As in the human larynx, it is the movement of air through the syrinx that enables the membranes here to vibrate, creating sound as the bird exhales. The pitch of notes is controlled by rings of cartilage that tighten or loosen to vary the sounds produced.

An organ called the interclavicular air sac also plays an important role in sound production, and birds cannot sing without it. The distance over which bird calls can travel is remarkable—up to 3 miles (5km) in the case of species such as the American bittern *(Botaurus lentiginosus),* which has a particularly deep, penetrating song. High, shrill notes can also carry long distances. Diminutive wrens produce a very loud song relative to their small size.

Song complexity also varies greatly among types of backyard birds. Species such as doves seem content to repeat a few simple phrases with little variation that human ears can detect. In contrast, songbirds, such as thrushes (Turdidae), have several hundred different phrases in their repertoire. These are combined in myriad different ways to produce a song that is constantly changing.

COURTSHIP DISPLAYS

Many birds rely on their breeding finery to attract their mates. The bright or bold colors of male birds are designed to warn off rival males and attract females. It is usually the female that selects her mate. She bases her choice not only on her potential mate's appearance but also on his singing talents, and in some cases, on his ability to demonstrate nest-building or food-providing skills. Species such as pine siskins *(Carduelis pinus)* present their mates with food to show their ability to provide for their young.

Some types of birds, although not generally backyard species, assemble in communal display areas known as leks, where hens witness the males' displays and select a mate. A number of game birds, such as sage grouse *(Centrocercus urophasianus),* as well as some hummingbirds, establish leks. The male of the bowerbird species of Australia builds an elaborate bower of grass that he decorates with items of a single color, such as blue.

PAIR BONDING

Many male and female birds form no lasting relationship, although the pair bond may be strong during the nesting period. It is usually only in long-lived species, such as eagles and waterfowl, such as swans, that a lifelong pair bond is formed. However, there are exceptions among smallish backyard birds—blue jays, for example.

Pair bonding in long-lived species has certain advantages. The young of such birds are slow to mature, and are often unlikely to nest themselves for five years or more. By remaining for a time in a family group, the adults can improve the long-term survival prospects of their young.

Below: *An American bittern* (Botaurus lentiginosus) *is well disguised in a reed bed. In spite of being solitary by nature, these waders have a remarkable territorial call, which booms out across the marshes, and has led to species becoming known locally as "thunder pumpers." The boom is created by use of the gullet to amplify sound, similar to a voice box.*

NESTING AND EGG LAYING

Birds vary in their nesting habits, some constructing very simple nests and others making elaborate ones. All birds reproduce by laying eggs, which are covered with a hard, calcareous shell. The number of eggs laid at a time—known as the clutch size—varies between species, as does egg coloration.

Most birds construct their nests from vegetation, depending on which materials are locally available. In coastal areas, some seabirds use pieces of seaweed to build theirs. Artificial materials, such as plastic packaging, twine, or Styrofoam, may be used by some birds in their nests.

Different types of birds build nests of various shapes and sizes, which are characteristic of their species. Groups such as finches build nests in the form of an open cup, often concealed in vegetation. Most pigeons and doves construct a loose platform of twigs. Swallows are among the birds that use mud to construct their nests. They scoop muddy water up from the surface of a pond or puddle, mold it into shape on a suitable wall, and then let it dry and harden like cement.

The simplest nests are composed of little more than a pad of plant material, resting in the fork of a tree or on a building. The effort entailed in nest construction may reflect how often the birds will nest. The platforms of pigeons and doves can disintegrate easily, resulting in the loss of eggs or chicks.

Above: *Hummingbird nests are tiny cups of vegetation, bound with cobwebs and disguised with lichen. They are usually sited on a horizontal branch. Two eggs are laid.*

Above: *A red-bellied woodpecker* (Melanerpes carolinus) *carves a nest. Tree holes offer fairly safe nest sites, although predators, such as snakes, may be able to reach them. Eggs laid in cavities do not need camouflage, and so are often white.*

However, if disaster hits the nest, the pair often breed again within a few weeks.

Cup-shaped nests are more elaborate than platform nests, being usually made by weaving grasses and twigs together. The inside is often lined with soft feathers. The raised sides of the nest cup lessen the likelihood of losing eggs and chicks, and also offer greater security to the adults during incubation. The hollow in the nest's center is created by the bird compressing the material here before egg laying begins.

Suspended nests enclosed by a domed roof offer even greater security. They are much less accessible to predators because of their design and also their position, often hanging from slender branches.

NEST SITES

Many birds use tree holes for nesting. Woodpeckers (Picidae) are particularly well equipped to create nesting chambers, using their powerful bills to enlarge holes in dead trees. The diameter of the entry hole thus created is just wide enough to let the birds enter easily, which helps to prevent the nest being robbed.

Some birds rely on the safety of numbers to deter would-be predators, building at communal nest sites that may be occupied by successive generations. Pine siskins *(Carduelis pinus)* are among the American birds that nest communally, in this case in the conifer forests of the north.

Other birds, such as cowbirds *(Molothrus)* and the European cuckoo *(Cuculus canorus),* simply lay and abandon their eggs in the nests of other species. The foster parents-to-be do not seem able to detect the difference between their own eggs and that of the intruder, so they do not reject the cowbird or cuckoo egg. They incubate it along with their own brood, and

Below: *A songbird chick hatches in the nest. Birds' nests are located in secluded sites, such as in trees or dense shrubs. If detected, they should be left undisturbed.*

feed the foster chick when it hatches out. The young imposter often ejects the other eggs or nestlings from the nest.

Birds that nest on the ground in open country, such as the horned lark *(Eremophila alpestris)* and lark bunting *(Calamospiza melanocorys)* are especially vulnerable to predators and rely heavily on their fairly drab colors as camouflage.

Some birds return to the same nest site each year, but many birds simply abandon their old nest and build another. This may seem a waste of effort, but it actually helps to protect the birds from parasites, such as blood-sucking mites, which can otherwise multiply in the confines of the nest.

MATING

For most birds, mating is a brief process. The male usually mounts the female, twisting his rump so that the cloacas, or body openings, of the two birds touch for a second. Spermatozoa swim up the hen's reproductive tract, and fertilize the ova at an early stage in the process. Generally, only one mating is required to fertilize a clutch of eggs. Hens can also lay unfertilized eggs if no male is around, but these eggs will not hatch however long they are incubated. The period between mating and egg laying varies according to species. In small birds, the interval may be as little as ten days, while in larger species such as owls, it may be several months.

THE REPRODUCTIVE SYSTEMS

The cock bird has two testes located within his body. Spermatozoa pass down the vas deferens, into the cloaca and then out of the body. Insemination occurs when the vent areas of the male and female bird are in direct contact during mating. Cock birds do not have a penis for penetration, although certain groups, such as waterfowl, may have a primitive organ that is used to assist in the transference of semen in a similar way.

Normally only the left ovary and oviduct of the hen bird are functional. Eggs pass down through the reproductive tract from the ovary.

1 Testes	8 Isthmus
2 Kidneys	9 Egg with shell
3 Vas deferens	contained in
4 Male cloaca	the hen's
5 Ova	reproductive tract
6 Infundibulum	10 Female cloaca
7 Magnum	

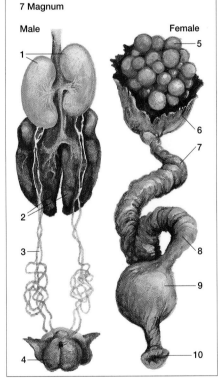

EGG SIZE AND COLOR

The size of eggs produced by different species of birds varies dramatically. An ostrich's egg is thousands of times heavier than the eggs that are laid by wrens or hummingbirds. The coloration and markings of a bird's eggs are directly

linked to the nesting site. Birds that usually breed in hollow trees produce white eggs, because these are normally hidden from predators and so do not need to be camouflaged. The pale coloration may also help the adult birds to locate the eggs as they return to the nest, thus lessening the chances of damaging them. Birds that build open, cup-shaped nests tend to lay colored and often mottled eggs that are camouflaged and so less obvious to potential nest thieves.

CLUTCH SIZES

The number of eggs laid at one time varies according to species, as does the number of clutches produced in a year. Birds such as bushtits *(Psaltriparus minimus)* lay one or two clutches of 5–13 eggs. In contrast, female American robins *(Turdus migratorius)* produce two or three clutches of 3–6 eggs in a season. Birds' breeding habits are linked to the food that will be fed to the nestlings. For example, bushtit nestlings are fed on tiny insects, which are most abundant in spring and summer. Robin nestlings are reared on berries and earthworms, found throughout the year.

Below: *Ostriches lay the largest eggs in the world, weighing up to 3lb 5oz (1.5kg). In comparison, a chicken's egg, shown in front of the ostrich egg, looks tiny. The egg nearest to the viewer is a hummingbird egg. These tiny birds lay the smallest eggs in the avian world, weighing only about one-hundredth of an ounce (0.35g).*

HATCHING AND REARING CHICKS

Birds are vulnerable to predators when breeding, especially when they have young in the nest. The chicks must be fed frequently, necessitating regular trips to and from the nest, which makes it conspicuous. The calls of nestlings represent a further danger, so the breeding period is often short.

Most birds incubate their eggs to keep them sufficiently warm for the chicks to develop inside. Larger eggs are less prone to chilling during incubation than small eggs, because of their bigger volume. In the early stages of the incubation period, when the nest may be left uncovered while the adult birds are foraging for food, eggs can withstand a lower temperature. Temperature differences also account for the fact that, at similar altitudes, incubation periods tend to be slightly longer in temperate areas than in tropical regions.

The eggshell may appear to be a solid barrier, but, in fact, it contains many pores, which are vital to the chick's well-being. These tiny holes let water vapor and carbon dioxide escape from the egg and let oxygen enter it to reach the embryo.

INCUBATION TIMINGS

The incubation period often does not start until more than one egg has been laid, and sometimes not until the entire clutch has been completed. The interval between the laying of one egg and the next varies— finches lay every day, whereas birds such as gannets may lay only one egg every six

Below: *A fertile chicken's egg, showing the development of the embryo through to hatching. 1 The fertilized egg cell divides to form a ball of cells that gradually develops into an embryo. 2 The embryo develops, nourished by the yolk sac. 3 The air space at the rounded end of the egg enlarges as water evaporates. 4 The chick is almost fully developed and ready to hatch. 5 The chick cuts its way out, and its feathers quickly dry off.*

days. If incubation does not start until egg laying has finished, the chicks will all be of a similar size when they hatch, which increases their overall chances of survival. Among species such as owls, incubation generally starts after the first egg is laid. This results in one chick that is larger than its fellows. This large individual often bullies its nestmates.

The cock and hen may share incubation duties, as in the case of most pigeons and

Above: *Spring sees the onset of the nesting season, when parent birds work hard to gather food, such as insects, for their chicks.*

doves, or just one member of the pair may incubate. Among backyard birds, this is usually the hen, but there are exceptions in the wider bird world. For example, in ostriches *(Struthio camelus)* and most other large flightless birds, it is the cock bird who incubates the eggs and cares for the

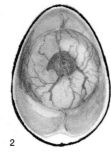
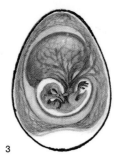

1   2   3   4   5

NEST PARASITISM

This occurs on a worldwide scale, including among cowbirds (*Molothrus* species) of North America. The males do not establish breeding territories, but mate with females at random. The females lay a single egg in the nests of host species, such as vireos and orioles. The rapid development of the cowbird's egg is vital to the chick's survival. It hatches first, and monopolizes the food supply brought by its foster parents, leaving the natural offspring of the host to face starvation. The success of the cowbirds' nesting strategy is such that the populations of some host species have declined.

Below: *A brown-headed cowbird chick* (Molothrus ater) *is fed by a yellow warbler* (Dendroica petechia). *The foster parents will continue to feed the cowbird, even when the impostor dwarfs them in size.*

resulting chicks. Anis (*Crotophaga*) breed communally, and all members of the group share the task of incubation. Incubation periods vary among bird species, ranging from as few as 11 days in the case of American cowbirds, to more than 80 days in some albatrosses (Diomedeidae).

HATCHING

When hatching, the chick uses the egg tooth on the tip of its upper bill to cut through the inner membrane into the air space at the blunt end of the shell, which forms as water evaporates from the egg. In this way the chick starts to breathe

atmospheric air for the first time. About 48 hours later, it breaks through the shell to emerge from the egg.

Chicks hatch out at various stages of development, and are accordingly able to leave the nest sooner or later. Species that remain in the nest for some time after hatching, including finches (Fringillidae), hatch in a blind and helpless state and are entirely dependent on their parents at first. Birds in this group are known as nidicolous. If not closely brooded, they are likely to become fatally chilled. In contrast, species that leave the nest soon after hatching, known as nidifugous, emerge from the egg and are able to move around on their own at this stage. They can also see and feed themselves almost immediately. The offspring of many game birds, such as pheasants, as well as waterfowl and waders, are nidifugous, which gives them a better chance of survival, because they can run to escape from predators. Young waterfowl cannot take safely to the water at first, however, because they lack the oil from the preen gland above the base of the tail to waterproof their feathers.

REARING AND FLEDGING

Many adult birds offer food to their offspring, even some nidifugous species. This can be a particularly demanding period, especially for small birds that have relatively large broods. Titmice (*Parus* species), for example, must supply their offspring with huge quantities of insects. They may feed their chicks up to 60 times an hour, as well as keeping the nest clean by removing feces.

Young birds usually leave the nest from about 12 to 30 days after hatching. However, some species develop much more slowly. Among birds generally, albatross chicks are particularly slow developers, spending up to eight-and-a-half months in the nest.

Above: *The broad and often colorful gape of chicks lets parent birds feed their offspring quickly and efficiently. Weak chicks that are unable to raise their heads and gape at the approach of a parent will quickly die from starvation.*

When they first leave the nest, many young birds are unable to fly, simply because their flight feathers are not fully functional. If these feathers are not completely unfurled from the protective sheaths in which they emerged, they cannot function effectively. The strength of the wing muscles also needs to be built up, so it is not uncommon for young birds to rest on the sides of the nest, flapping their wings occasionally, before finally taking to the air for the first time. Chicks that are unable to fly immediately after fledging remain reliant on the adults, especially the cock, for food until they become fully independent. It is a common sight to see immature songbirds following a parent around the backyard, begging for food.

Below: *Chickadees (*Parus *species) are typical of many birds that leave the nest before they are able to fly effectively. The young are fed by their parents during this critical time after leaving the nest—a period that can last up to 3–4 weeks.*

BIRD BEHAVIOR

The field of bird behavior, or avian ethology as it is known, is very broad. Some patterns of behavior are common to all birds, whereas other actions are very specific, just to a single species or even to an individual population. Interpreting behavior is a fine art, and of special interest to eager bird-watchers.

All bird behavior essentially relates to various aspects of survival, such as avoiding predators, obtaining food, finding a mate, and breeding successfully. Some behavior patterns are instinctive, while others develop in certain populations of birds in response to particular conditions. Thus the way in which birds behave is partly influenced by their environment as well as being largely instinctual.

AGGRESSION

Birds can be surprisingly aggressive toward each other, even to the point of sometimes inflicting fatal injuries. Usually, however, only a few feathers are shed before the weaker individual backs away, without sustaining serious injury. Conflicts of this type can break out over feeding sites or territorial disputes. The risk of aggressive outbreaks is greatest at the start of the breeding season, when the territorial instincts of cock birds are most aroused. Size is no indicator of the potential level of aggression, because some of the smallest birds, such as wrens and hummingbirds (Trochilidae), can be extrememly ferocious.

Below: *A dispute breaks out between American goldfinches over food. Birds often fight with wings outstretched as they seek to batter their opponent into submission.*

Above: *A gila woodpecker* (Melanerpes uropygialis) *is feeding on a cactus flower. These desert-dwelling woodpeckers will bore into larger cacti to create a nest site.*

Age, too, plays a part in determining behavior, since young birds often behave in a very different way to the adults. Some forms of bird behavior are relatively easy to interpret, while others are a great deal more difficult to explain.

ADAPTING BEHAVIOR

One of the first studies documenting birds' ability to adapt their behavior in response to changes in their environment involved blue tits *(Parus caeruleus)* in Great Britain. The study showed that certain individuals learned to use their bills to tap through the shiny metallic foil covers on milk bottles left on doorsteps to reach the milk. Other blue tits followed their example, and in certain areas householders with milk deliveries had to protect their bottles from the birds. In addition, the tits concerned demonstrated the ability to distinguish bottles containing creamy milk from ones holding skimmed milk from the colors of their tops. The study showed that the birds directed the overwhelming majority of their raids at bottles containing the creamier milk.

The way in which birds have learned to use various types of backyard feeders also

Above: *In birds such as starlings* (Sturnus vulgaris), *preening may serve to reinforce bonds between individuals, as well as keeping the feathers clean.*

demonstrates their ability to modify their existing behavior in response to new conditions when it benefits them. A number of new feeders on the market designed to thwart squirrels from stealing the food exploit birds' ability to adapt in this way. The birds have to squeeze through a small gap to reach the food, just as they might to enter the nest. Once one bird has been bold enough to enter in this fashion, others observe and soon follow suit.

PREENING

Although preening serves a variety of functions, the most important aspect is keeping the feathers in good condition. It helps to dislodge parasites and removes loose feathers, particularly during molting. It also ensures that the plumage is kept waterproof by spreading oil from the preen gland at the base of the tail.

Preening can be a social activity, too. It may be carried out by pairs of males and females during the breeding season, or among a family group. This behavior is seen in a variety of birds, including members of the finch family. In some cases, preening may be a prelude to mating.

BATHING

Preening is not the only way in which birds keep their plumage in good condition. Birds often bathe to remove dirt and debris from their plumage. Small birds sometimes wet their feathers by lying on a damp leaf during a shower of rain, in an activity known as leaf bathing. Other birds immerse themselves in a pool of water, splashing around and ruffling their feathers.

Some birds, especially those found in dry regions and deserts, prefer to dust bathe, lying down in a dusty hollow known as a scrape and using fine earth thrown up by their wings to absorb excess oil from their plumage. They then shake themselves thoroughly and preen their feathers to remove the excess oil.

SUNBATHING

This may be important in letting birds synthesize vitamin D3 from the ultraviolet rays in sunlight, which is vital for a healthy skeleton. This process can be achieved only by light falling on the bird's skin, which explains why birds ruffle their plumage at this time. Some birds habitually stretch out while sunbathing, while others, such as many pigeons, prefer to rest with one wing raised, leaning over at a strange angle on the perch.

MAINTAINING HEALTH

Some people believe that when birds are ill, they eat particular plants that have medicinal properties, but this theory is

Below: *A wren is sunbathing. Many birds tend to sunbathe with their wings outstretched and often an open beak.*

very difficult to prove. One form of behavior that does confer health benefits has been documented, however: it involves the use of ants. Instead of eating these insects, some birds occasionally rub them in among their feathers. This causes the ants to release formic acid, which acts as a potent insecticide, killing off lurking parasites, such as mites and lice. Blue jays *(Cyanocitta cristata)* and also starlings (Sturnidae) and Eurasian blackbirds *(Turdus merula)* are among the species that have been observed using insects in this way.

Members of the crow family have also been seen perching on smoking chimney pots or above outdoor fires, ruffling their feathers and letting the smoke penetrate their plumage. The smoke is thought to kill off parasites in a process that confers the same benefits as anting.

Above: *When bathing, birds frequently dip down and use their wings and tail to splash the water. This ensures their whole body receives a wetting.*

DISPLAYS

Birds often signal their intentions to one another using displays, or ritualized gestures. Such actions are used in courtship, to coordinate flock behavior, and also to reinforce territorial claims and resolve disputes. A songbird wanting to warn another off a food source will fluff itself up and spread its wings to look as big as possible. Its rival may indicate submission by crouching low to minimize its size.

Below: *A red-winged blackbird menaces another using a typical threat posture, with feathers fluffed and wings outstretched.*

MIGRATION

Some birds live in a particular place all year round, but many are only temporary visitors. Many species fly north to temperate or even polar latitudes to breed in spring, and return south in fall. They have a wide distribution, but are seen only in specific parts of their range at certain times of the year.

Many species of birds take long seasonal journeys. The birds that regularly undertake such movements using specific routes are known as migrants, and the journeys themselves are known as migrations. Migrations are different from so-called irruptions, when flocks of certain types of birds suddenly move to an area where conditions are more favorable.

Birds migrate to seek shelter from the elements, to find safe areas to rear their young, and, in particular, to seek places where food is plentiful. Birds such as waxwings (Bombycillidae) irrupt to a new location to find food when supplies become scarce in their habitat, but such journeys are less frequent and are irregular.

The instinct to migrate dates back millions of years, to a period when the seasons were often much more extreme, which meant that it was difficult to obtain food in a locality throughout the year. This forced birds to move in search of food. Even today, the majority of migratory species live within the world's temperate

Below: *Many birds, such as tanagers* (Piranga *species) migrate after molting. Damaged plumage can make the task of flying harder and more hazardous.*

Above: *Ruby-throated hummingbirds migrate long distances considering their tiny size, mainly wintering in the tropics.*

zones, particularly in the Northern Hemisphere, where seasonal changes remain pronounced.

ROUTES AND ALTITUDE
The routes that the birds follow on their journeys are often well defined. Land birds try to avoid flying over large stretches of water, preferring instead to follow coastal

routes and crossing the sea at the shortest point. For instance, many birds migrating between North and South America prefer to fly over the isthmus of Central America. Frequently, birds fly at much greater altitudes when migrating. Cranes (Gruidae) have been recorded flying at 16,400 feet (5,000m) when crossing mountainous areas, while geese (Anatidae) have been observed crossing very high mountain ranges. Even if the migratory routes are known, it is often difficult to see migrating birds because they fly so high.

SPEED AND DISTANCE
Migrating birds also fly at greater speeds than usual, which helps to make their journey time as short as possible. The difference can be significant. Migrating barn swallows *(Hirundo rustica)* travel at speeds between 1.8 and 8.7mph (3–14kmh) faster than usual, and are helped no doubt by the greater altitude, where the air is thinner and resistance is less.

Some birds travel huge distances on migration. Arctic terns *(Sterna paradisea)* are renowned for covering distances of more than 9,300 miles (15,000km) in total, as they shuttle between the Arctic and Antarctic. They fly an average distance of 100 miles (160km) every day. Among backyard birds, barn swallows fly south from North America as far as Argentina to overwinter. Experienced birds may cover about 185 miles (300km) a day during their long journey. However studies suggest that as few as 25 percent of young swallows manage to complete the round trip and return to their birthplace.

Size does not preclude some birds from migrating long distances. The tiny ruby-throated hummingbird *(Archilochus colubris)* flies over the Gulf of Mexico from the eastern United States every year, a distance of more than 500 miles (800km).

PREPARING FOR MIGRATION
The migratory habits of birds have long been the subject of scientific curiosity. As late as the 1800s, it was thought that

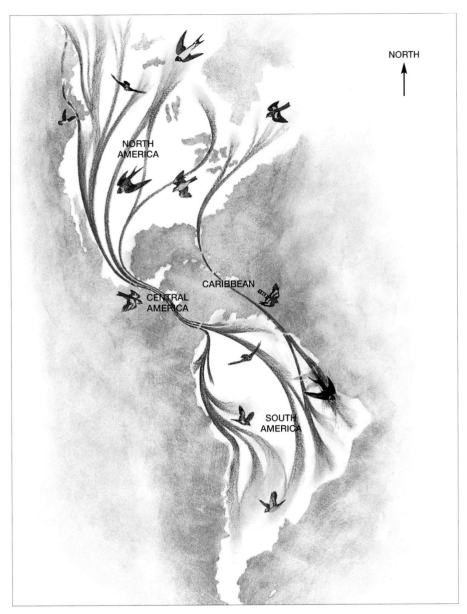

NORTH

NORTH
AMERICA

CARIBBEAN

CENTRAL
AMERICA

SOUTH
AMERICA

Above: *This diagram illustrates the main migratory routes in the Americas, where birds fly either down the Central American isthmus, or across the Caribbean via the local islands. In following traditional routes over or close to land, the birds avoid long and potentially hazardous sea crossings.*

barn swallows hibernated in the bottom of ponds because they were seen skimming over the pond surface in groups before disappearing until the following spring. Now we know that they were probably feeding on insects to build up energy supplies for their long journey ahead.

Even today, the precise mechanisms involved in migratory behavior are not fully understood. We do know that birds feed up before setting out on migration, and that various hormonal changes enable

them to store more fat in their bodies to sustain them on their journey. Feeding opportunities are likely to be more limited than usual when birds are migrating, while their energy requirements are, of course, higher. In addition, birds usually molt just before migrating, so that their plumage is in the best condition to withstand the inevitable buffeting that lies ahead.

NAVIGATION

Birds use both learned and visual cues to orient themselves when migrating. Young birds of many species, such as swans, learn the route by flying with their elders. However, many young birds set out on their own and reach their destinations successfully without the benefit of experienced companions, navigating by instinct alone. Birds such as

swifts (Apopidae) fly mainly during daytime, whereas others, including ducks (Anatidae), migrate at night. Many birds fly directly to their destination, but some may detour and break their journey to obtain food and water before setting out again.

Experiments have shown that birds orient themselves using the position of the Sun and stars, as well as by following familiar landmarks. They use the Earth's magnetic field to find their position, and thus do not get lost in cloudy or foggy weather, when the sky is obscured. The way in which these factors come together has, however, yet to be fully understood.

BANDING BIRDS
Much of what we know about migration and the lifespan of birds comes from banding studies carried out by ornithologists. Bands placed on birds' legs let experts track their movements when the ringed birds are recovered again. The rings are made of lightweight aluminum, and have details of the banding organization and when banding was carried out. Unfortunately, only a very small proportion of ringed birds are ever recovered, so the data gathered is incomplete. However, now other methods of tracking, such as radar, are also used to follow the routes taken by flocks of birds, which supplement the information from banding studies.

Below: *A tracking device has been attached to the leg of a swan. The colored band can help experts to identify individual birds from some distance away.*

SURVIVAL

The numbers of a particular species of bird can vary significantly over time, affected by factors such as the availability of food, climate, disease, and hunting. When the reproductive rate of a species falls below its annual mortality rate, it is in decline, but this does not mean it will inevitably become extinct.

For many birds, life is short and hazardous. Apart from the risk of predation, birds can face a whole range of other dangers, from starvation and disease to either deliberate or inadvertent human persecution. The reproductive rate is higher and age of maturity is lower in species that have particularly hazardous lifestyles, such as titmice (Paridae). In such species, adult birds often breed twice or more each year in rapid succession.

RISING AND FALLING NUMBERS
Some birds have a reproductive cycle that is geared to let them increase their numbers rapidly under favorable conditions. In regions where rainfall is low or erratic, for example, seed-eating birds multiply quickly when the rains come. Rainfall not only ensures the rapid germination of the grasses that often form the basis of their diet, but also replenishes rivers, lakes, and other water sources. During periods of drought when food and

Above: *Predatory birds, such as barn owls (Tyto alba), do well in years when conditions favor prey, such as rodents, letting them multiply. In years when rodent populations are lower, there is less food for barn owl adults and their young.*

Below: *As grain eaters, pigeons in rural areas worldwide have benefited from the spread of agriculture, while in cities, food scraps are available in trash. These opportunists have also adapted to other changes in their environment, for example, the chance to roost on power lines.*

water become harder to find, the same bird populations may plummet, but they can grow again rapidly when conditions become more favorable.

Regular falloffs in populations can occur on a cyclical basis in the case of predatory birds, such as owls, that feed mainly on one type of food, such as rodents. In years where conditions favor rodents, the parent birds are able to rear more chicks. When rodent numbers decline, the owls' breeding success plummets, only to recover when the rodent population rises again.

GROUP LIVING
Living within a group offers several major advantages to birds such as starlings (Sturnidae) and pigeons (Columbidae). Flocks of birds are able to exploit large supplies of food as they become available. Birds that live in flocks also find their mates more easily than other birds. Another advantage is the safety of numbers. An aerial predator, such as a hawk, will find it harder to recognize and target individuals in a flying mass of birds, although stragglers are still likely to be picked off.

Coloration can increase the safety of birds in flocks. In Florida, there used to be feral budgerigar flocks made up of multicolored individuals. The different colors reflected the diversity of color varieties that were developed through domestication. Today, however, green is by far the predominant color in such flocks, as it is in genuinely wild flocks, simply because predators found it much easier to pick off individuals of other colors. Greater numbers

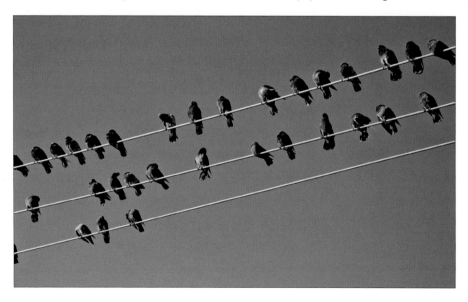

CRYPTIC COLORATION

Camouflage, also known as cryptic coloration, enables a bird to hide in its natural surroundings. It offers distinct survival benefits in concealing the bird from would-be predators. Cryptic coloration has the effect of breaking up the bird's outline, letting it blend in with the background in its habitat. Posture and, in particular, keeping still can also aid concealment, because movement often attracts the attention of potential predators.

Below: *Camouflage lets birds, such as this cactus wren, forage while remaining undetected by enemies. However, cryptic coloration is also useful to predators, such as owls.*

urban areas, road systems, mines, farms, and other developments worldwide has greatly reduced the amount of wild habitat that is available to birds. In North America, the modernization of agriculture has led to the creation of larger fields in some areas, and also increased use of chemicals, both of which have had serious consequences for many species of native birds.

However, the expansion of agriculture has not always had a negative effect on bird populations. In arid areas, the expansion of farming has resulted in the greater availability of food and water in what was formerly more barren country, which has enabled some types of crop- and seed-eating birds to spread.

Other birds have benefited more directly from human intervention, as is the case with the common starling *(Sturnus vulgaris)*. These birds have spread across North America following their introduction from Europe in the late 1800s. Similarly, game birds, such as pheasants and partridges, introduced from the Old World, are now found across large areas, and frequently reared for sport shooting. In some instances, more survive than would otherwise be the case, thanks to the attention of gamekeepers who provide food, and also help to curb predators in the terrain where the birds are released.

ENVIRONMENTAL CHANGE

In the last decade or so, scientists believe that global warming has started to affect habitats worldwide, producing generally warmer conditions and in some regions, making extreme weather events, such as droughts, more common. Research shows

Above: *Meadowlarks (*Sturnella *species) have generally benefited from the spread of agriculture. However, they often nest in hay fields, where their nests are sometimes destroyed by harvesting machinery.*

that this has started to affect birds' breeding habits and migration patterns. Some species appear to be benefiting from environmental changes. However, birds that reproduce slowly are likely to be highly vulnerable to any changes in their surroundings, whether caused by climate change or other factors, such as habitat loss, hunting, or disease.

Below: *Group living provides safety in numbers for birds, such as red-winged blackbirds (*Agelaius phoeniceus*). These birds spend much of the year in a flock.*

of the green budgies survived to breed and pass on their genes to their descendants, and so green became the dominant color within the feral flocks.

Group living also means that when the flock is feeding and at its most vulnerable, there are extra eyes to watch out for predators and other threats. Within some flocks, individual birds may take it in turns to act as sentinels and screech loudly at any hint of danger.

EFFECTS OF HUMANS

It is generally assumed that human interference in the landscape is likely to have harmful effects on avian populations. In the last century or so, the expansion of

BIRDS IN TOWNS AND CITIES

*Some birds display a remarkable ability to adapt to modern life, settling in the heart of towns and cities.
They use buildings for nesting and, in the case of predatory birds, as vantage points for hunting, like
they would trees or rocky crags in the wild. All this means that cities can be great places to watch birds.*

Cities tend to be slightly warmer than
the surrounding countryside, and this
warm microclimate offers a number of
advantages for birds. Drinking water is
less likely to freeze in cold weather, and
in spring, insects are more abundant at
an earlier time, as plants bud and grow
more quickly because of the warmth.

RESIDENTS AND VISITORS
Some birds live permanently in cities, taking
advantage of parks, whereas others are
regular visitors, flying in to roost at night
from outlying areas, or pausing here on
migration. Old, low-rise buildings can offer
a snug and relatively safe retreat for birds
that roost in flocks, whereas birds of prey

Above: *Out of all birds, the feral pigeon
(Columba livia) has adapted best to urban
life to the extent that it is now a common
sight in cities around the world, including
in North America.*

Above: *Some species introduced from
the Old World, such as starlings and house
sparrows* (Passer domesticus) *do well in
urban parks and backyards.*

Below: *City parks offer the best chance of
viewing a wide range of species in urban
environments, particularly if a pond or lake
offers a habitat for species such as ducks.*

seek the inaccessible ledges of high-rise
buildings. The abundance of feral pigeons
(Columba livia) in urban areas attracts
peregrine falcons *(Falco peregrinus)*,
proving that these predators are just as
adaptable as their prey. The falcons may
keep pigeon populations in check but,
if not, pigeon numbers can also be curbed
by feeding them with corn, which acts
as a natural contraceptive.

Migrating birds pass through cities and
suburbs on occasions, for example flocks
of common starlings *(Sturnus vulgaris)*.
These congregate not just in city parks,
but also roost on buildings and tree-lined
streets when breaking their journey,
creating a noisy chatter and plenty of mess.

BENEFITS AND DANGERS
Life above the bustle of city streets
generally offers predatory species a fairly
safe existence, compared with more rural
areas where they risk being shot illegally.
However, there are still dangers lurking
on city streets. Homes or high-rise office
buildings with large expanses of glass can
lure birds to a fatal collision.

Right: *Many bird species thrive in towns
and cities. There are plenty of places
for perching, nesting, and rearing young.
However, the spread of cities also causes
many avian populations to decline by
altering neighboring habitats. When
new development encroaches on
surrounding land, it becomes hard
for many birds to find food.*

**TIPS FOR OBSERVING BIRDS
IN TOWNS AND CITIES**
• Early morning is a good time to
view birds at close quarters in cities,
before many people are out and
about to disturb avian residents.
• Join the local ornithological society
to gain insight into the more unusual
species that have been observed in
your town or city.
• If you venture outside the backyard to
watch birds, do not forget about the
dangers of traffic in your enthusiasm.

Typical sightings in towns and cities,
depending partly on location:
• Pigeons and doves
• Sparrows and juncos
• Jays and crows
• Finches and titmice
• Ducks and moorhens

1 House sparrows
2 Starlings
3 Peregrine falcon
4 Feral pigeons
5 Common crows
6 Mallards
7 Moorhen
8 Black-headed gulls

BIRDS IN RURAL BACKYARDS

A wide variety of birds are likely to be seen in rural backyards. As well as the species that naturally visit in search of food among the trees and shrubs, the addition of feeding stations will help to draw birds to rural backyard settings. As many as 40 species have been observed regularly visiting bird tables.

Tidy, immaculately manicured backyards generally support less bird life than well-established yards with plenty of mature shrubs that provide cover and can be used for roosting and nesting. If there are stands of trees nearby, or even just lining the road outside, the variety of birds will increase, and larger species will become more common. Artificial nest sites, such as nest boxes of various types and sizes, can also help to increase the variety and numbers of birds that visit your backyard.

Birds face a major danger in backyards in the guise of the domestic cat. Huge numbers of individuals fall victim to these

Above: *Bird feeders help to attract birds, such as blue jays, into backyards by providing them with additional food sources. These supplies are especially valuable during the months of cold weather.*

Above: *Bluebirds (*Sialia *species), such as this eastern bluebird, bring welcome color to backyards in spring and summer. These are members of the thrush family (Turdidae). The males are the most brightly colored.*

TIPS FOR OBSERVING BIRDS IN RURAL BACKYARDS
• Positioning a bird table near a window will let you watch birds from inside the house, but be careful to site it well away from cover where cats can lurk and ambush birds.
• Keep a pair of binoculars handy indoors so you can get a good view of the bird table and any unexpected visitors to it, plus a notepad to record any unusual birds you see.
• You can encourage invertebrate-eating birds to visit your backyard by creating a wild area or by establishing a compost pile where invertebrates can multiply.
• Try to avoid using insecticides in your backyard, because these reduce the food available for birds.
• Ordinary slug pellets will poison slug eaters, such as thrushes. Use pellets that are described as safe for birds instead.

Typical sightings in rural backyards, depending on location:
• Titmice and chickadees
• Thrushes and cardinals
• Finches
• Sparrows and juncos
• Grackles and starlings

pets annually. The majority of the casualties are young fledglings, which lack the awareness and caution of adult birds. In areas where the cat population is especially high, there may be local declines in bird numbers. However, studies suggest that bird populations do not seem to be adversely affected by cats overall.

HELPERS AND PESTS
Birds are often regarded as gardeners' friends because they help to control the number of invertebrate pests in backyards. For example, titmice (Paridae) eat aphids on rose bushes, and thrushes (Turdidae) hunt snails. At certain times of year, however, some birds can themselves become pests. Pigeons (Columbidae), in particular, often dig up newly planted seeds and eat them before they can germinate, unless the seeds are protected in some way. Later in the year, some species eat ripening berries.

RESIDENTS AND VISITORS
Some songbirds are resident in backyard settings throughout the year. Others are temporary visitors, migrating to warmer climes for the winter period. For example,

swallows, warblers, and hummingbirds frequent backyards in many parts of North America for only spring and summer, and then head south for winter. Meanwhile, winter migrants from farther north, such as redpolls and pine grosbeaks, may appear in backyards at about the same time.

Studies provide clear evidence that actual shifts in the behavior and distribution of birds are currently occurring because of the availability of backyard habitats and the provision of food and nest boxes there. For example, the American robin (*Turdus migratorius*) has moved from its traditional woodland haunts into backyards, where it is now a common sight.

Right: *In many respects, rural backyards offer an ideal habitat for birds. Food is readily available in these surroundings, as well as trees and shrubs, which provide good opportunities for roosting and nesting. Unfortunately, backyards can often be dangerous places for birds to visit, thanks to the popularity of cats as pets. Nor are cats the only danger. Woodpeckers and corvids, such as jays and magpies, will raid the nests of songbirds in springtime to take both eggs and chicks.*

1 Downy woodpecker
2 Purple martins
3 Eastern bluebirds
4 Cardinal
5 Blue jay
6 Purple finches
7 Common grackles
8 Ruby-throated hummingbirds
9 Eastern phoebe
10 Black-capped chickadees
11 Tufted titmouse

WOODLAND BIRDS

If your home lies near a woodland habitat, be it a forest plantation, countryside grove, or even a tree-lined avenue in a city center, your backyard will be visited by woodland birds. However, many of these species are very shy and secretive by nature, which can make them difficult to observe.

Bird life is more prolific and varied in and near deciduous, broad-leaved woodlands than in coniferous forests, largely because of greater feeding opportunities in the former setting. Nonetheless, some species manage to thrive in coniferous forests.

DECIDUOUS WOODLANDS

A wide variety of food types exists for birds in deciduous forests. The species here may eat all kinds of foods, ranging from seeds to berries and invertebrates, depending on the time of year. Deciduous woodlands are more open than coniferous ones, particularly in winter when trees have lost their leaves. This means that there is a significant understory of vegetation and insects are more plentiful. Migratory birds feed in these woods in summer. Ground birds may be found here along with wood warblers, owls, and woodpeckers. In spring, woodland birds gather in clearings

Below: *The yellow warbler (Dendroica petechia) is one of North America's most common warblers. These birds will nest in backyards with mature trees and take suet, baked goods, and raisins from bird tables.*

to display and mate. However, in winter these leafless woods provide less shelter and food for birds, and so at this time these birds often visit backyards.

CONIFEROUS WOODLANDS

Birds such as crossbills thrive in coniferous woodlands. Their curving bills let these members of the finch family extract the seeds from pinecones effectively. Other species, including woodpeckers and corvids, such as jays, may prepare for the cold winter weather by burying stores of nuts or hiding them in trees.

Owls are frequently found in coniferous forests, preying on the rodents that can be plentiful there. However, owls may also be forced to hunt elsewhere if the numbers of their prey plummet, following a shortage of pinecones. Evergreen coniferous forests provide shelter all year round for birds, but here, too, food supplies

Below: *Black-capped chickadees will nest in wooded backyards in spring. These birds spend the winter months doing the rounds of bird feeders, surviving on handouts, such as peanuts and sunflower and mixed seeds.*

TIPS FOR OBSERVING WOODLAND BIRDS
• Spring is a good time to watch woodland species, before the trees are covered in foliage, providing concealment for birds.
• In summer, woodland trees teem with invertebrates, which attract insectivorous birds in search of prey.
• Stand quietly in wooded areas and listen. Hidden among foliage, woodland birds use song to announce their presence to others. Such species are as frequently detected by sound as by sight.

Typical sightings in backyards with or near wooded areas, depending on location:
• Woodpeckers and flickers
• Finches and grosbeaks
• Nuthatches
• Wood warblers

are far from guaranteed. There are barren years when the trees do not produce as many cones as usual, forcing the birds to abandon their regular haunts and seek food elsewhere, including in backyards. These unpredictable movements, known as irruptions, occur when birds, such as waxwings, suddenly appear in large numbers outside their normal range, searching for food. They later disappear just as suddenly as they arrived, and may not return again for years.

Right: *Deciduous woodlands offer an ideal habitat for birds during the warm months of the year, providing food, excellent cover, and a variety of nesting sites. Selective planting can help to recreate these conditions in your backyard to attract woodland species. During winter, life in deciduous woodlands can become much harsher. Once the leaves have fallen, the birds will be much more conspicuous and food is likely to be scarce.*

1 Black-capped chickadee
2 Goshawk
3 Pileated woodpeckers
4 Long-eared owl
5 White-breasted nuthatch
6 Pine siskins
7 Yellow warbler
8 Winter wren
9 Hermit thrush

AQUATIC BIRDS

Some birds are drawn to backyards with or near ponds and streams because of feeding opportunities, while others seek sanctuary from would-be predators in these surroundings. Aquatic species can be attracted to your backyard by the presence of even a small water feature, such as a pond.

A wide variety of birds haunt streams, ponds, and lakes, but not all are easy to observe because of their camouflage. The dense plant growth often found by water also provides concealment.

FINDING FOOD

Many predatory birds hunt in wetland habitats, including backyard ponds, swooping low over the water to seize fish by day or even at night. Some fish-eating birds, notably kingfishers (Alcedinidae), dive to seize their prey, which they may feed to their young in nest sites built into the banks of streams. Other hunters rely on different strategies to catch food. Herons (Ardeidae) lurk by the water's edge and seize fish that swim in range of their sharp, powerful bills. Rails (Rallidae) and bitterns often forage by slow-flowing or still water with well-established reed beds, but these birds are shy by nature. Their mottled plumage and slim body shape make them hard to see.

NESTING

Some birds are drawn to ponds, bogs, or streams in backyards not so much by food but by the nesting opportunities there.

Below: *Moorhens* (Gallinula chloropus) *are more commonly seen by the water's edge than in open water. Long toes spread their weight as they walk across boggy ground.*

Above: *Carolina wood ducks* (Aix sponsa) *will use duck nest boxes near ponds in backyards. These rank among the most common waterfowl in North America.*

Swallows *(Hirundo rustica)* collect damp mud from the water's edge to make their nests, and may also catch midges flying above the water surface. Ducks, geese, moorhens, and other birds that actually nest by ponds and streams seek seclusion when breeding. They hide their nest away, or make it hard to reach by choosing a spot surrounded by water.

Swans and geese have been known to nest by large ponds in backyards. Mute swans *(Cygnus olor)* construct large nests, which restricts their choice of sites. Both sexes defend the nest ferociously. These largish birds are capable of inflicting painful blows with their wings on intruders, so be careful not to venture too close.

Above: *Belted kingfishers* (Ceryle alcyon) *may venture into backyards with ponds in search of fish and other prey. Despite their bright colors, they are difficult to see.*

Right: *Reed beds or dense plant growth by the edge of ponds or streams in parks and backyards provide cover for aquatic birds. The slender shape of some freshwater birds lets them move easily through thick vegetation, avoiding detection. Fortunately, birds swimming into open water will be much easier to see.*

TIPS FOR OBSERVING AQUATIC BIRDS

• Patience is essential when watching aquatic birds, because many are shy and easily frightened away.
• Plant cover can make bird-watching difficult, but can also provide concealment for bird-watchers.
• Always be careful near water. If you have a water feature in your backyard, you may need to install protection to ensure children will not be in danger if they are drawn to the water's edge.

Typical sightings in backyards with or near ponds, lakes, or streams, depending on location:
• Coots and moorhens
• Belted kingfisher
• Ducks, including wood duck, teal, wigeon, and mergansers
• Geese and swans

1 American crows
2 Starlings
3 Black-billed magpie
4 Feral pigeons
5 Herring gulls
6 Coots
7 Mallards
8 Tufted ducks
9 Mute swan
10 Wigeons
11 Northern pintails
12 Wood duck
13 Goldeneyes
14 House sparrow

WATCHING BIRDS

Thanks to their widespread distribution, birds can be seen in virtually any location, even in the center of cities. You do not need any special equipment to watch birds, but a pair of binoculars will help you to gain a better insight into avian behavior by letting you study birds at close range.

Observing the birds that visit your backyard can give hours of pleasure. It will also let you build up a detailed picture of the species that frequent your area. You may be surprised at the variety of visitors. Some species visit on a daily basis, others at only certain times of year. As you become an experienced bird-watcher, you will become attuned to seasonal changes that occur through the year, as birds molt, court a mate, nest, and raise their families, and as migrants depart for warmer climes in fall and return again in spring.

Birds may be observed at any time of day, with the early morning being a prime time of feeding activity. You may be able to observe bird behavior from behind the cover of tall vegetation in the backyard, or from the house, particularly if you position a bird table or feeder nearby. Alternatively, you can construct your own hide.

GETTING A GOOD VIEW
Binoculars can be purchased from bird preserves, camera stores, and similar outlets, but it is important to test them

Above: *Binoculars provide a close-up view of birds, letting you observe details of anatomy, plumage, and also behavior that cannot be seen with the naked eye. They will also help you find shy species.*

first, particularly as they vary significantly in price. When buying binoculars, you need to consider not only the power of magnification, but also how closely they can be focused, especially as you are going to use them at home, where the bird table is likely to be relatively close. Of course, you can also take them on bird-watching ventures farther afield, for example, to local parks, woods, or wetlands. There, you will be able to observe different birds and probably a greater variety of species than can be seen at home.

FIELDSCOPES
As well as binoculars, dedicated bird-watchers often use birding telescopes, called fieldscopes. These are ideal for use indoors or in hides because they can be mounted in various ways, using either a clamp fitting or a tripod. Fieldscopes are equipped with lenses similar to those in binoculars, but are more suited to long-term use, when you are watching a nest or the bird table for example, as you do not have

---

DRAWING BIRDS FOR REFERENCE

1 *Sketching birds is relatively straight-forward if you follow this procedure. Start by drawing an egg shape for the body, with a smaller egg above, which will become the head, and another to form the rump. A center line through the head circle will form the basis for the bill. Now add circles and lines to indicate the position of the wings and tail. Add lines for the legs and then sketch in the feet and claws.*

3 *Colored pencils will let you add more detail after you have erased any unwanted pencil markings.*

2 *Use an indelible, fine-line, felt-tip pen to ink in the shape of the bird that you have drawn previously in pencil, avoiding the unwanted construction lines.*

4 *If you take a number of prepared head shapes with you when bird-watching, you can fill in the detail quickly and easily, enabling you to identify birds later.*

to keep holding the scope while waiting for birds to appear. Instead, set up the scope trained on the nest or feeder, then simply be patient until the birds appear.

MAKING NOTES

When observing birds in the backyard or farther afield, it is always useful to have a notebook handy to write down details and make sketches. When sketching, proceed from a few quick pencil lines to a more finished portrait as time allows. Water-soluble pencils are helpful for coloring sketches, because the colors can be spread using water and a small paintbrush.

If you see a bird you cannot identify, jot down the details quickly in your notebook. Note any sound the bird makes, and also its colors and markings. Notice the length of neck and legs, and the shape of the bill. Assess the bird's size in relation to familiar species, and try to decide which family you think it belongs to. Your notes can then be compared with a field guide or other sources of information to identify the bird.

Above: *Taking notes will enable you to build a comprehensive picture of all the birds that visit your backyard at different times of year. Note the date and time, as well as the species and sex of birds if you know them.*

Above: *To get a really close-up view, you can buy a special camera for installing inside a nest box. This provides a wonderful opportunity to observe behavior without disturbing either the chicks or their parents.*

MAKING A TEMPORARY HIDE

1 Making a hide does not need specialized equipment—just a large cardboard box, paints, stakes, and a little creativity.

2 Open out the cardboard box and paint it. The pattern or color is not important; your body shape will be hidden behind it.

3 Preparing the hide can be a lot of fun and is something that the whole family or friends and neighbors can join in with.

4 To support the cardboard, drive a few stakes into the ground until they are firm enough to support the weight of the hide.

5 Hides are traditionally made of dull-colored material, some with military-style camouflage. In the case of a backyard hide, the color is

rarely important. Backyards are often full of extreme contrast, so why not design a colorful hide that children will love to make?

ATTRACTING BIRDS TO YOUR BACKYARD

Birds are a delight in backyards at all times of year. In spring and summer, their singing provides pleasure, while in winter their colorful plumage helps to brighten dull days. Urban and suburban backyards can be havens for wild birds, especially if you put out food and water. Birds will soon come to know it as a food source and it will become a regular stopping-off point. If nest boxes are provided, birds may well set up home, too. There is immense pleasure to be had from knowing that you are helping wild bird populations to thrive and from watching the species that come to feed.

Left: *In spring, the provision of suitable food and also nesting materials may help many types of birds to rear their young successfully.*

Above: *Feeders containing different foods placed at varying heights in the yard will help to attract a greater variety of birds.*

Above: *Northern cardinals are among the bird species that benefit from the provision of seeds and nuts in feeders.*

Above: *Planting shrubs, such as holly, will attract berry-eating birds in winter, when they are most vulnerable to the elements.*

BIRDS IN DOMESTIC BACKYARDS

Birds have always lived around people. As human settlements developed, birds were happy to move into buildings that provided cosy roosts and also food scraps. The art of domesticating wild birds has a long history, although in the early days this was generally because birds were seen as a source of food.

Pigeons were probably the first birds to be domesticated, because they were good to eat, their food requirements were simple, and they were prolific breeders. Both the Egyptians and the Romans built towers for pigeons on their rooftops, designed with internal ledges on which the birds could roost and nest.

The Native Americans had a different reason for inviting wild birds to share their homes. They used bottle-shaped gourds to make nest boxes for purple martins, whose massed presence helped to deter vultures from raiding the meat left out to

Below: *Birds will make use of even the smallest urban spaces. This compact courtyard area contains a small tree, a mixture of flowers, herbs, vegetables and climbers, and an open-front nest box postitioned in a sheltered place on the wall.*

dry in the sun. Nest boxes made from gourds are still widely used today, and east of the Rocky Mountains much of the entire purple martin population lives in sites provided by humans.

HISTORY OF BEFRIENDING BIRDS

It was not until fairly recently that people began to encourage birds into their backyards purely for the joy of watching them. The English naturalist Gilbert White noted in his diary for June, 1782, that his brother Thomas had nailed up scallop shells under the eaves of his house, with the hollow side facing upward against the wall, for martins to nest in. This strategy proved successful, as the martins began to move in almost immediately.

In the early 19th century, the pioneering naturalist Charles Waterton, who turned his estate in England into a nature preserve,

Above: *Swallows are among the species that establish their own homes on buildings, forming mud nests under eaves.*

developed stone nest boxes for barn owls and built a tower for jackdaws, similar to a dovecote. Baron von Berlepsch was an early popularizer of nest boxes in Great Britain. In the late 19th century, he spent much time experimenting, eventually originating a design that replicated a natural woodpecker's nest, consisting of a section of tree trunk that had been hollowed out at one end, an entry hole that went into this chamber from the front, and a wooden lid with an attachment for hanging it at the back. This simple design was effective, and similar nest boxes are still used today. Since then, designs for nest boxes and birdhouses have burgeoned, ranging from purely functional structures to ornate miniature versions of their owners' homes.

PLANNING A GARDEN FOR BIRDS

If you want to make your backyard a haven for wild birds, it is important to take the birds' needs into account throughout the planning and installing process. A long-established backyard with mature trees, flowering plants, and a diverse selection of shrubs, surrounded by a thick

Above: *Pyracantha, also known as firethorn, shelters birds from the elements. In fall, the scarlet berries provide food.*

Above: *Sunflowers provide blazing color in backyards, and many types of birds feed on the oil-rich seeds.*

hedge, is ideal, and if your house is old it probably has plenty of nooks and crannies in its walls that are good for roosting.

Not everyone is lucky enough to have such perfect conditions, but if you are considering making some changes, it is not difficult to improve on what you have. An urban backyard may not get as great a variety of visitors as a rural one, but it has some advantages. City air is warmer so there is less risk of frost. The birds are also used to people, so will allow close observation.

CHOOSING PLANTS FOR BIRDS

You will need varied vegetation to attract insects, a vital food source for birds that are nesting. The best plants are ones that will produce plenty of berries, seeds, and nuts. Birds need cover for protection, so hedges are perfect. Hawthorn and pyracantha are a good choice: these shrubs provide shelter from wind and rain; are good for nesting; and in fall, their berries make fine pickings. If possible, keep one part of your backyard wild. If you can find room for a tree, plant a native species that the birds are adapted to. Shrubs, such as elder, produce berries

Right: *This garden is ideal for attracting birds. It contains shrubs and hedges for protection, a variety of flowering plants for seeds and insects, and a lawn where you can sit and observe your feathered friends.*

that are enjoyed by dozens of species. A fruit tree, such as apple or pear, will benefit both you and the birds.

Many border plants attract butterflies, moths, and bees, which the birds feed on in the summer, as well as providing seeds in fall. Good choices include cornflowers, Michaelmas daisies, cosmos, marigolds,

zinnia, bee balm, penstemon, Queen Anne's lace, and sunflowers, whose seeds are irresistible to nuthatches and finches.

A lawn is ideal for observation. Water the grass regularly in dry weather to bring earthworms to the surface. Let the grass grow long around trees—the weeds will provide seed for finches.

STRUCTURES TO ATTRACT BIRDS

By providing a range of feeding, nesting and watering structures and distributing them around the backyard, you can attract a wide range of bird species. Tables, feeders, nest boxes, birdhouses, roosts and birdbaths are also beautiful structures in their own right, and will enhance any yard.

Seeing birds regularly visiting your backyard is enormously rewarding, and the inclusion of a few simple structures will ensure that your yard is attractive to birds.

BIRD TABLES

A bird table is the most obvious and effortless way to attract birds into your backyard. Winter is the best time to set one up, when the natural food supply is scarce and the ground is too hard for the birds to penetrate with their beaks.

A bird table may be supported on a post or brackets or it may hang from a branch. It needs a roof to keep the rain off and a rim to prevent the food from being blown away. Other additions, such as a scrap basket, seed tube, or water port, may be incorporated into the design.

FEEDERS

Pet and garden suppliers stock a huge range of feeders for different types of nuts or seeds. These are useful, because seeds are otherwise easily scattered and blown away. Some of the designs that are readily available are squirrel proof. Mesh feeders are designed to dispense nuts, while feeders made of plastic tubing are designed for seeds.

There are also feeders that are designed to be stuck onto a window. Provided you do not mind the birds making a mess of your window and walls, these will enable you to study your avian visitors at close proximity. As an alternative to buying feeders, you can try making your own, using the ideas for constructing inexpensive versions given later in this book.

NEST BOXES

Simple nest boxes are generally designed to hang from a tree or wall. Store-bought boxes may be made of plain wood, preserved with creosote, or rustic-looking hollowed-out logs fitted with roofs. It is generally best to choose a box that is designed with a specific type of bird in mind. The all-important factor is the size of the entry hole to admit nesting birds.

If you are building your own nest box, wood is probably the best material to use, although if it is thinner than $\frac{5}{8}$ inch (15mm), it may warp and will not provide much insulation. Old floorboards are a good source of timber if you can get them, because they are well seasoned. Softwood is easier to work with, but hardwoods, such as oak, are longer lasting. Exterior or marine plywood can be used in any situation.

Wherever possible, use the wood with the grain running vertically. This will help the rain to drain off. Glue all joints before screwing them together, or use galvanized nails, which are better for damp conditions because they will not rust easily.

The most important thing is that the box is warm and dry, but not so airtight that condensation becomes a problem. Some birdhouse builders drill small holes high on the sides of the box to create ventilation and lessen condensation. There is still plenty of room for improvement with traditional designs and materials, so feel free to experiment.

BIRDHOUSES

These are ornamental versions of nest boxes. They have a dual purpose, providing a safe nest site for birds and also satisfying your aesthetic need to decorate the backyard. Designs ranging from plain to highly ornamental are available from bird preserves, pet stores, and garden centers and are usually post-mounted. The important thing to check when buying

Left: *Many types of roofed bird tables can be purchased inexpensively. Better still, you can construct your own.*

Above: *A post-mounted dovecote provides a sheltering place for pigeons, and also makes an attractive addition to the backyard. Choose a site that is protected from prevailing winds, rain and too much sun.*

a birdhouse is that it will fulfill the needs of the type of birds you want to attract. Each of the projects featured here indicates the typical inhabitants that it is designed for, but you also need to consider local breeds.

ROOSTS

Most birds sleep at night with their beaks hidden under one shoulder, their heads tucked in, and their feathers puffed up to keep them warm. They need regular roosting places that are protected from the elements and from predators. Birds will often use nest boxes for this purpose, so do not despair if your house or box has not been selected for a nest site—it is still probably being used as a roost or shelter, so it will be doing an important job, and possibly saving birds' lives in severe weather conditions, including icy temperatures and storms.

BIRDBATHS

Birds get much of the water they require from their food, but they still need supplies to supplement this. Seed eaters, in particular, need plenty of drinking water

Right: *These cosy woven roosts provide a place for birds to sleep or shelter from inclement weather. They are inexpensive and look attractive tucked between the branches of a tree.*

to compensate for the lack of moisture in their diet. Most birds drink by dipping their beaks into the water, then tilting their heads back, although pigeons are able to suck water up through their bills. Because birds do not sweat, they need another way to keep cool. They lose moisture by opening their mouths and panting.

The main purpose of providing water for birds is not for drinking but for bathing. All species need to keep their feathers in good condition for both flight and insulation, and baths are just as important in wintertime as they are in summer. If their

Above: *Birds need regular bathing to keep their feathers in good condition. During winter, break any ice regularly and never put antifreeze into the water.*

plumage is not properly maintained, birds will not survive the cold winter nights. In frosty weather, it is vital to check daily that your birdbath has not frozen over.

A design for a birdbath with an ingenious anti-freezing device has been included in this book. It is important never to put antifreeze or salt into the water—this can kill birds.

FEEDING TIMES AND BOX LOCATIONS

When providing tables, feeders and nest boxes in your backyard, it helps to understand birds' daily rituals, preferred feeding times and food types so that you can get the best results. It is also important to choose appropriate sites for your nest boxes, to maximize their safe use and minimize aggression.

In North America, common feathered visitors include cardinals, juncos, titmice, chickadees, finches, mourning doves, and American robins. Depending on location, wrens, sparrows, thrashers, crows, grackles, towees, and mockingbirds may also pay regular visits to backyards.

Migration makes for interesting changes. At the end of winter, some of your regulars will return to the countryside or migrate to more suitable breeding grounds. You may suddenly notice the odd bird that has never visited your backyard before: it may be looking for food to fuel its journey, or it may have been swept off course by bad weather. During the winter, there will be many visitors looking for food, but come spring, the battle for territory will begin, limiting the number of birds in your yard.

DAILY RITUALS
Birds wake up just before dawn, when they sing with great gusto. The dawn chorus involves many different species and lasts about half an hour, heralding the daylight.

Breakfast is a good time to observe birds' behavior, when they often quarrel over food. You will soon start to notice a

Below: *Blue jays* (Cyanocitta cristata) *enjoy eating from bird tables, particularly if there are oak trees nearby, and their playful behavior is always entertaining to watch.*

pecking order. The first birds to visit the backyard may be thrushes and blackbirds, who come to scan the lawn in search of earthworms and soft grubs. They hunt quietly and carefully, pausing between hops and watching for their prey. Starlings, who may appear later, seem to stab at the ground until they find a tasty morsel.

Birds have two important daily activities. The first is to find and eat food, which is done throughout the day; the second is to take care of their feathers. These must be kept in perfect condition for both flight and insulation. After bathing comes preening. Birds collect fatty oil

Above: *Although wonderful to watch, fledglings must learn to survive, so any human intervention is not a good idea.*

from the preen gland at their rump and smear it over the feathers before stroking them back into place.

WHAT TO FEED WHEN
Birds will quickly come to depend on your support, so once you have enticed them into the backyard, you need to make sure that they continue to thrive. It is important to maintain supplies of food and water throughout the winter. The birds will appreciate fresh food on the table first thing in the morning, or at least at a regular time. If you need to go away, fill up your feeder and leave fat balls to sustain your avian visitors until your return.

Birds need food with a high fat and carbohydrate content, as they may lose up to 10 percent of their body weight overnight in bad weather. Suet, cheese, and bacon rinds will help them build up their energy reserves. Crows, starlings, titmice, and woodpeckers particularly like these.

The shape of a bird's beak roughly indicates its diet. Finches have hard, thick beaks that are designed to crack and crush. They feed mostly on grain and seed.

Above: *Be careful that nest boxes are mounted high enough on trees so that there is no danger of animals, such as cats, reaching the box, especially when there is a ledge attached to the outside.*

Warblers and wrens, with their slender, soft beaks, eat caterpillars, grubs, and other insects. Gulls, starlings, and blackbirds have general-purpose bills, which let them eat a little of everything. Whatever the species, they all enjoy culinary variety, and kitchen scraps are always welcome.

Bread is the food most commonly put out for birds, but it is not particularly good for them. If you do give it, soak it first in water or, even better, fat. In fact, any dried foods—especially fruits—should be soaked. Never give birds dry, shredded coconut or uncooked rice. These will swell up in their stomachs and can kill. Kitchen leftovers, such as baked potatoes and spaghetti, are good, because they are soft enough for birds to eat but difficult for them to pick up whole to fly away with. Keep some of your windfall apples and pears in storage for winter, when they will be most welcome on the bird table. Do not worry if birds don't visit your feeder immediately— it may take up to two weeks for a bird table to be accepted by the neighborhood bird population.

SITING AND MAINTAINING BOXES

When choosing sites for your birdhouse and other accessories, there are several points to keep in mind. Will birds be left in

Above: *Feeders containing seeds, peanuts, or chopped fruit can be used to attract birds such as chickadees (*Paridae family*) to your backyard. These small, lively birds have considerable agility.*

peace there? It is not a good idea to erect a table, nest box, or birdbath where children play or where the pet cat tends to prowl. Birds must have shelter nearby to which they can flee if danger threatens.

Place nest boxes in sites where they are protected from the prevailing wind, rain, and strong sunlight. If you put a box on a tree, notice which side of the trunk has more algae growing. This will be the wet side, so place the box on the opposite side. If you angle the box slightly forward, it will give more shelter to the occupants.

Be careful not to damage the tree by banging nails into it; special securing devices are available for this purpose. Boxes do not have to be rigidly mounted, as long as they are secure. Nest boxes that hang from a wire or string work well and may well offer better protection from predators, such as cats.

The best time of year to put up nest boxes is in fall. The boxes can then act as roosts during the winter and be ready for early spring when the birds start choosing their breeding sites. During winter, you can insulate the boxes with cotton, straw, or wood shavings for roosting birds, but remember to remove this padding before nesting begins in the spring. Cleaning out birdhouses and nest boxes after the

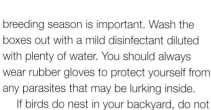

breeding season is important. Wash the boxes out with a mild disinfectant diluted with plenty of water. You should always wear rubber gloves to protect yourself from any parasites that may be lurking inside.

If birds do nest in your backyard, do not be tempted to sneak a peak—the shock may cause the mother to abandon her brood, or the chicks to leave the nest prematurely. The best help you can give nesting birds is to leave them undisturbed.

AVOIDING AGGRESSION

To discourage fighting, do not overdo the number of boxes you set up in your backyard. Species such as titmice can be very territorial and aggressive with other members of their species. A bird's territory is the finite area that it will defend for either feeding or breeding, or both. If a bird does not manage to establish its own territory, it will be unable to nest or breed, and may even die of hunger.

The gestures birds make to communicate with one another are known as displays. To show aggression, a bird will puff up its feathers, raise its wings, and point its beak at its rival to look menacing. To show submission, a bird will crouch down and sleek its feathers in. Fights most commonly occur when a newcomer arrives in the territory of an established group, and the stranger's status needs to be evaluated. Occasionally, birds will fight to the death.

Below: *Water can be provided for birds in small backyards by hanging up bowls or attaching containers or troughs to a wall.*

BACKYARD MENACES

In the last hundred years or so, birds generally have been threatened by changes to or loss of the wild habitats where they feed and breed. In backyards and parks, feeding and nesting birds may be at risk from menaces, such as cats, squirrels, and predatory birds, including hawks and magpies.

Most of the songbirds that visit backyards die young through either predation or natural causes, such as cold. The average life expectancy for an adult songbird is less than 2 years. This compares to a potential lifespan of 7 or 8 years for titmice, 12 years for sparrows, and up to 20 years in the case of larger species, such as blackbirds and starlings.

It is not only winters that are perilous; summers claim as many lives, and breeding time is as dangerous as migration. If you encourage birds to visit your backyard, it is also your duty to protect them, especially from "unnatural" predators, such as cats.

PREDATORY BIRDS
Birds of prey, such as hawks and falcons, including the American kestrel, can be a danger to backyard birds. Most falcons approach fast and low, appearing as if out of nowhere to seize small birds in midair. American kestrels mostly hunt on the

Below: *Corvids, such as the black-billed magpie, are omnivorous, with a diet that includes songbirds' eggs and nestlings in the breeding season.*

ground. A number of falcons are known after their favored prey. For example, the merlin is also known as the pigeon hawk. The pererine falcon is called the duck hawk. In the 1950s and 1960s, populations of falcons, hawks, eagles, and other predatory birds declined due to use of the powerful pesticide DDT, but many species staged a recovery after DDT was banned. Scientists have estimated that a breeding pair of falcons may need to kill as many as 2,000 small birds to raise their family.

Members of the crow family, known as corvids, are a danger to nesting birds worldwide. In springtime, crows, jays, and magpies raid songbirds' nests to steal eggs and nestlings. Magpies in particular have been known to conduct systematic raids, returning to raided nests after a suitable interval to take replacement clutches. These habits make magpies and their kin unpopular with songbird lovers. However, there is no hard scientific evidence that predation by corvids has any long-term effect on populations of songbirds.

Providing thick cover for nesting birds, such as dense shrubs and hedges, increases their chance of survival. You can also put wire mesh over the nest entrance to exclude corvids while letting small nesting birds enter. This is best done once

Above: *The American kestrel* (Falco sparverius) *is also known as the sparrow hawk after its favorite prey, the house sparrow* (Passer domesticus).

the eggs are laid and the birds start incubating, or there may be a danger that the parent birds might abandon the nest.

Woodpeckers (Picidae) have been known to drill into nest boxes with their long, sharp bills, or simply reach inside to steal the nestlings. Enclosed nest boxes for small birds, such as titmice, can be protected by backing the nest hole with a metal plate drilled with a similar-size hole.

RATS, MICE, AND SQUIRRELS
Food left on the ground encourages rats and mice, which will take every opportunity to steal and eat birds' eggs. The rodents are attracted to surplus food, so do not put out too much at any one time. If you store bird food outdoors, do so in a strong, sealed container. This will also help to prevent the food from being spoiled by moisture.

The gray squirrel is a menace to songbirds both in North America and now in parts of Europe, where it was introduced in the 1800s. With keen intelligence, acrobatic skills, and sharp teeth and claws, these rodents are a menace on bird feeders

Above: *A gray squirrel displays the acrobatic skills that make it a menace at bird tables. Feeders that are enclosed by a stout wire cage can help thwart such raids.*

and tables. Mounting tables on smooth, slippery posts, which can be made from plastic drainpipes, will prevent squirrels and also cats and rats from clambering up to steal food. A number of squirrel-resistant feeders can also be purchased nowadays. These usually consist of a feeder enclosed by a strong wire cage designed to admit small birds but exclude squirrels. However, these rodents are very destructive, and have been known to bear away the whole feeder, so they can attack it at their leisure! Some bird lovers resort to providing the squirrels with their own supply of nuts in the hope they will leave bird feeders alone.

Gray squirrels not only steal birds' food but also raid nest boxes to steal eggs and young birds. A metal plate around the entrance hole will help to prevent squirrels from enlarging the hole by gnawing. Tree-mounted boxes can be fitted with smooth protective collars of plastic projecting from the entrance hole, or be mounted on a slippery backplate. Some people take the precaution of building an internal ledge underneath the entrance hole of the box, so that the nestlings have somewhere to hide if a predator trespasses.

CATS

The single biggest threat to backyard birds is not any wild mammal but the much-loved domestic cat. In Great Britain, for example,

the cat population exceeds 7 million, of which at least 2 million are feral cats living in the wild and hunting for survival. Scientists estimate that between 30 million and 75 million birds are killed by cats each year in Great Britain alone. Because the higher figure only represents each cat killing a bird every month or so, it is credible. Unlike magpies and squirrels, domestic cats kill adult birds, which is more likely to have an impact on bird populations.

If you have a cat, put a bell on its collar to alert the birds to its presence, or keep it inside while the birds are at their morning feed. Alternatively, a pet dog let out at the same time will help to deter visiting cats. To prevent cats from killing in your backyard, position feeders and bird tables out in the open, where felines cannot use the cover of shrubs to stalk their prey. Make sure nest boxes are sited in places cats cannot reach. You can also put chicken wire or nylon mesh around a box, as long as there is room for the birds to get in and out.

PROTECTION FOR WILD BIRDS

In every part of the world, there are organizations that are involved with the protection and conservation of wild birds, and all are happy to answer queries. Contact local groups for information about the birds in your area.

In North America and many other areas, including Great Britain and other European countries, it is against the law to kill, injure, or capture wild birds, or to remove or destroy their eggs. Contact the local police

Above: *Mice and even rats can be surprisingly acrobatic, raiding food sources high above the ground with the help of a nearby shrub or tree.*

or a conservation organization, such as the American Bird Conservancy, if you see or suspect someone is killing or trapping birds or stealing eggs. We can all play a part in helping to ensure that these remarkable creatures survive in all their variety, despite losses to their natural habitats.

Below: *The cat's natural agility and hunting instincts make it a formidable predator. Attaching a bell to a collar will alert birds to the cat's presence before harm is done.*

FEEDING BIRDS

The simplest way to attract birds to your backyard, or even window box, is to put out food for them, particularly during the months of winter when natural food becomes much scarcer. However, you may also provide appropriate food for backyard birds throughout the year if you want.

Whatever feeding method you decide upon, be consistent. A wasted journey to an empty bird table uses a bird's precious energy supply, especially as winter progresses and food becomes more difficult to find. Ideally, feed birds twice a day in winter: once in the early morning and again in the early afternoon.

In spring and summer, feeding can still be helpful, but do follow rules for safety and hygiene. Do not use peanuts unless they are in a mesh container; this will prevent the larger pieces, which can choke baby birds, from being removed. In summer, avoid fat cakes; the fat will melt and become very messy, and can also glue birds' beaks together.

Below: *Roofed bird tables will keep birds— and the food provided—dry in wet weather. This one was made from pieces of fallen wood collected from the forest floor.*

Above: *Lard cakes studded with seeds appeal to many varieties of bird, including this starling (Sturnus vulgaris).*

Above: *Ground feeders provide food for birds that forage for seeds at ground level, such as dunnocks, finches, and thrushes.*

BIRD TABLES

Ideally, a bird table should be placed approximately 6½–10 feet (2–3m) from a bush or tree, which can provide safety for birds in case of danger, and at least 16½ feet (5m) from the house. Many birds are nervous of open sites, but they can have accidents flying into house windows, and may be scared away by the movement of people inside the house. Window stickers featuring birds of prey are available. When stuck to the window panes, these indicate the presence of an otherwise invisible surface and will deter smaller birds from flying too close to the house.

A bird table gives you a clear view of feeding birds, and offers the birds some protection against predators and the elements. Use wood that has not been treated with wood preservative if you are making your own table. A roof will keep the food and feathered visitors dry. If you do not make a roof, drill a few holes in the floor of the table for drainage. A small lip around the edge of the food table can prevent lighter food items from being blown away by wind. The bird table must be cleaned

Above: *When snow covers the ground, small birds are at serious risk of dying from hypothermia. Backyard foods, such as sunflower and peanut hearts, can be vital in these conditions to species like goldfinches. Your bird table may well be visited by a flock of these foraging birds.*

from time to time and any food that is past its best should be removed. An adequate supply of water should be provided all year round, but this can be as simple as a bowl of water placed on the surface of the table, or a separate facility.

GROUND STATIONS

Birds such as grackles, thrushes, and American robins are habitual ground feeders. Finches, sparrows, buntings, and doves may also be attracted to ground feeding stations—a wooden or plastic hopper secured to a strong base. Place ground stations away from the bird table, so that the food is not contaminated by droppings from the birds above.

HANGING FEEDERS

Chickadees, titmice, and other species that are adapted to feeding in trees will benefit from a more challenging feeder. These small birds can cling upside down from various types of hanging feeders, and may be joined by siskins and nuthatches. Many types of feeder are available, or you can

Above: *Seed balls and strings of nuts are a welcome supplement to the meager diet that is available to many birds in winter. Remember to keep a supply of fresh water on hand, because dried food does not contain enough natural moisture.*

make or adapt your own, using the projects shown in this book. Some foods are also suitable for hanging without a feeder, for example, peanuts in their shells, popcorn garlands, and fat cakes on strings.

Right: *Hanging feeders offer an easy challenge to species with natural acrobatic abilities, such as titmice (Paridae). In this way, suspended feeders can provide an added spectacle at the bird table.*

WHAT TO FEED BIRDS

As warm-blooded or endothermic animals, birds have to expend considerable energy maintaining an even body temperature. This process is particularly costly in terms of energy in cold weather, so when temperatures drop toward freezing point, providing food for birds is especially important.

Like many wild creatures, birds enjoy a range of foods. Many of these are easy for bird lovers to obtain. Leftovers are a valuable but variable commodity. Seeds are very useful and can be supplemented with such items as pinhead oatmeal or porridge oats, golden raisins, shredded suet, and toasted bread crumbs. Other popular items for the bird table include cracked corn, canned corn, and fruit, broken into pieces.

The greater the variety of foods that can be provided, and the more types of feeder, the better. Whatever you decide to place out for the birds, make sure that you stick to natural foods, rather than chemically altered or processed items, such as margarine. Keep food fresh—leave out only enough for a day or two—and never let food or feeding debris accumulate because it can spread disease.

FAT PRODUCTS
The best types of base for fat cakes are lamb and beef fats, either in natural form or as processed suet. Because these are

Below: *A live feeder can help a variety of birds, including bluebirds, that rely on invertebrate prey to feed their young.*

Above: *A coconut section filled with seeds and melted fat is a good way of providing supplementary food for small, clinging birds.*

hard, they do not melt too readily in warm weather, which can potentially glue birds' beaks together. Manufacturers add enticements to their fat cakes, but you can easily make your own at home with a mixture of seeds, fruits, and nuts following the recipes on the next pages.

LIVE FOOD
Some birds, bluebirds in particular, can benefit from supplements of live food, such as waxworms and mealworms, including during the springtime when their breeding cycle is in progress. The worms can easily be purchased from pet stores or by mail order, and can be placed on tables or in specialty feeders.

SEEDS AND GRAINS
Use best-quality seeds from a reliable source, not sweepings or waste seeds, because these are neither of interest nor of nutritional value to the birds. Black sunflower seeds rather than the striped variety are the favored food of many

species. The skins of this type are the thinnest of all sunflower varieties, making them easy for the birds to open. All types of sunflower seeds are safe for young birds to eat, so they may be offered all year round. Canary seeds, melon seeds, hemp seeds, small wheat, kibbled and flaked maize, corn kernels, and oatmeal are all good sources of nutrition. The exact mixture of seeds you put out can be fine-tuned to attract particular species of birds to your backyard. You can consult a specialty catalog for more details.

UNSALTED PEANUTS
Buy only high-quality "safe nuts," marked as such by a reputable ornithological organization or similar body, to ensure that the nuts are free from lethal toxins. Whole peanuts are best avoided during the nesting season because of the danger they pose to nestlings. They should be chopped, if left on a table, or placed in a mesh peanut feeder from which adult birds can take only small fragments.

Below: *A string of peanuts provides nutrition and can also look attractive if hung in a well-chosen site, such as this.*

COMMON BIRD FOODS

The variety of seed and other food supplements for birds that are commonly available in stores or by mail order has increased vastly in the last few years. All have their own merits and will be preferred by different types of birds. Trial and error will show what goes down best with the feathered population in your local area, but here are some ideas.

Mixed seeds
Consists of various seed types for a wide range of birds, but can be of variable quality.

Black sunflower seeds
More commonly known as the "oil sunflower," this seed—as its name suggests—is rich in oil and ideal for feeding a range of birds in winter.

Striped sunflower seeds
This type of seed has a lower oil content than the black variety, and is useful in the springtime when natural foods become more abundant.

Niger
Also called thistle seed, this tiny black birdseed is high in calories and oil content, and is quickly devoured, especially by finches of various types.

Grain
Consists of any commercially grown crops in the grass family, including wheat, millet, maize, and oats.

Bread
This is eaten by many species. Wheat bread is best, but whatever type you offer, make sure that it has been thoroughly soaked to avoid the danger of it swelling in birds' stomachs.

Dried and fresh fruits
Always popular, dried fruit should be soaked as for bread. Fresh fruits, especially pears and apples, are enjoyed by some types of thrushes. These fruits are particularly useful in winter.

Split coconuts
Hanging on a string, a section of coconut offers good value for money and provides delightful entertainment when titmice come to feed. Once the flesh has been stripped, the shell can be filled with a wholesome mixture of nuts, seeds, and melted fat.

Fat ball
A ball of suet into which other dried foodstuffs have been incorporated. It is usually hung in nets or special feeders.

Suet cake
The block type of suet food contains a mixture of seeds that provides a balanced diet for many species. It is ideal for feeding birds if you are away for any period, although the fat content can sometimes attract scavenging mammals, such as rats, to the table.

Fruit suet treats
Mainly for bird tables or feeders, this suet-base cake is best made with moist, dried fruit and peanut granules, and is popular with larger birds.

Dried mealworms
These freeze-dried grubs are an excellent source of protein for invertebrate-eating birds.

Peanuts
In their shells, peanuts can be strung on thread or wire, but do not use multistrand thread because birds may get their feet caught in this. Do ensure the nuts are fresh—moldy ones produce a toxin that kills many backyard birds.

Hazelnuts
Wedged into tree bark, hazelnuts will appeal to nuthatches, which will enjoy hammering them open.

Cheese
Grated cheese is a popular food with some types of songbirds.

Leftovers
Household foods, such as hard-boiled eggs, baked potatoes, uncooked pastry, and stale cake and cookies are all widely available choices that birds will enjoy. Feel free to experiment, being careful not to offer dehydrated, spicy, or salty foods, because these can be dangerous.

Grit for digestion
Although not actually foodstuffs, grit, sand, and gravel aid digestion, particularly for seed eaters.

Mixed seeds

Black sunflower seeds

Niger

Dried fruit

Fresh fruit

Fat ball

Suet cake

Fruit suet treats

Dried mealworms

Peanuts

Cheese

Leftovers

SWEET TREAT

This prettily shaped treat will look attractive in the backyard and make feeding the birds more fun, especially if you want to interest your children in bird-watching. You can also mold fat treats in empty yogurt containers, but remember to let the mixture cool before filling.

YOU WILL NEED
3oz (75g) lard
pan
shelled nuts
seeds
berries
wooden spoon
twine
heart-shaped mold
raisins
dried cranberries
tying wire
wire cutters
bowl of water
ribbon

TYPICAL FEEDERS
starlings
titmice
nuthatches
waxwings

Above: *Starlings love sweet foods, and may drive away competing visitors to this treat.*

1 Place the lard in a pan and slowly melt it over a gentle heat. When the lard has completely melted, stir in a generous mixture of shelled nuts and seeds and also some berries.

2 Lay a doubled piece of twine in the bottom of the mold and spoon in the nut-and-seed mixture, embedding the twine within it. Smooth the top of the treat and let stand to cool completely.

3 Thread raisins and cranberries alternately onto a piece of tying wire long enough to surround the heart-shaped treat. Twist the ends together and soak the wreath in water to plump up the fruit.

4 When the treat is set, turn it out of the mold and tie the twine to the twisted ends of the wire so that the heart is suspended in the middle of the wreath. Tie a ribbon over the join to hide it.

OTHER SWEET TREATS
These simple recipes are designed to bring birds flocking to your backyard and ensure a healthy, satisfied bird population. For both, you will need a filling made with nuts, seeds, and dried fruit, and either granola or cooked rice.

Orange sunrise mixture
Prepare a mixture of granola, fruit, nuts, and seeds for the filling. All these ingredients should be fully soaked to rehydrate before mixing. Cut an orange in half, and remove the flesh to create a hollow. Fill with the mixture.

Bejeweled apple
An apple stuffed with colorful, nutritious goodies is a visual as well as a nourishing feast. Hollow out an apple that is past its best. Fill it with a mixture of cooked rice, seeds, rehydrated dried fruit, and berries. Make sure the fruit has been thoroughly rehydrated before adding.

FAT TREAT

When the weather gets colder, backyard birds keep warm by eating high-energy foods, such as this hanging fat, fruit, seed, and peanut snack. The design will suit acrobatic birds, such as titmice. You can make several and crumble one on to the bird table, too, for less agile species.

YOU WILL NEED
package of suet
pan
wooden spoon
bird seed
raisins
fresh peanuts
aluminum foil
scissors
household string
yogurt container or plastic plant pot

TYPICAL FEEDERS
titmice
sparrows
finches
starlings
woodpeckers

Below: *When hung from a tree, this tasty fat treat makes an attractive backyard decoration in its own right.*

1 Melt half a package of suet in a pan on a low heat. Keep it on the heat until the suet is melted. Stir until the fat turns clear.

2 Take the pan off the heat. Add mixed bird seed, broken-up peanuts, and a few raisins. Stir the mixture, then let it cool.

3 If using a plant pot, cut out a circle of aluminum foil to fit inside the bottom of the pot to cover the drainage holes.

4 Twist a length of string to make a thick cord. Tie a knot at one end. This will stop the snack from falling off when hanging.

5 Hold the knot at the bottom of the pot with the string upright. Now spoon the fat-and-seed mixture into the pot. When the pot is full, firm the mixture down with the back of the spoon. If you have more mix, repeat with another pot.

6 Stand the pot outside to let the mixture cool and set. When it has set and is hard, remove the snack from the pot by squeezing the pot sides carefully. Peel off the foil base. Now hang the treat from a branch using the loop of string.

FESTIVE TREATS

These treats will bring color to your backyard on dark days of the year, and provide birds with the sustenance they need most in cold weather. The ideas described here will make good presents for friends who are already bird lovers, or they can be the start of an engrossing hobby.

CRANBERRY WREATH

To make this wreath, you will need glazed sliced cranberries, a length of wire, string, and a pretty ribbon. Thread the cranberries onto the wire to form a ring. Twist the ends together and tie a loop of string at the top to hang the wreath. Now add the ribbon tied into a bow at the top.

CRANBERRY TERRINE

This delectable treat is quick to make. Melt down some lard or white fat in a pan. Place a layer of rehydrated cranberries into the bottom of an individual oval pan. Slowly pour over just enough melted fat to secure the berries in place. Let it cool and set. When set, add more melted fat to form another layer. Let this cool and set before adding the final layer of berries, secured with a little more melted fat. Let it set, and remove by inverting the pan. Run a little warm water over it to aid release.

NUT AND BERRY LOAF

A festive loaf will delight the birds in midwinter. Soak brown bread crumbs in water until soft. Mix in rehydrated

berries, seeds, and nuts. Grease an individual loaf pan, and add the mixture, pressing down well. Bake in a moderate oven for about 15 minutes, or until the top is golden brown and the loaf leaves the sides of the pan. Let cool slightly, remove from the pan, and cool on a wire rack.

GIFT BASKET

A basket of bird food makes a thoughtful gift. You will need several different types of food. Roll plastic containers diagonally in squares of wax paper to form bouquetlike cones. Put a different type of bird food in each. Recipes for additional bird treats can also be included, or a decorative container to hold water.

Left: Bags containing different varieties of bird food make a great gift, packed into an attractive wooden basket.

Above: *A wreath of glazed, sliced cranberries will be appreciated by the feathered community.*

A BIRD BORDER

Winter is the time of year when birds most need our help. A border planted with birds in mind can be a real lifeline during this period, providing a diverse array of foods, including seeds, berries, and even the odd overwintering insect among the vegetation. The border will also provide color throughout the year.

A bird border does not have to be wild or overgrown, but can look attractive all year round. There are few absolute rights or wrongs when you plan one, but growing a wide variety of plants to attract wildlife in general will offer backyard birds food and shelter, helping them both survive winter and feed their hungry fledglings the following spring. Think of your bird border as a roadside café, a place where birds can feed and rest before moving on.

CHOOSING A SITE
Some species of birds are much more sensitive to disturbance than others, particularly during the nesting season. For this reason, it is usually best to set aside a quiet area for a bird border. The ideal backdrop might be a hedge or line of berry-bearing shrubs. If you are planting against a fence or wall, clothing it with climbing plants and shrubs can turn it into a "living boundary" that will provide cover and nesting sites. Bird borders can be made on any scale, with even a small one proving useful, although the more space and diversity you can devote to such a feature, the more birds will benefit.

Below: *Songbirds, such as American goldfinches, appreciate the abundant seeds produced by the large seed heads of sunflower plants* (Helianthus annuus).

CHOOSING PLANTS
Depending on where you live, it is often best to include a range of native plants in your border, and you should try to include as many different kinds as possible. In the illustration shown opposite, a formal backdrop has been created by using a hedge made of yew *(Taxus baccata),* although beech *(Fagus sylvatica),* holly *(Ilex aquifolium),*

Below: *Rudbeckia (black-eyed Susan) brings color to a bird border in fall. The conical seed heads provide food for birds.*

Above: *Barberry* (Berberis *species) is an ideal plant to include in a bird border, offering nestlings much-needed protection from predators in spring, as well as a rich crop of berries in fall.*

and privet *(Ligustrum* species) are equally effective, all providing good shelter for birds. If space permits, try a less formal hedge of native shrubs, pruned on only one side in alternate years to provide an excellent source of food and nectar, as well as nesting and shelter.

Trees are also extremely useful, but large forest species, such as oak *(Quercus),* are often too large for most backyards. If choosing trees for a town garden, make sure you use smaller examples. Mountain ash *(Sorbus aucuparia),* holly *(Ilex aquifolium),* and crab apple *(Malus* 'Red Sentinel') will provide perches and shelter, and are an excellent food source when in fruit.

A range of shrubs will provide cover from predators and the worst of the weather. Native species might come top of the list, but it is equally important to consider a range of evergreen and deciduous types to give variety and hiding places in winter. The barberry *(Berberis*

thunbergii atropurpurea) is an attractive semievergreen whose thorny branches offer protection to small birds from the likes of cats. Firethorn *(Pyracantha coccinea)* offers similar protective cover for larger birds, and both have berries that can be eaten over winter. The Oregon grape *(Mahonia aquifolium)* is a slightly shorter, evergreen, prickly leaved shrub with berries that ripen in summer, while both elder *(Sambucus nigra)* and black currant *(Ribes nigrum)* are deciduous species that attract many insects and bear summer berries.

Ideally, in addition to these woody plants, you should aim to plant a range of annual and herbaceous plants. Natives are very useful but, if you want a more ornamental look, choose a range of showier species that will attract insects in spring and summer, and later produce good seed heads to help feed small birds.

Lastly, you might want to leave some space in your border for a birdbath and feeders, providing food supplies when natural sources run low.

Above: *Songbirds, such as northern cardinals, use the dense vegetation provided by shrubs in borders as nesting sites.*

Above: *The downy woodpecker usually feeds on wood grubs and other insects, but occasionally eats fruit in winter.*

BIRD BORDER

A good bird border needs to provide a range of food throughout the seasons. The plants featured here are chosen to either attract insects or bear fruit in the summer, or are rich in seeds and/or fruit in the winter months. It also includes a range of trees, shrubs, and smaller herbaceous plants.

1 *Polygonum bistorta*— Common bistort
2 *Artemisia vulgaris*— Mugwort
3 *Helianthus annuus*— Sunflower
4 *Sorbus aucuparia*—Rowan
5 *Berberis thunbergii atropurpurea*—Barberry
6 *Achillea millefolium*— Common yarrow
7 *Oenothera biennis*—Evening primrose

8 *Lavandula angustifolia*— English lavender
9 *Ribes nigrum*— Black currant
10 *Sambucus nigra*— Elderberry
11 *Pyracantha coccinea*— Firethorn
12 *Ilex aquifolium*—Holly
13 *Angelica sylvestris*— Wild angelica
14 *Amaranthus caudatus*— Love-lies-bleeding

15 *Myosotis arvensis*— Field forget-me-not
16 *Mahonia aquifolium*— Oregon grape
17 *Malus* 'Red Sentinel'— Crab apple
18 *Taxus baccata*—Yew
19 *Dipsacus fullonum*—Teasel
20 *Solidago virgaurea*— Golden rod
21 *Lunaria annua*—Honesty
22 *Viburnum opulus*— Guelder rose
23 *Tanacetum vulgare*—Tansy
24 *Melissa officinalis*— Lemon balm
25 *Ribes uva-crispa*—Gooseberry
26 *Cotoneaster horizontalis*— Rock cotoneaster
27 *Fragaria vesca*— Wild strawberry

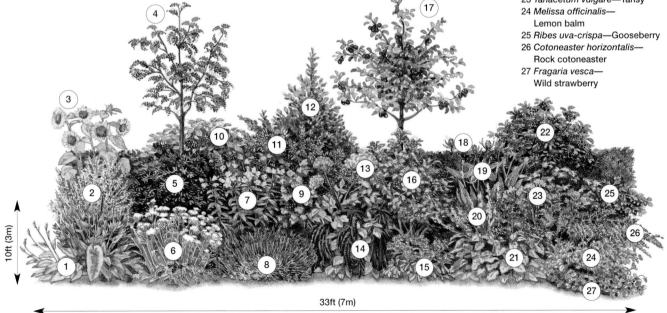

A WILD AREA FOR BIRDS

A wild corner of the backyard offers the closest substitute to a natural habitat for birds and, if designed properly, can be very attractive. However, a wild backyard should not be thought of as a low-maintenance option and be left to become completely chaotic. Regular maintenance is still required.

Wild backyards differ from other styles of wildlife gardens primarily because they use only native plants. It is precisely because of this that more traditional gardeners sometimes deride them, regarding them as little more than weed patches. But many native plants are not only supremely beautiful, they are also well adapted to the site and particularly soil conditions of the area. In addition, many provide cover for birds and food, such as seeds and berries.

Thankfully, recent years have seen a reversal of the traditional form of gardening, with native plants now being commonly seen in an ornamental setting. With a little imagination they can form an immensely attractive display. Avoid plants that are known to be invasive—there are always less troublesome, attractive alternatives. Native plants also offer certainty that they are excellent choices for local birds in terms of their food value.

Below: *Wildflower areas are more accessible if paths are mown through. Several species of butterflies will lay their eggs alongside the mown paths, producing caterpillars that feed many young birds.*

Above: *Seed eaters, such as cardinals, house finches, and this tufted titmouse, find a wealth of food in wild backyards.*

MAINTENANCE
Always choose a range of plants that will flower and also provide foods, such as seeds and berries, over as long a period as possible. When it comes to maintenance, most native plant species are no different from other backyard plants. However, here

Above: *In dappled shade areas, a mass of spring bulbs, such as wild garlic, offers a welcome early supply of nectar for insects.*

the general effect can be somewhat untidy. Fallen plant debris harbors many overwintering insects, which are eaten by birds. Those dead flowers in the borders are often a rich source of seed for birds in winter. The real difference in making a wild area is that you will have created a refuge for birds and a host of other creatures, using a rich diversity of native plants, many of which are becoming increasingly rare in the wild.

Below: *Many different butterflies are attracted to wild backyards, where they feed on nectar from flowers. Their caterpillars provide food for birds.*

WILD BACKYARD

A design for a wild backyard has to be as well thought out as a formal design. Care should be taken to include as many different habitats as possible, especially wildflower meadows and deciduous trees, which support myriad insects to feed birds. Short-cut grass areas are kept to a minimum. Deadwood is left in place to harbor more insect food for birds.

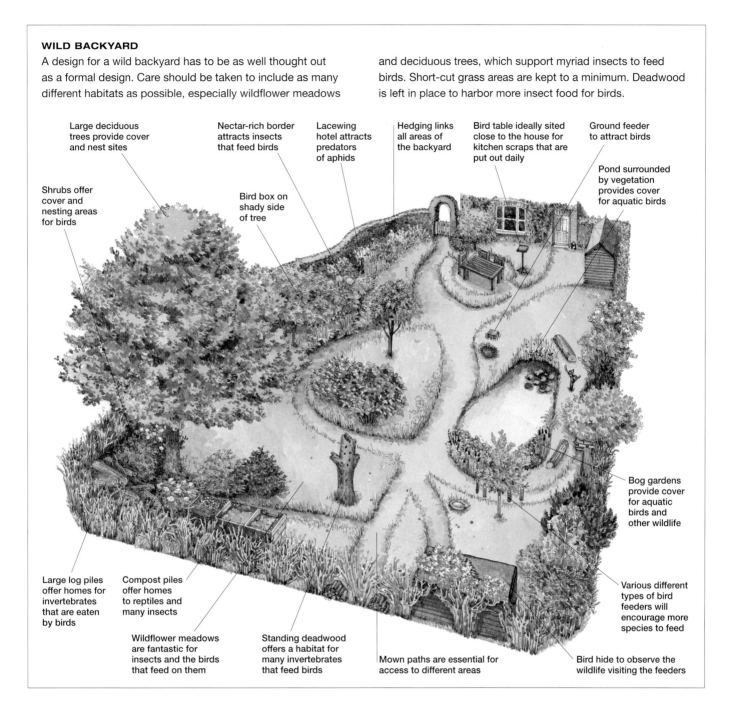

Large deciduous trees provide cover and nest sites

Nectar-rich border attracts insects that feed birds

Lacewing hotel attracts predators of aphids

Hedging links all areas of the backyard

Bird table ideally sited close to the house for kitchen scraps that are put out daily

Ground feeder to attract birds

Shrubs offer cover and nesting areas for birds

Bird box on shady side of tree

Pond surrounded by vegetation provides cover for aquatic birds

Bog gardens provide cover for aquatic birds and other wildlife

Large log piles offer homes for invertebrates that are eaten by birds

Compost piles offer homes to reptiles and many insects

Wildflower meadows are fantastic for insects and the birds that feed on them

Standing deadwood offers a habitat for many invertebrates that feed birds

Mown paths are essential for access to different areas

Various different types of bird feeders will encourage more species to feed

Bird hide to observe the wildlife visiting the feeders

Above: *Water lilies provide walkways for moorhens and a landing pad for damselflies, dragonflies, and frogs.*

Right: *Letting short grass regenerate can result in areas rich in Queen Anne's lace, its seeds feeding birds in fall.*

LAWNS FOR BIRDS

In many backyards, grassy areas all too often consist of manicured lawns, which are of only limited benefit to birds and other wild creatures. With just a few changes to the way we maintain our lawns, however, we can transform them into superb wildlife habitats.

The most common use of grass in the domestic backyard is in a lawn. These often carefully tended features mimic grassland in certain respects but, in many ways, the traditional lawn is different from its wild counterpart. In its close-cropped, well-tended state, a lawn might look good to humans, but as a habitat for birds it does not offer much. Changing a lawn from what is effectively a green desert into a thriving habitat often involves little more than outlawing the use of fertilizers, pesticides, and weed killers and reducing the amount of mowing you do. This will have an almost immediate benefit for birds and other wildlife, but it may take some years before the full effects appear. And the time saved maintaining the lawn can be spent more usefully elsewhere in the yard.

THE IMPORTANCE OF LONG-GRASS AREAS

There is a simple truth where grass in your backyard is concerned. If a lawn is less frequently mown and not walked on wherever possible, it soon becomes richer in invertebrates that are eaten by birds. Indeed, long-grass habitats are some of the most useful undisturbed areas in the yard and are very simple to provide. Where space is limited, they may be restricted to strips of uncut grass alongside a hedge, or around the base of a tree. However, if space allows, they can form more extensive

areas. Whatever the size of a long-grass area, they are an important, sheltered habitat and may provide cover for birds and a range of other creatures. Insects, such as bumblebees or other wild bees, often prefer to nest in longer grass, while grasshoppers or the caterpillars of moths will feed on the grass leaves and small creatures, such as spiders and beetles, move in to eat them. All these species provide food for invertebrate-eating birds, while seed eaters, such as finches, pigeons, cardinals, titmice, and sparrows, may also search the area for food.

Below: *The California poppy has attractive blue-green foliage and orange flowers. It will grow well in poor but well-drained soil.*

Above: *Spring and summer are the most spectacular time for meadows. Flowering reaches its peak at this time and the sight is truly stunning.*

WILDFLOWER MEADOWS

Lawns that are converted into miniature wildflower meadows can be an important refuge for declining wildflowers, and are an excellent habitat for many insects and spiders that are eaten by birds. Lawns in full sunlight are especially useful, attracting solitary bees and butterflies, and flowering plants, such as poppies, coneflowers, and rudbeckia, are excellent food plants that provide food for both bugs and birds.

TYPES OF GRASS

In nature, grassland is a rich and varied habitat that is molded by the effects of geography, climate, soil, and, in many cases, human intervention. Choosing the right type of grassland for your needs will depend on all these factors. Where you live will automatically decide the first three, but the last factor is your choice, depending on what you want for your backyard.

Prairie is a term used to describe the vast areas of flower-rich grassland that once clothed North America, and is similar

Below: *Pigeons and doves are seed eaters that may find rich pickings in long grass. Other birds feast on insects that lurk there.*

Above: *Lawns provide good hunting grounds for birds that feed on invertebrates, such as earthworms and snails, including this grackle* (Quiscalus quiscula).

to the European steppe. The soils in these wild habitats are often richer than those found in artificial meadows, and they are often full of colorful flowering plants that provide seeds for birds. Many of these are now familiar backyard plants. The effect is potentially relatively easy to establish in most backyards, because it depends on rich soil, with similar mowing regimes to those used in meadows.

Short grass, sometimes called downland turf, is most commonly seen in temperate regions. It is usually the result of grazing livestock and the consequent short-cropped turf contains a multitude of flower species. It is the closest model to

Below: *Wildflowers and some insects, such as this hummingbird hawkmoth, provide color in backyards, as well as food for birds.*

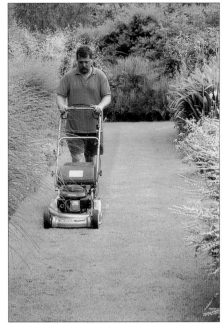

Above: *Traditionally, lawns in backyards are kept short by frequent mowing. Although this keeps the grass healthy, it results in a poor wildlife habitat.*

the modern backyard lawn, and can be maintained by regular (if infrequent) cutting by a mower on a high setting.

Hay meadows are a traditional way of managing grassland for the hay that is cut in the summer months and stored for animal fodder. The long grass frequently harbors many species of wildflower during spring and early summer, creating an extremely attractive habitat. Wildflower seeds are eaten by birds, such as finches.

Traditional forms of management often resulted in poor soil that reduced the vigor of the grasses and favored the growth of wildflowers. Sadly, modern intensive agriculture has seen a severe decline in these habitats and consequently in many wildflower species that benefit birds.

Wet meadows or flood meadows are largely similar to hay meadows, except that they are subject to seasonal flooding, usually in winter, and consequently harbor different species of birds. All types of meadow can be established in backyards to benefit birds, but they need to be situated carefully and cut during summer, when they are not that attractive. Also note that they can be hard to establish on lawns that have been previously well fertilized.

Marginal grassland is a term used to describe remnants of grassland plant communities that survive on field margins, roadsides, or waste ground. These areas are often a last, vital refuge for grassland birds and also native flower species and their dependent wildlife that were formerly common in the area. The same effect can be created in your backyard by leaving a wild grassy area at the bottom of a hedge. In terms of maintenance, all you need to do is cut the grass back every year or two, preferably in late winter.

Below: *Even when you intend to let the grass grow, short-cut paths provide access and create vegetation of different heights that benefits insects. Some insects lay their eggs by paths, providing food for birds.*

PLANTING A WILDFLOWER MEADOW

*An area of long grass is a valuable habitat, providing cover for birds, insects, and other wildlife.
Wildflower meadows and flowery lawns are actually easier to create than you might think. You
can add wildflowers by reseeding an area or by planting pot-grown plants into existing grass.*

The first step in transforming an existing lawn is to think about what you want it for, and how much you want to change. If it is important to keep the same amount of lawn, the simplest approach may be to change to wildlife-friendly maintenance. Alternatively, reduce the area of short-cut lawn to a minimum, with wildflowers.

CHANGING AN EXISTING BACKYARD LAWN
Assuming that you intend to keep some lawn, the simplest change is to let flowering plants colonize it. Reduce the frequency of cutting, and stop fertilizing, using pesticides and weed killers, or watering it. The initial

effect may be hard to see, but low-growing, broad-leaved plants will soon begin to get a foothold. Even letting areas on a clover-rich lawn have a flowering break for a week or two will help the bees.

CREATING A WILDFLOWER LAWN
Most grassland wildflowers grow best in full sun and open spaces with minimal root competition from trees, so choose your site accordingly. New lawns are best grown

Right: *Insect-eating birds and seed eaters, such as this chipping sparrow, will benefit from a wildflower meadow, which will also enhance the diversity of your backyard.*

PREPARING THE GROUND AND SOWING WILDFLOWER MEADOWS

1 Start the project by marking out the area you intend to convert to a wildflower meadow. It is best to use a rope or hose to establish flowing lines and curves.

2 Once you have finalized where the edge of the meadow is to be, cut the line in the existing sod using a half-moon edging tool, following the line made by the rope.

3 Lift the existing sod, digging deep enough to remove all grass plants. Plants growing in wildflower meadows prefer nutrient-poor substrate and little topsoil.

4 Once the sod has been lifted and removed, lightly cultivate the whole area with a fork, before raking it to produce a light, crumbly seed bed ready for sowing.

5 Mix the wildflower seeds into the grass seeds before sowing to make it easier to distribute evenly. Lightly sow the mix at a rate of ½ ounce per square yard (15g/m^2).

6 The grass and wildflower seedlings will soon emerge, and the light sowing rate ensures that the grass does not swamp the less vigorous wildflowers as they develop.

from seeds that are either bought premixed or that you mix yourself. Ideally, the mixture will produce about 60–80 percent grass coverage, with the remainder being filled with wildflowers. The seed mixture should be sown sparingly to avoid the grasses outcompeting the wildflowers, at a rate of ½ ounce per square yard ($15g/m^2$) or less.

You can make an existing lawn richer in flowering plants that will benefit birds by overseeding in fall with a mixture of wildflower seeds. To overseed an area, cut the grass as low as possible and rake away the debris, leaving bare patches of soil. The seeds are mixed with some fine, dry sand, and thinly sown over the bare patches and then raked in lightly.

The results from overseeding can be variable, and many gardeners prefer to plant container-grown wildflowers directly into an existing lawn. Mow the lawn early in the season and scrape or use bare patches for planting into. Arrange the young plants in groups of three to nine for the best effect and maximum chance of success. Once planted, the lawn can be mown on a high setting every two to three weeks in the first year to reduce the competition from grasses. The following year, the lawn can be mown less often.

MOWING LONG GRASS

The amount of time and effort a bird-friendly lawn needs will vary. Shorter lawns need little change to their maintenance because the basic method of mowing remains the same, albeit less frequent.

Long grass is trickier, not least because it can be a fire hazard during dry weather. Always site an area of long grass at least 20 feet (6m) away from buildings or other

TOP PLANTS FOR A WILDFLOWER MEADOW
For a pretty, low-maintenance wildflower meadow, a mixture of native, European, and Asian species produces good results. The flowering plants listed below provide color, shelter, and food for birds and insects. Some native grasses are also listed.

FLOWERING PLANTS
Black-eyed Susan (*Rudbeckia* species) The many types of rudbeckia produce long-lasting, yellow, daisylike flowers.

California poppy *(Eschscholzia californica)* This perennial produces yellow to orange flowers from February to September, and later fruits containing numerous small black seeds.

Coreopsis (*Coreopsis* species) Plains coreopsis and lanceleaf coreopsis both yield attractive yellow or red flowers.

New England aster *(Symphyotrichum novae-angliae)* Has flowers with deep purple or pink petals and yellow centers.

Purple coneflower *(Echinacea purpurea)* Produces lavender or purple flowers with red-orange, cone-shape centers.

Queen Anne's lace/Wild carrot *(Daucus carota)* This pretty plant has a delicate filigree head of dainty flowers in summer—an excellent source of food for insects.

GRASSES
Broomsedge *(Andropogon virginicus)* Reaches a similar height to little bluestem and also turns orange in fall. These two species may be seeded together or separately.

Little bluestem *(Schizacyrium scoparius)* This grass reaches a height of up to 3 feet (90cm) tall, and turns an attractive orange color in fall.

Sheep fescue *(Festuca ovina)* This grass reaches a maximum height of about 2 feet (60cm) tall, and has an attractive bluish color all year.

Black-eyed Susan

Purple coneflower

Queen Anne's lace

Sheep fescue

combustible items. A buffer zone of conventional lawn can be made more attractive by cutting the first strip of lawn next to the tall grass on the highest mower

setting, and reducing this by one setting on each consecutive strip, so that the longer grass blends in gradually.

Mowing a margin between long grass and features, such as flower borders, also means that the grass will not collapse onto them following rain or storms. If you have a large lawn, mow a pathway through it so you can watch ground-feeding birds and other wildlife without having to trample on the tall grass. Frequently mow areas you want to keep as paths.

Hay and water meadows are usually best cut after they have stopped flowering, although, if space allows, you can try leaving some areas of long grass uncut until late winter to provide shelter for birds and hibernation sites for insects. When you do cut the grass, remove all the clippings, usually after letting them lie for a day or two, to let any wildlife escape.

PLANTING WILDFLOWERS INTO EXISTING GRASS

1 Set out small wildflower plants grown in pots, and, once positioned, cut out and remove a plug of sod before planting.

2 The wildflower plants, once planted into the grass, have a head start and are able to compete with the surrounding grass plants.

HEDGES FOR BIRDS

Widely used as boundaries and dividing features in agricultural and also urban landscapes, hedges are important habitats for birds and many other creatures. Properly managed, they provide shelter and food for birds, and are home to many once-common and often beautiful wildflower species.

A hedge can be defined as a boundary of closely planted woody shrubs or trees. The earliest known use of the word dates back to Anglo-Saxon times. The Anglo-Saxons of western Europe used hedges as a way of defining ownership of land, but their hedges were unlike those of today, being more like a rough fence, and often containing as much deadwood as living material. Ancient hedges were made up of many plants that benefit birds, such as hawthorn *(Crataegus monogyna)*—haw means "hedge" in Old Saxon—and roses.

In times gone by, farming was less intensive and hedges were just another place for birds and other animals to shelter and forage. In both the Old and New World, land clearance, intensified agriculture, and growing populations later put pressure on wild habitats, and hedges became a refuge for many native birds and other species. In this way, mature hedges are now a tangible link with the wildlife that once inhabited the woodland edge and open spaces, containing a rich variety of birds and other animals, and a multitude of plant species, both woody and herbaceous. Hedges are often a prime habitat in their own right.

Below: *Hedges are often rich in seed- and berry-producing shrubs that provide an ideal food source for overwintering birds.*

THREATS TO TRADITIONAL HEDGES

The intensification of agriculture in recent decades, coupled with the introduction of large machinery, has meant that many areas that were traditionally managed using hedges as part of the rural landscape have been transformed beyond recognition.

Machinery, such as tractors and combine harvesters, work most efficiently in large fields, and hedges were seen as taking up valuable land that could produce crops. In addition, hedges in the United States contained a lot of barberry *(Berberis),* and this was identified as the alternative host species of the wheat rust *Puccinia graminis*, which is a serious fungal disease of commerically grown wheat.

The net effect of this was that farmers on both sides of the Atlantic were encouraged to remove hedges. In doing so, a rich and vital habitat was removed from the landscape. In the case of European hedges, the rich legacy of over a thousand years was lost in some cases, leaving birds and other wildlife in a precarious position. Backyards became one of the few places where hedges remained common, and as such they are a valuable resource for birds.

Above: *Even where a more formal effect is required, you can choose hedging plants that benefit birds and other wildlife.*

HEDGES AND WILDLIFE

The traditional approach to hedges in backyard settings has been to cultivate a tight-cropped and controlled shape with many closely planted specimens of the

Below: *Hedge species, such as this hawthorn, have abundant spring blossom that attracts insects, and in turn birds.*

same species. But while highly decorative, these have limited appeal to wildlife. Some birds are able to find shelter in the dense growth, but the range of species is limited, as is the likelihood of finding much food.

A more wildlife-friendly approach lies in planting a mixed hedge. Remember that a mosaic of plant species will favor a wider range of wildlife. Choose plants that provide food in the form of nectar-rich flowers and berries for overwintering birds. Hawthorn *(Crataegus)*, wild roses *(Rosa)*, holly *(Ilex)*, and elder *(Sambucus)* are good all-round choices. You could also consider planting shrubs, such as cotoneaster,

TYPES OF HEDGE

Hedges are diverse, partly as a result of their function but also because of how they are maintained.

Mixed hedges Simply, a mixed hedge is one where the intention is to grow a range of species and provide a habitat that has the maximum species diversity. This type of hedge is most like a natural woodland edge.

Single-species hedges These hedges are common, especially in backyards, where their intention is to provide a consistent backdrop or feature. They can be useful for birds provided that a suitable species is chosen.

Formal hedges Found in highly manicured yards and cut with a smooth face, the high frequency of their cutting and general absence of flowers or fruits mean that formal hedges are less useful for birds.

Informal hedges As the name suggests, these are hedges where the cutting regime does not entail frequent cuts or a smooth face or finish. They can be planted as single- or mixed-species hedges.

Dead hedges These barriers consist of dead branches and twigs that are firmly staked in place. Climbers are left to ramble through them and provide excellent shelter for birds.

barberry and pyracantha, which produce plenty of berries for the birds.

Resident birds will appreciate hedges for shelter and also breeding. For this reason, wildlife hedges should not be trimmed in the nesting season, from early spring to late summer. Human impact can be further lessened by cutting back (not too tightly) only one side of the hedge in alternate years. Ideally, hedges should be lightly pruned in late winter so that birds can take advantage of the insects, fruits, and buds during the cold months, and then again in summer and fall.

Hedges are especially important habitats because they share key characteristics with two other habitats—woodlands and open fields—providing corridors for wildlife, and

Above: *Tanagers (Thraupinae), such as this western tanager, seek the cover of trees and hedges to feed on insects and berries, and also to provide refuge from predators and the elements.*

letting species disperse and move from one habitat to another. Always let the hedge bottom—the portion where the base of the hedge adjoins another habitat, such as grassland—become overgrown with grasses and flowers. The bottom is characteristically the dampest and most fertile area, and often proves to be the part richest in wildlife. Plants also find it difficult to spread across open fields, and "traveling" along the base of a hedge is their only realistic option.

Below: *The bottom of hedges often provide a refuge for woodland flowers. The same area is also rich in birds and other wildlife that find refuge there.*

Below: *Honeysuckle is a good example of a hedge climber that is useful for birds and other wildlife, such as moths, and is also ideal as an ornamental plant.*

PLANTING A WILDLIFE HEDGE

A wild hedge can be a real boost to a bird-friendly backyard. The best usually consist of mixed plant species that provide nesting sites and year-round cover for birds. They may also produce flowers and berries. Single-species hedges provide less variety, but may still be useful if managed properly.

When deciding what kind of hedge will most benefit birds and other wildlife, you should also consider your own needs. If the hedge is also to provide security or a barrier, or if you need a certain height, then check the plants' possible dimensions. Also note that a wildlife hedge will not be frequently pruned, and can grow both tall and wide in a single season.

The most bird-friendly hedges include a range of four or five species in varying numbers. The exact species will vary considerably according to the conditions,

but any plants chosen should always be compatible in their maintenance requirements when grown as a hedge.

CHOOSING HEDGE PLANTS

Start by walking around and observing your neighborhood, looking at the hedges and seeing what plants are growing well. Try to choose at least half of your plants from locally indigenous species because they will often be the ones that will prove most valuable to native wildlife. If possible, when looking at other hedges growing locally,

Above: *Some grosbeaks are birds of hedges and woodland edges. They benefit gardeners by eating insect pests.*

make notes about the range and types of wildlife they attract. A single-species hedge can be useful, if only because all the plants will have the same maintenance requirements. For plants that flower and set fruit, you can try escallonia, elder, or barberry, all of which attract insects and birds. Traditional agricultural hedges mainly consist of up to 80 percent of one species, such as hawthorn, but will usually also contain other trees and shrubs. This creates a variety of blossom, berries, and scent with a range of niches that make such a hedge the best choice for birds. If you have a large backyard, this type of hedge may be appropriate, but for a typical suburban neighborhood, a single-species hedge may be more aesthetically pleasing.

SETTING OUT AND PLANTING A HEDGE

1 Start by leveling your previously prepared ground, using a rake to ensure that there are no rises and dips on the row.

2 Consolidate the ground to make sure there are no void spaces by lightly treading the area with a flat foot, not your heel.

3 Rake the ground level, either with a rake or using the back of a fork. It is always best to start planting into level ground.

4 Using a spade to make a planting pit, slide the roots down into the hole, ensuring all are covered.

5 Using the heel of your boot, make sure the plant is firmly planted, with no air spaces around the stem.

6 Use guards to protect the stems from rabbits. These also shelter the young plants from the wind.

PREPARATION AND PLANTING

When planting a wildlife hedge, prepare the soil properly beforehand. Dig a trench at least 20 inches (50cm) wide, and mix plenty of organic compost and a general fertilizer such as blood, fish, and bone, at around 2 ounces per square yard (50g per m²). Refill the trench and let it settle for a few weeks before planting. Hedges are usually planted as either single rows of plants, about 1 foot

CUTTING A HEDGE

1 Once the hedge begins to outgrow its setting, it must be cut. This should be done before or after nesting time.

2 Set out a line of canes every 7ft (2m) or so to mark the line you want to cut, thereby producing a good face.

3 Before cutting the top, set out a string line to mark the desired height and ensure that a straight line is maintained.

4 Even for neat wildlife hedges, the finished cut should not be too tight as it will still preserve a somewhat informal look.

(30cm) apart, or as staggered, double rows with the same distance between the plants and rows. When planting, peg out a line of string to keep the hedge straight. Species such as beech and hawthorn *(Crataegus)* are best planted at a 45-degree angle to encourage thick growth at the bottom.

To stimulate dense, twiggy growth, trim off one-half to two-thirds of the total height of the hedge and then, for the first two or three years, remove at least half of the new growth during the winter period. Mulch the bottom of the rows annually, and apply an organic feed just before you mulch.

MAINTAINING YOUR HEDGE

Once established, trim your hedge every second or third year, but avoid doing so when birds are nesting. The ideal time is in late winter, making nuts and berries available to birds for the longest possible period. Try cutting opposite faces of the hedge in alternate years where space is restricted, or if a slightly more formal shape is desired, because this will produce some flowers and fruit each year.

The best shape for a wildlife hedge is an "A" shape, because the sloping sides let light and rain reach the bottom of the hedge. An established hedge, say four to five years old, can be enhanced by planting climbers that benefit birds, such as honeysuckle *(Lonicera),* roses *(Rosa),* and clematis. However, be careful, because planting climbers before the hedge is well established can result in the hedge being overwhelmed and strangled. You can also plant wildflowers at the bottom of hedges to provide extra cover for birds.

TOP HEDGE PLANTS FOR BIRDS

Any hedge has potential as a wildlife habitat, but the species described here are among the most useful to the widest range of birds.

Blue mist *(Caryopteris clandonensis)* This shrub, growing to 4 feet (1.2m), bears blue flowers that attract bees.

Chokecherry *(Prunus virginiana)* This tree, growing to 20 feet (6m), produces clusters of white flowers and black fruit.

False indigo *(Amorpha fruticosa)* This shrub, growing to 8 feet (2.4m), has delicate foliage and clusters of purple flowers. A favorite with insects.

Fernbush *(Chamaebatiaria millefolium)* A dry-tolerant shrub up to 8 feet (2.4m), it attracts bees and insect-eating birds.

Golden currant *(Ribes aureum)* This attractive shrub, growing to 6 feet (1.8m), has fragrant yellow blossoms. It is a good understory plant for moist areas.

Gooseberry *(Ribes leptanthum)* This understory shrub, growing to 5 feet (1.5m), flowers in early spring. The fruits are enjoyed by many birds.

Mulberry *(Morus* species) This tree, growing to 49 feet (15m), has glossy foliage, and produces multiple sweet berries that attract birds and wildlife.

New Mexico locust *(Robinia neomexicana)* This thorny shrub, growing to 10 feet (3m), produces large clusters of magenta blossoms.

Russian sage *(Perovskia atriplicifolia)* This silvery-gray shrub, growing to 4 feet (1.2m), bears purple flower spikes throughout the summer, which attract insects and insect-eating birds.

Silver buffaloberry *(Shepherdia argentea)* This large shrub, growing to 10 feet (3m), is an excellent hedge plant that yields bright berries in fall.

Wild plum *(Prunus americana)* This shrub, growing to 8 feet (2.4m), yields abundant white flowers that attract insects, and later, edible fruit. It also provides cover for nesting birds.

Blue mist   Gooseberry   Mulberry   Russian sage

WOODLAND AREAS FOR BIRDS

Wooded areas provide a rich and varied habitat for birds and other wildlife. Woodland varies greatly, depending on location and the tree species within it. In many cases, it is also a product of the way in which it has been managed. A wooded area in your backyard can benefit many kinds of birds.

Vast areas of the earth's surface are still covered with trees. Natural, undisturbed woodlands are one of the most diverse habitats found anywhere on the planet. There are many different types of woodlands. Each type harbors a different community of birds and other wildlife,

Below: *Trees are tall, long-lived plants that form a dense shady habitat. Ground-cover plants only grow in springtime before the trees form their leaves.*

which is important if you want to create a woodland area in your backyard.

Almost all woodlands can be divided vertically into a series of layers called stories, which contain different plant species. The tallest and most dominant trees form the topmost layer, called the canopy. The canopy can either be closed, in the case of dense woodland, or more open, with sunlight penetrating between the trees. Beneath the canopy is a layer of less dominant tree species, called the

Above: *American redstarts are seen in wooded backyards. Their preference for the second-growth woodlands that cover much of the country means they are widespread.*

understory, and beneath that is a layer of smaller, woody plants and immature trees called the shrub layer. The ground layer, or forest floor, is covered to a greater or lesser extent with a layer of herbs. The soil is continuously enriched by the decomposing leaves, shed from trees either throughout the year, in the case of evergreens, or in fall, in the case of deciduous trees.

Below: *Fallen leaves and seed cases often form a dense layer on the woodland floor. These slowly break down to release nutrients for trees and other plants.*

Above: *Taking a long time to die, trees often become full of deadwood, which in turn provides a habitat for invertebrates.*

Above: *Clearings in woodlands, such as this one alongside a path, often attract birds and other wildlife.*

TYPES OF WOODLAND

Broad-leaved woodlands contain a greater variety of birds than any other wooded area found outside the tropics. They are dominated by trees with wide, flat leaves. There is considerable variation between broad-leaved woodlands in different locations in respect of the birds and other wildlife they contain. The trees here mostly lose their leaves in fall in order to survive harsh winter weather.

Coniferous woodlands grow naturally in northern parts of North America, Europe, and Asia. The trees here are mostly adapted to a cold, harsh climate and a short growing season. Coniferous woodlands are less productive in terms of birds than deciduous woodlands, but nonetheless support species such as woodpeckers, owls, and crossbills.

Temperate rain forests grow in areas with warm summers and cool winters, and can vary greatly in the diversity of plant life they contain. In some, conifers dominate, while others are characterized by broad-leaved evergreens. The largest tracts of these forests lie along the northwest coast of North America, but they are also found in southwest South America, New Zealand, and Tasmania. Small, isolated pockets of temperate rain forest grow in other areas. Despite their rarity, these are amazingly diverse natural habitats and home to some of the world's most massive trees.

TRADITIONAL MANAGEMENT

In many areas where woodland once formed extensive cover, much has now been removed and the vast majority that remains has long been managed by people. Despite the loss of ancient "wildwoods," the remaining managed woodlands prove to be excellent habitats for birds, whose exact nature depends on the system of management employed.

Coppicing is a traditional method of woodland management, by which young tree stems are cut down to 1 foot (30cm) or less from ground level to encourage the production of new shoots. This is done repeatedly through the life of the tree and results in a habitat that transforms from a clearing into a woodland habitat. Many familiar woodland birds, such as jays and woodpeckers, are well adapted to these woodlands. Pollarding is a similar system but involves cutting the branches from a tree stem 6 feet (2m) or so above ground level. Pollarding was mostly practiced in wood pastures and grazing areas where cutting above head height protected the new shoots from being damaged by browsing animals.

THE BEST WOODLAND FOR BIRDS

The ability of woodland to support birds and other wildlife varies considerably. The age of a woodland and the variety of plant species it contains have a part to play, as does the way the wood has been managed. Generally, open woodland, especially when deciduous, is more accessible than closed woodland to species that browse and graze, and tends to be richer in ground-level plants.

The woodland floor is often rich in species that feed on decaying plant matter. Deadwood is also important for many insects that live in rotting wood and feed birds. Where the greatest concentrations of wildlife occur will vary greatly according to the type of woodland, but the richest areas always tend to be those that border other habitats, for example, at woodland margins. Fortunately, the latter woodland type is the easiest to recreate in a backyard.

Below: *Clark's nutcrackers visit backyards with conifers. They sometimes wedge pinecones into bark crevices to pry out the seeds with their slender beaks.*

PLANTING TREES AND SHRUBS

Trees and shrubs form the essential framework of any backyard, providing cover for a variety of birds, as well as nesting sites that are well above the ground and safe from ground-dwelling predators. The secret to success in planting lies in careful ground preparation, stock selection, and planting.

When selecting plants, always choose trees and shrubs that are vigorous, healthy, and suitable for the site conditions or intended usage. They should always be free from any obvious signs of damage, pests, or disease. If you are buying bare-rooted stock, make sure that the roots never dry out before planting, and keep them covered at all times—even a couple of minutes left exposed to cold or drying winds can cause a lot of damage. You should plant them as soon as possible; if the soil is frozen or waterlogged, plant them in a temporary bed of soil mix, at

a 45-degree angle (this is called heeling in), and keep them moist until you are in a position to be able to plant them.

PREPARING THE GROUND
Despite what is written in many books and guides, organic additives, such as soil mix, can be a mixed blessing if they are incorporated into soil at planting time. An enhanced soil mix does improve the soil

Right: *Nuthatches are woodland birds, feeding on seeds and insects. The white-breasted variety visits wooded backyards.*

PLANTING AND STAKING TREES

1 Container-grown trees should be thoroughly watered an hour before you plant them. Soak really dry ones overnight.

2 Clear any weeds and cut any suckers coming from the roots, because these may slow the tree's top and root growth.

3 Once you remove the pot, tease out any encircling roots to encourage root spread in the soil and to prevent root-balling.

4 Dig the planting pit and ensure that it is deep enough for the root-ball. Check by lying a spade or fork on its side.

5 Backfill the pit, firming the soil with a heel every 3 inches (8cm) to make sure it is well planted and has no large air pockets.

6 Drive the stake in at an angle to avoid damaging the roots. Face the stake into the prevailing wind for stronger root growth.

7 Secure the stem of the tree, using a tie nailed on to prevent movement. To avoid chafing the stem, use one with a spacer.

8 The tree should remain staked for about a year, during which time the tie must be checked and loosened.

MULCHING A TREE

1 Young trees growing in grass are often slow to establish due to competition from the surrounding plants.

2 Remove the sod around the tree. Create a cleared circle around the stem of the tree that is 3 feet (1m) in diameter.

3 Thoroughly water the ground, then apply a layer of mulch to a depth of about 2 inches (5cm) on the cleared circle.

4 The tree must be kept clear of weeds and vegetation for around 4 or 5 years. Water thoroughly in dry conditions.

but also causes the plants to become "lazy." Simply, the roots like soil mix better than the surrounding soil and circle around as if in a pot, resulting in an unstable "corkscrew" growth pattern known as girdling. Avoid this by applying organic matter across the surface after planting. This creates more natural conditions and encourages insects, including beetles. Apply fertilizers only if really needed, after planting but before mulching.

WHEN TO PLANT

Plant deciduous species during early winter, when they are dormant. Evergreens, on the other hand, tend to do well if planted either in early fall or late spring. Trees and shrubs growing in containers can be planted throughout most of the year, provided that the ground is kept sufficiently moist, although they, too, will generally establish best in the cooler months. Never plant when the soil is frozen, excessively dry, or waterlogged, because this may damage the roots and lower stem. Make planting holes big enough, adding one-quarter to one-third of the diameter again of the root spread. Check that the plant is at the same depth as it was before.

STAKING AND PROTECTION

Large shrubs and trees require staking to prevent them from blowing over in their first season. Smaller, more vulnerable stock is protected by putting it in a tree or shrub shelter that helps stems thicken, promotes rapid upward growth, and protects plants from rodents and sometimes deer attack.

TOP TREES FOR BIRDS

If you have the space, trees are a valuable feature for birds, and by choosing the species carefully, you can greatly enhance the wildlife potential of your backyard.

Apples and crab apples *(Malus sylvestris)* These are a familiar fixture in many backyards. The older varieties are best, supporting diverse insects on the leaves and stems. The buds are eaten by some birds, as is the fruit. The tree is of most use to birds if left largely unpruned.

Oak *(Quercus robur)* While this long-lived tree has outstanding value for birds, it is too large to grow in most backyards. There are over 600 species, enjoying different climates, and some are the richest habitat trees available for insects and birds.

Pine *(Pinus nigra* and *P. radiata)* Pines are among the best conifers for birds, offering a source of seeds that are taken by many species. The dense crowns are used by nesting birds, such as owls. These trees are an excellent choice for dry soils, although they eventually grow very tall.

Red mulberry *(Morus rubra)* The mulberry produces berries throughout the summer that are eaten by at least 40 different bird species. This is an ideal tree for moist, fertile soils. Keep it clear of pathways and patios, because the fruit can be messy.

Rowan *(Sorbus aucuparia)* A medium-sized tree that is well suited to the smaller backyard. There are numerous closely related species and cultivars. Birds visit rowan trees but rarely make them a permanent habitat. Insects love the flowers, while birds, especially thrushes, often feed on the attractive, bright red berries in the fall.

Sugar maple *(Acer saccharum)* This maple fruits between early summer and fall. It attracts birds, such as pileated woodpeckers, as well as numerous insects. In fall, the leaves provide spectacular color, ranging from yellow through orange to deep red.

Crab apple   Oak   Pine   Sugar maple

CREATING WOODLAND EDGES

Woodland edges are found where forests and woodlands give way to more open areas. These are potentially highly productive habitats for birds, offering a wide range of foods, shelter, and breeding sites for species that are usually restricted to wooded areas.

Woodland is most diverse at its edges, either at the treetops of the upper canopy, where there is plenty of light, or adjoining another habitat. Here, species from both areas meet and share the space. The exact nature of the edge is largely dependent on the adjoining habitat. Often this is grassland or cultivated land but, equally, it can be marsh or open water. Either way, the

woodland produces an abundance of growth each year during the growing season. This leads to a rich organic layer deposited over the soil that produces very fertile ground, both within and just beyond its limits. Most backyards, even relatively large ones, do not have room for an area of naturalized woodland, but you may be able to accommodate a group of several small

or medium-size trees, which will support many insect species and provide food and perches for birds.

SITING A WOODLAND EDGE

A woodland edge is easier to recreate than you might think. Even if space is limited, shrub borders fulfill some of the role of a woodland edge, and, if managed correctly,

Above: *Woodland edges are home to a great abundance of plants, such as this blackberry, which thrive in dappled shade areas. Birds feed on the summer fruits.*

Left: *Where trees and shrubs give way to grassland, the mosaic of different habitats is naturally rich in plants and birds.*

REMOVING A TREE STAKE

1 Start by removing any nails that were used to secure the tie to the stake, then unbuckle the tie. Do this carefully and avoid pulling at it because this can potentially damage the bark of the tree.

2 Gently loosen the tie by feeding the belt back through the spacer block that was used to prevent the tree's stem from chafing on the stake. Check the stem for any sign of damage.

3 Remove the stake by gently rocking it back and forth until it can be pulled upward. If it is too firmly in the ground you might have to cut it off with a saw, being careful to avoid the stem.

Above: *Pileated woodpeckers regularly visit backyards near woods, and may appear more often if you plant a woodland edge.*

hedges can also attract woodland-edge species. Choose a strip along an edge of the backyard facing the sunniest direction. This means you will minimize shade on the rest of the yard while the woodland-edge border gets the benefit of sunshine, which will widen its appeal to a greater range of birds. Alternatively, make it face the afternoon sun. This will, of course, cast shade on your backyard in the morning, but this need not be a problem. The plants often benefit most from the afternoon sun, especially in the cooler seasons. When choosing a site

Below: *Planting a mixture of trees and flowering shrubs in narrow strips mimics the edge of a woodland. You should remove tree stakes after one year.*

TOP WOODLAND EDGE PLANTS FOR BIRDS

Woodland edges are naturally rich in flowering and fruit-bearing species, many of which provide vital food for a variety of birds, insects, and other wildlife.

CANOPY PLANTS

Apples and crab apples *(Malus)* Deciduous, small, shrubby, spring-flowering tree with abundant round, fleshy, applelike fruits that follow large, cup-shape, white, pink-flushed flowers that attract bees. A food source for many insects and birds.

Box elder *(Acer negundo)* A small, usually fast-growing and fairly short-lived maple whose winged seeds are sometimes eaten by birds and other animals. The sugary sap is sometimes eaten by songbirds.

Rowan *(Sorbus)* This group includes the familiar rowan tree or mountain ash *Sorbus aucuparia,* which becomes heavily laden with bright red berries that are enjoyed by birds in the late summer and early fall. A versatile genus with many species and cultivars.

SHRUB LAYER

Rose *(Rosa)* Roses can be extremely attractive shrubs. If possible, plant a wild species and choose single flowers over double types, because these are best for visiting insects. The hips that follow the flowers are often eaten by birds.

Rubus An important group of bird-friendly shrubs that includes the common blackberry *(R. fruticosus).* Care should be taken when choosing this because it can easily become very invasive. Many other species and cultivars are good garden specimens.

Viburnum A very varied group of plants that includes a wide range of species and hybrids, with good wildlife value and an attractive appearance. Choose varieties with berries, such as either arrowwood *(V. dentatum)* or blackhaw *(V. prunifolium),* to provide food for birds.

Crab apples   Rowan   Rose   Viburnum

for your border, do not forget to discuss your plans with neighbors, whose backyards may be affected by the shade the trees will cast. A wall or a fence is the ideal back boundary for your woodland edge because it can provide support for some of the climbing plants that benefit birds.

PLANTING AND MAINTAINING A WOODLAND EDGE

Plant a woodland edge so that there is a general increase in height from the front to the back of the area or border, thereby letting light reach all the plants. The tall plants at the back are called the "canopy edge" plants. In a narrow border, you will need around one canopy tree for about every 17 feet (5m). Choose smallish, sun-loving woodland trees, particularly those that bear berries to feed birds. The plants in front of this are the shrub layer, with the

herbaceous layer forming the lowest layer at the front. Growing under the canopy trees, these layers can include both sun-loving and shade-tolerant plants because the canopy trees cast very little shade on the border. There is always room for variety, though, and many smaller, more shade-loving plants, such as early perennials and bulbs, can easily be planted among the taller woody plant species.

Surprisingly, managing an area of your backyard like a woodland edge takes far less time and work than you might imagine. Once planted, you just need to keep the area well watered until everything is established. You should also keep an eye on the border for the next few years, making sure that no one plant is dominating and smothering the others. Eventually, though, the area should need little or no maintenance.

PONDS FOR BIRDS

No wildlife-friendly backyard would be complete without a pond, which provides a bathing and drinking site for birds and a habitat for many other creatures. With its aesthetic appeal, a pond makes a worthy addition to any design, but where space is limited, even the smallest patch of water can be useful.

The term "pond" is surprisingly vague, there being no clear distinction between a large pond and a small lake. The average backyard pond is relatively small, but a well-designed pond can attract a greater variety of wildlife than any other single feature in the backyard.

WILDLIFE VALUE

A pond provides not only a drinking and bathing site for birds, but also a breeding site for amphibians and for a whole host of insects, such as dragonflies, that spend part of their life here. In addition, it is the sole habitat for a range of other creatures, from water snails that spend their life underwater to pond skaters that skim across the surface.

Below: *Even a relatively small area of water can be an attractive backyard feature, which results in a surprisingly diverse habitat for birds and other creatures.*

Above: *Aquatic birds, such as coots and moorhens, may take refuge in backyards near wetlands or with water features.*

Right: *Ponds are full of interest, often revealing curiosities, such as this empty dragonfly larva case in the summer.*

PLANTS FOR WETLANDS
Natural wetlands contain both open water and wet ground, with different plant species living on the margins and in deep water.

Marginal or emergent plants These plants have roots and sometimes stems that grow in shallow water, but with shoots, leaves, and flowers above the water surface.

Oxygenators These important plants live beneath the surface and enrich the water with oxygen.

Water lilies and deep-water aquatics The roots of these plants are submerged, the leaves are on the surface, and the flowers are either on or above the surface.

Free-floating plants The leaves and stems are free-floating on the water surface. The roots are submerged and the flowers grow on or just above the water.

Bog plants These are plants that prefer to grow in permanently wet or waterlogged ground. Some species that flourish on pond margins can also be grown as bog plants.

Ponds should be shallow at one end to provide a bathing area for birds, and if possible have wet, muddy margins to attract birds needing a drink. Ponds also provide a unique visual focus, and have a restful quality that is hard to match.

POND PLANTS
Plants are essential to the health of any small area of water, enabling the habitat to achieve a correct water balance and provide surface cover on otherwise open water. Without them the water would, over time, probably start to resemble a thick pea soup, as algae—small, mostly microscopic, plantlike organisms—will start to grow prolifically and ultimately color the water. Plant leaves have the double action of absorbing both carbon dioxide and minerals from the water, which in turn starves the algae. Many natural bodies of still or slow-moving water have extensive cover of floating plants, and their sides are also shaded by larger, bankside or shallows vegetation.

In a backyard pond, it is easy to recreate this by ensuring that there are plenty of submerged plants. About half the surface should be covered with foliage and the margins should have plants that are capable of surviving immersion in shallow water in order to achieve this balance. This will keep the water clear and will also make the pond attractive for birds and a host of creatures that are either regular visitors or residents.

Above: *Pond dipping will help you to assess what wildlife you have in a pond. It is also a great way to interest children in wildlife.*

BOG GARDENS
Usually specially constructed areas, bog gardens provide permanently waterlogged soil. They are often made in conjunction with a pond, and can support a range of unusual plants normally found in wetland habitats. Bog gardens are an important element of any mosaic, and can be a vital refuge for aquatic birds, such as coots and moorhens, and also amphibians, which will relish the cool, damp shelter.

POND PLANTINGS
Ideally, a pond profile will include shallow areas as well as deeper water. In the deeper reaches, the vegetation consists of plants able to live permanently underwater or those with roots that send up leaves, which float on the surface. Shallow water will support plants capable of tolerating waterlogged conditions, and the remainder are free-floating on the surface.

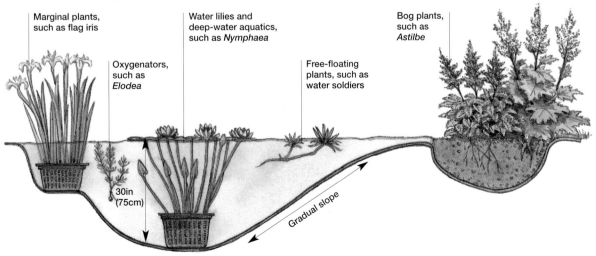

MAKING A POND

A pond is a real boost to a wildlife-friendly backyard, providing a watering hole for birds and a habitat for other wildlife. Ponds are relatively easy to construct, but need to be properly sited and designed to be useful habitats. Care and attention at the planning stage will boost the wildlife potential of your backyard.

When choosing a site for your pond, look for an attractive, sunny place, sheltered from the prevailing wind. Try to avoid a site that is shaded by trees because they will cut out light, and their leaves will drop into the water, enriching it with nutrients and organic debris. This promotes algae in the warmer months. In any backyard where a water feature is planned, child safety is of paramount importance. If there is any risk that young children might fall in, consider delaying your plans until they are older. Children love water and aquatic life, but you should always weigh the risks.

THE SHAPE AND SIZE OF A POND

As a general rule, 43 square feet ($4m^2$) is the minimum area needed to create a balanced environment, with marginal shelves at least 10 inches (25cm) wide to support containers of emergent plants. Create the outline using sweeping curves with no sharp bends; a figure eight or a kidney shape is ideal for smaller ponds. Then draw a rough cross section of the pond to check how much depth you will get for your width. Aim to get at least 2 feet (60cm) and ideally 3 feet (90cm) or more in the deeper reaches to benefit a range of

Above: *A sizable pond may attract mergansers. These slender ducks are called sawbills because their beaks have jagged edges for holding onto slippery fish.*

wildlife. The slopes should drop at a rate of one-third of the equivalent distance traveled across the top to assure stability.

CHOOSING A LINER

For small ponds, molded or fiberglass pools can be used but are limited in terms of design, and do not always look very

natural. A flexible liner, such as butyl rubber, is generally considered the best (if most expensive) option, although UV stabilized vinyl can be a cheaper alternative. Both these materials are prone to puncture, and care must be taken to line the hole with soft sand and/or an underlay, such as old carpet (made of natural fibers), to avoid this. The liners are easy to lay, and can also be used when creating bog gardens.

HIDING THE EDGE

Both flexible and rigid liners need to be hidden if you want to promote a natural effect. There are many ways of doing this.

A cobbled edge is easily achieved by setting some large stones or cobblestones into a bed of sand/cement that has been laid on the liner, both below and above the eventual water surface on a shallow slope. The stones form a firm base, and other loose stones can be piled on and between them with the gaps providing sheltering space for small animals, while also providing a gently sloping "beach" for birds to approach the water and drink.

A drystone wall, or alternatively a loose rock pile set on a mortar base on the liner, just below the water, can act as a retaining

CREATING DRINKING SHALLOWS

1 The shallow areas of ponds are important to let birds drink, but they can become muddy traps for smaller creatures and offer little protection or shelter for visitors.

2 Start by placing some larger stones or rounded rocks both in the shallow water and on the bank, arranging them in small groups of varying sizes to create a natural-looking effect.

3 Once the larger stones have been placed, the spaces between them should be filled with round cobblestones to create both shallow stony pools and drier beach areas.

4 The finished effect is very ornamental, and the strong shoreline provides hiding places for smaller creatures, as well as a basking area and safe drinking site for birds.

wall for nearby planting, with the niches between the stones providing shelter for amphibians. Walls or rock features are best placed at the back of the pond so that they create a reflection on the water surface.

A planted edge is also an option with a "planting pocket" being built on the liner. This involves running the liner roughly

4 inches (10cm) above maximum water level, and then burying it in the soil around the edge. It provides a simple and natural effect, with the overhanging plants hiding the edge, but the liner will show when the water level drops, and there is always the added danger of damaging a flexible liner when mowing or gardening near the pond.

Concrete or stone slabs laid on a sand/ cement bed over the edge of the liner are a somewhat formal solution, but are very practical if you want to view the water up close. Try to avoid this all the way around, though, as very small animals, such as young frogs, may have difficulty climbing in and out over the stone edge.

PUTTING IN A PLASTIC LINER FOR A POND

1 Start by marking out the outside edge of the pond using stakes or canes, and then mark out the locations of any shallow margins with spray paint.

2 Once marked out, begin digging the pond, starting with the deeper areas first, before digging out the margins and finalizing the edge of the pond.

3 Once you have excavated all of the pond to the required depth, establish the slopes on the side of the pond and the planting shelves within it.

4 To gain nicely smooth sides to the excavated pit, line the whole of the bottom and sloping sites with graded stone-free sand, fabric, or old carpet.

5 Carefully lift the liner over the pit. Do not drag it because sharp stones may puncture it. Secure the corners using bricks or stones and start to fill the pond with water.

6 As the liner fills with water, it will mold to the shape you have excavated. Once the pond is nearly full, cut the edge of the liner, leaving a generous overlap.

7 As the water level continues to rise, fold the liner to create an even finish and avoid any unsightly creases across the pond bottom or sloping sides.

8 Once the water is almost up to the top, bury the edges of the liner by cutting and then lifting the sod edges of the pond, and laying the liner under the cut sod.

9 The new pond can now be filled to the brim, then planted with various wetland species. Shallows can be created using stones of varying sizes.

PLANTING A POND

Naturally occurring ponds and wetlands are rich in plant life, much of which is specially adapted to grow in waterlogged ground, shallow water, or even under the surface. By including a range of these plants, you will greatly improve the look of your water feature and also its value for birds and other wildlife.

Surprisingly, new ponds can seem initially stark and lifeless. Plants will provide the magic to bring them to life and, once surrounded by vegetation, the whole feature becomes more attractive both to us and to birds and other wildlife.

To create a natural look, you can put a layer of soil on top of the liner for plants to root into, and creatures to hide in. This has the disadvantage, however, of introducing nutrients that can cause algal growth, and often means that you must be prepared to cull the plants regularly because aquatic plants can spread rapidly and choke the pond. Most people minimize

the problem by using special aquatic plant containers that curtail excessive growth. Most pond plants are perfectly happy in clay loam. Provided you ensure that the soil used is free of pesticides or pollutants most heavy types are fine, but the best idea is to buy a proprietary brand. The planting is mostly the same as for other potted plants, but the soil needs to be firmed down more than usual, and it is a good idea to spread gravel or cobblestones on top of the soil to keep the pot stable and keep the soil in the pot. The best time for planting is late spring as the water warms up. Do not give plants a shock by plunging them into icy water.

Above: *Water lilies, such as this* Nymphaea alba, *are a beautiful addition to any pond. Frogs are often seen on the leaves.*

CHOOSING POND PLANTS

When selecting aquatic plants, there are three different types of plant that you will need to attract wildlife. All are essential to a healthy pond because they constitute the range of habitats needed to support a diverse wildlife community.

Oxygenators spend the whole year submerged. These plants supply a steady infusion of oxygen, which is needed by the aquatic creatures that breathe through their gills. Oxygenators often grow densely and serve as egg-laying sites, nurseries, and cover for many aquatic animals. The second type are the deep-water aquatics,

PLANTS USUALLY BEST AVOIDED
These plants can become invasive in a backyard pond and, if they escape into the wild, can become a severe problem in natural ponds, lakes, and waterways. Avoid using them in favor of native species or noninvasive plants.
Note: If these plants are already in the pond, they should be disposed of carefully to prevent their spread either here or elsewhere.

- Australian swamp stonecrop (*Crassula helmsii*)
- Fairy moss (*Azolla filiculoides*)
- Floating pennywort (*Hydrocotyle ranunculoides*)
- Curly waterweed (*Lagarosiphon major*)
- Parrot's feather (*Myriophyllum aquaticum*)
- Kariba weed (*Salvinia*)
- Water hyacinth (*Eichhornia crassipes*), a particularly invasive species
- Water lettuce (*Pistia stratiotes*)

FILLING A POND BASKET AND PLANTING IT UP

1 Pond plants are best planted in specially made crates. These are lined on the bottom with gravel and filled with specially formulated soil mix.

2 Once the bottom is covered with stones and soil, put your plants in the crate. Fill around the remaining gaps with more of the aquatic soil mix.

3 When the soil mix is up to the height of the top of your plant root-ball, dress the soil mix surface with more gravel to help keep it in place.

4 The pond plants should quickly establish in their new surroundings and will soon send up new shoots and flowers above the surface.

RENOVATING A BOG GARDEN

1 Thoroughly weed the bog garden, being especially careful to remove all the roots of any persistent perennial weeds or unwanted plants.

2 Retain any useful specimens and dig in some organic matter to enrich the soil. Take a note of any bare areas to calculate numbers of new plants needed.

3 Dig over the whole area to be planted, then set out the new plants and decide the best arrangement before planting them in their final positions.

4 Once the area is planted, give the garden a thorough watering to help the plants settle in. Take a note of all species planted in case replacements are needed.

Above: *Small sections of oxygenating plants, such as this* Elodea, *can be tied with a stone and placed into the pond to grow and start to oxygenate the water.*

which have roots and stems in the deeper reaches, but with floating leaves and flowers. These are very important because they help to shade the water in summer. Too much light entering the water can cause algae to multiply. Ideally, you need to cover about half the surface of the pond with these plants. Water lilies *(Nymphaea)* are a big favorite, being very decorative, relatively easy to grow, and available in a wide range of colors and sizes. Other plants are also available, but you must ensure that the species chosen are not too vigorous for your pond size. Entirely free-floating species include duckweed *(Lemna),* water fern *(Azolla),* and water hyacinth *(Eichhornia crassipes),* but these can be invasive and may be best avoided.

The third class of aquatic plants, marginal or emergent plants grow in shallow water at the edge and offer shade and cover for birds and other animals, while greatly enhancing the visual appeal. They are also used by dragonflies and nymphs to crawl out of the water and pupate.

MARSH AREAS
Bog gardens mimic areas of marshy ground found in wetlands. They provide ideal cover for amphibians because the soil in these areas is always wet. The need for permanently wet ground means they are lined in a similar way to a garden pond. Many species of marginal plants are equally at home in a bog garden, and careful planting in such situations can help hide the division where the water stops and the bog garden starts, thereby enhancing its look.

TOP PLANTS FOR WILDLIFE PONDS
There are various types of wetland plants. They are split into categories to make it easy to select the correct plants for different areas of the pond or wetland.

EMERGENT PLANTS
Arrow arums *(Peltandra)*
Arrowhead *(Sagittaria)*
Bulrush *(Scirpus)*
Cattail *(Typhaceae)*
Pickerelweed *(Pontedaria cordata)*
Smartweed *(Polygonum)*
Spike rush *(Eleocharis)*

MARGINAL PLANTS
Blue flag *(Iris versicolor)*
Buttonbush *(Cephalanthus occidentalis)*
Cardinal flower *(Lobelia cardinalis)*
Forget-me-not *(Myosotis scorpiodes)*
Joe-pye weed *(Eupatorium dubium)*
Sweet flag *(Acorus species)*

Bulrush Cattail Blue flag Cardinal flower

SUBMERGED PLANTS
Water celery *(Vallisneria americana)*
Waterweed *(Elodea canadensis)*

FLOATING PLANTS
Duckweed *(Lemna)*
Pondweed *(Potamogeton)*
Water lily *(Nymphaeceae)*

Water celery Waterweed Duckweed Water lily

ATTRACTING INSECT-EATING BIRDS

Insects offer a rich source of protein for birds and their young. Insectivorous birds are a familiar sight in backyards particularly in summer, when their activities help to control pests. Many of the species seen are summer migrants that visit to feast upon the abundance of insect life that appears at this time.

Insects and small invertebrates constitute an important food source for birds and particularly their young, especially in areas where insects are most plentiful. Swallows, martins, and swifts pursue their insect meals while flying, often swooping down in pursuit, while woodpeckers can sometimes be seen—and more often heard—making holes in wood to find grubs. Even the starlings that walk across your lawn are systematically searching for insects.

INSECT EATERS

Typical species Swallows, swifts, martins, wrens, woodpeckers, warblers, nuthatches, flycatchers.

Backyard benefits Insect eaters benefit gardeners by eating many pests. Incoming migrants help tackle the rocketing summer population.

Migratory species For insectivorous birds, with their high mobility, migration is the rule rather than the exception. For some, such as swallows and swifts, the journey covers thousands of miles.

Natural diet Insectivorous birds will often take a range of invertebrates. Because they gain most of their moisture from their food, they drink less frequently than seed eaters.

Resident species Very few insectivores remain as residents in higher latitudes. Those that do—mostly small birds, such as wrens—are very susceptible to cold and, therefore, limited to mild regions.

Supplementary diet Mealworms are an excellent supplement and can be offered in a simple dish or a special feeder. In addition, many food suppliers now provide dried food for insectivores.

HABITAT PREFERENCES

While some birds are entirely insectivorous, others, including many common songbirds, catch insects only when raising young. Some of these feed their offspring entirely on insects, but a small percentage of their own food is also insects. This trait has the obvious advantage that they do not have to change their preferred habitat and can remain in the backyard all year.

Some larger birds eat insects as part of their diet when these are plentiful, but revert to other foods at other times of the year. Swallows, on the other hand, are an example of a group that feed almost exclusively on insects throughout the year. They must, therefore, make radical shifts in their habitat through the year by migrating vast distances to follow seasonal "gluts" of their prey in different areas.

FEEDING STRATEGIES

Although there are many different species of insect-eating birds, they often adopt similar strategies for catching their prey. Most have fine, narrow beaks, although even this can vary greatly according to

Below: *Barn swallows* (Hirundo rustica) *migrate vast distances to follow seasonal abundances of insects.*

Above: *Wrens are among the smallest backyard birds, but are voracious predators of insects in the summer months.*

species. Ecologists, therefore, tend to divide insectivorous birds according to their hunting habits, or guilds.

These guilds consist of groups of species that, although not necessarily closely related, behave in similar ways. Leaf gleaners, such as warblers, pick insects off leaves, whereas bark gleaners, such as nuthatches, pick them off tree trunks. Woodpeckers are wood and bark probers because of their ability to dig out their prey from within the branch.

The air salliers, including flycatchers, sit on a perch waiting for their prey to pass,

Above: Several species of woodpeckers, flickers, and sapsuckers visit backyards. All feed on wood-boring grubs.

whereupon they fly out and catch insects on the wing. The final guild includes swallows, martins, and swifts—gleaners of aerial plankton. These eat a large number of small insects while on the wing. In reality, however, most birds opt for more than one strategy, particularly if food becomes scarce. Most insectivorous birds will

PLANTS TO ATTRACT INSECT-EATING BIRDS
Baccharis (*Baccharis* species)
Buckthorn (*Rhamnus californica*)
Elderberry (*Sambucus mexicana*)
Monkeyflower (*Mimulus* species)
Oaks (*Quercus* species)
Sage (*Salvia* species)
Wild lilac (*Ceanothus* species)
Willow (*Salix* species)
Yarrow (*Achillea* species)

Sage

Wild lilac

Willow

Yarrow

THREATS
Pesticides Increased use of pesticides in both urban and rural settings means that insects are now relatively scarce. Many surviving insects carry small traces of poison, which can accumulate in the bodies of insect-eating birds.

Predation Small birds are vulnerable to predation from larger species, both birds and mammals. Domestic cats are a danger in urban backyards, and both squirrels and large birds, such as magpies, will take eggs and the young in the breeding season.

Territory If food becomes scarce, small birds are generally less able to compete with larger birds and become seasonal insectivores. Many will need larger territories as a result, and the effort of defending this may use a lot of energy.

Urbanization Insect-eating birds often find it difficult to find enough food in particularly developed areas. The lack of suitable vegetation means that insect prey is often relatively scarce. Vehicular pollution in the environment can also limit insect populations.

consume several different kinds of insect, often switching their preferences through the season according to the abundance of species available.

MIGRATORY SPECIES
Birds that feed exclusively on insects often face seasonal food shortages if they remain in one place, and that is why they travel in search of food. Swallows and flycatchers in northern parts of North America fly south in fall to spend winter in southern parts of the continent or in Central or South America. They do so because the cold, dark months in the north offer little reward in terms of insects. What is less easy to understand is why they should return. The answer is that northern areas offer a large seasonal glut of insects in summer. The birds move from place to place so that the climate is always warm and there is plenty of food.

Migrating insect-eating birds also prosper because there are often not many resident insectivorous birds in their summer feeding grounds. This means that the migrants have an abundant food supply without facing competition from too many residents. Furthermore, feeding and raising their young in northern latitudes means that they can use the longer hours of daylight to gather plenty of food, so they can potentially raise more young. A final advantage for migratory birds is that they avoid speciality predators trying to feed on them, because few of their predators make the same migratory journey.

Below: Milkweed is an excellent plant for attracting insects, such as bees and butterflies, which flock to the flowers in search of nectar. In turn, these creatures often become food for many birds.

ATTRACTING SEED-EATING BIRDS

Seed eaters include some of the most engaging of backyard birds. Changes in agriculture have caused a decline in these birds, many of which were once very common. Fortunately, the increasing popularity of backyard feeders has given the birds a lifeline, and many now prosper in a domestic setting.

The majority of birds using backyard feeders will be seed eaters for at least part of the year. However, comparatively few species are exclusively seed eaters, because most seed-eating birds hunt nutritious insects when they are feeding and raising their young. The main problem with being a seed eater is that the majority of seeds ripen in summer and fall. By the following spring, seed is in short supply and the birds must switch to a substitute food during winter or face a shortage. Feeding seed-eating species, therefore, helps them to survive this period, and ensures that they will be in peak condition for the breeding season in the spring.

HABITAT PREFERENCES

Recent years have seen a serious decline in many formerly common seed-eating birds. Intensification of agriculture has borne most of the blame, although realistically shortage of food is the root of the disaster. The seed eaters' numbers were previously probably artificially high as they prospered under traditional agricultural practices. If that sounds puzzling, note that large flocks

Above: *Although they have a variable diet, titmice are largely dependent on seeds during the cold winter months.*

of seed eaters were often seen feeding on winter stubble before moving on to land that was plowed in late winter to find weed seeds that had been brought up to the surface. Before the widespread use of herbicides, crops had many weeds that left seeds in the soil. It was these weeds that the seed-eating birds depended on, and

Above: *Goldfinches eat mostly seeds, but they will also consume other plant matter and insects through a season.*

modern agricultural efficiency has largely removed them. A second problem is that seed eaters can no longer feed on spilt grain in the stubble because fields are now plowed soon after the harvest.

Another traditional agricultural habitat that has declined is the hay meadow. Many meadows were rich in plant species, but it is actually how they are managed now that is important. In fact, meadows do not have to have a great variety of plants to be important for birds, but those that contain thistles and poppies are especially useful for seed-eating birds in summer.

Ironically, new housing developments that spread over what was once farmland may yet help save some of these birds. The increasingly popular habit of feeding seed-eating birds has provided them a lifeline, and many now prosper as a result. However, it is not the same for all species. The house sparrow, introduced from Europe and now found in many cities in the United States, was first attracted to towns when the only form of transportation was horse-drawn. The sparrows fed on grain spilled in the streets and lived around stables all over the cities. The advent of the car caused their numbers to decline across much of their original range, but they remain common in the United States.

SEED EATERS

Typical species Finches, including goldfinches and house finches, sparrows, buntings, titmice, cardinals, pigeons, and doves.

Backyard benefits Seed-eating birds are potentially beneficial when they switch to hunting insects in order to feed their young. Their habit of foraging seeds from the soil in winter also helps to reduce weed growth the next season.

Migratory species Some buntings, sparrows, and finches, such as the purple finch and pine siskin, tend to migrate in search of food and to avoid harsh northern winters. They do not always choose a regular destination, and only some birds may migrate.

Natural diet Seed-eating birds eat a range of seeds, including grain, nuts, and wildflowers. They will switch their preferences as a season progresses according to the availability of food.

Resident species Resident populations of seed eaters are dependent on the availability of food, and most non-migratory species move between breeding and wintering areas to forage.

Supplementary diet Many seed-eating birds are choosy about what they eat, and prefer oil-rich, high-energy food. The best includes black sunflower hearts (seed with the husks removed), white proso millet, niger (thistle), and good quality peanuts.

**PLANTS TO ATTRACT
SEED-EATING BIRDS**
Baccharis (*Baccharis* species)
Bunchgrasses (various genera)
Oak (*Quercus* species)
Sage (*Salvia* species)
Sunflower *(Helianthus annuus)*
Wild lilac (*Ceanothus* species)

Oak

Sage

Sunflower

Wild lilac

Always try to provide as much natural food as possible to ensure that you preserve birds' natural behavior patterns. Plants such as sunflowers *(Helianthus),* and a patch of wildflowers that includes thistles, tickseeds, coreopsis, and goldenrod will help to attract seed eaters.

Traditionally, feeding birds was limited to the winter, but recent evidence suggests that serious shortages are experienced in summer by many species when they are rearing their families. Summer feeding with sunflower hearts and other seeds can help the birds to lay more eggs and rear a

Below: *Hollyhock and mallow* (Alcea) *flowers attract insects in summer and develop seeds that feed birds in fall.*

healthier brood. However, note that not all commercial bird foods are formulated to meet all nutritional needs of seed eaters.

FEEDING STRATEGIES
The seed feeders generally have short, thick, strong beaks that are good for crushing or cracking open seeds. They can take some time to learn which foods are safe or good for them to eat. They often have an instinctive wariness about any change in their habitat, and you will need to be patient when you try to feed them. Seed eaters prefer their natural food sources, and when they come to the backyard for the first time they may not actually recognize supplementary foods.

Try offering black sunflower, white proso millet, niger (thistle), and peanuts, but remember that most of these foods are supplements and cannot always meet all of the birds' nutritional needs. Gradually add variety once they become accustomed to feeding at the site. They will soon overcome their caution and start to experiment.

Seed eaters are naturally more gregarious in winter, probably because of their tendency to form large flocks at this time. This helps them locate food and feed more efficiently than when alone, and also makes them less vulnerable to predators.

MIGRATORY SPECIES
Seed eaters tend to be resident species; however, buntings, such as indigo and painted buntings, and finches, such as pine siskins, do migrate in search of food, moving to areas where the climate is milder and food sources are more accessible.

Below: *Cardinals have a variable diet through the seasons but depend heavily upon small seeds during winter.*

Above: *Cornflowers do well in long grass, flower beds, or a pot in winter. Their seeds are ideal for smaller seed-eating birds.*

These winter migrants return to their breeding grounds in spring, although in some bird populations, only part of the population migrates. Other species simply move to lower ground.

THREATS
Competition Winter is a time when birds naturally flock, and this can cause aggression and tension. Birds at a winter feeder are forced together, and aggression is likely. Try to spread food around, and for aggressive species, you should put food out separately to avoid conflict.

Habitat loss Intensification of farming has meant that many species of once common birds are in serious decline due to loss of habitat and food sources. Oil-rich wildflower seeds are vital for these species, with many now remaining abundant only in backyards.

Herbicides Weed killers have been used with increasing regularity in North America, as in many other places, both to control crop weeds and also to improve the look of the backyard. However, letting some weeds flourish is vital for the survival of foraging seed eaters.

Predation The seed eaters' habit of feeding on the ground makes them vulnerable to attack by cats, especially where the latter can hide and wait under backyard bushes.

ATTRACTING FRUIT-EATING BIRDS

Fruit is an abundant and nutritious source of natural food, and one that many bird species have learned to exploit. In cooler climes, fruit tends to be a seasonal bounty, and so most fruit eaters in these regions alternate their diet, eating other foods when fruit is not available.

Berries grow on a wide variety of plants including trees, bushes, climbing plants, and even some herbaceous and ground-cover plants. When they are ripe, birds often descend on them and can clear a bush in a matter of hours, with some species of thrushes, warblers, and orioles switching substantially to a fruit diet from late summer into fall.

ROLE IN BACKYARDS

Birds and berries are a remarkable example of how plants and animals have evolved together, with one exploiting the other. The fleshy pulp of a berry is surprisingly nutrient-rich, and contains a good deal of starchy carbohydrate or sugars that conceal and protect the seed within. Most berries are also full of vitamins. The trade-off is simple. Birds benefit from the nutrients contained in the soft flesh. The berry-bearing plant benefits because birds spread its seeds in their droppings.

The major limitation for most birds with a fruit diet, however, is that it is not available for enough of the year. Late winter to midsummer is a time when there is precious little fruit around, and birds must find an alternative. Most fruit eaters switch

Below: *A tufted titmouse feasts on the red fruit of a crab apple* (Malus sylvestris). *This food is a favorite of many birds.*

FRUIT EATERS

Typical species Catbirds, thrushes, sparrows, finches, waxwings, titmice, vireos, orioles, and woodpeckers.

Backyard benefits Fruit-eating birds play an important role in dispersing seeds, and are useful in summer when they switch to eating insect pests.

Natural diet Fruit rarely provides all of any bird's diet for the whole year, but it does form an important part of some species' diet from midsummer into the colder months. Even fruit specialists occasionally take alternative food types.

Migratory species While there are fewer migrant fruit eaters, many bird species that move short distances in

winter will eat fruit in winter. Waxwings, on the other hand, are unpredictable in their movements but travel long distances in search of food.

Resident species Birds will often widen their territories to forage, and may even defend fruit sources. Many species flock together in winter and adopt a methodical feeding approach that is different to their summer behavior.

Supplementary diet Fruit-eating birds will happily take substitutes for fruit, provided they are able to recognize what it is. Pieces of broken apple and dried raisins may prove popular, and speciality suppliers now sell dried fruit especially for these birds.

to eating insects or other protein-rich foods in summer. Even when fruit is plentiful, many fruit specialists still supplement their diet with insects or other animal protein to ensure that they maintain a balanced diet.

HABITAT PREFERENCES

Fruit availability varies according to the season and, in most temperate climates, is available from midsummer until late winter. The fruit of the European cranberrybush *(Viburnum opulus)* or currants *(Ribes)* are short-lived and, if not consumed right away, will fall from the plant and rot. However, the fruit of the cotoneaster and holly *(Ilex)* remains on the plant for months, being a vital food reserve for much of the winter.

Always choose a range of plants that produce fruit over a long period. Remember that most species of fruit-eating birds have their favorites that they will take first, and that some fruit will remain on the plant for a long time before it is taken. Early fruiting bushes, such as currants and wild strawberries, are just as important as the late berries, and even a small backyard can accommodate some of these plants.

FEEDING STRATEGIES

Many songbirds switch from a summer invertebrate diet to a winter one based on berries. This change is especially important when cold weather arrives and frozen ground prevents resident species from

Below: *The scarlet berries of the rowan tree* (Sorbus aucuparia) *provide sustenance for many species of birds in fall.*

Above: *Elderberry is an excellent source of berries in midsummer. Such berries are enjoyed by catbirds, thrushes, and titmice.*

THREATS

Competition Even if there is plenty of food at the start of winter, harsh weather may force the birds to eat more of it and shorten the supply. In addition, migrants moving into the area compete for resources and visiting flocks may even strip an area clean.

Habitat loss Changes to the countryside caused by agriculture have meant that many native berrying shrubs have been destroyed, particularly when rows of hedges are removed from field margins, and bird numbers often fall as a consequence.

Poor fruit years In some years, the amount of fruit that sets on a tree or shrub will be considerably less than usual, mainly because the weather has damaged blossom or deterred pollinators. Shortages may occur the following winter.

Predation The tendency to seasonal fruit eating among many bird species often attracts them to settled areas where domestic cats are common predators. Ironically, the very shrubs they are feeding on often give cover to these ambush specialists.

foraging for earthworms, grubs, or fallen seeds. It is at this time of year, when food is short, that nourishing fruit is most vital.

Some birds tend to descend en masse to take berries when ripe. Starlings, for example, are highly systematic in their approach, methodically stripping bushes and trees from the top down. They also drop far fewer berries than other birds, and leave bushes picked clean. Thrushes, on the other hand, are well known for their

tendency to defend their territory, and will often defend a berrying tree or shrub against all others. This acts as a pantry that will see them through the winter, and, if hard times do not materialize, the birds gain a great advantage in having food to the end of winter, enabling them to nest early.

MIGRATORY SPECIES
As with most bird species, harsh winter weather is often a trigger for berry eaters to move south. While most only move short distances, a few species fly much farther. The movements of berry-feeding birds are linked to the availability of fruit. Possibly the most famous migratory berry eaters are the waxwings. In both North America and Europe, these beautiful birds leave their

forest homes and move to warmer climes, often descending on backyards to feast on berries. They are communal feeders, with individuals eating up to 500 berries each day, and in Holland they are called *pestvogel,* meaning "invasion bird," due to their habit of appearing suddenly and clearing away all the fruit.

The cedar waxwing of North America is equally fond of berries and also migratory. Flocks of these berry-eating birds show a high degree of cooperation when they feed. On trees or shrubs where slender twigs hold a supply of berries that only one bird can reach at a time, members of a flock have been observed lining up along the twig and passing berries from beak to beak so that each bird gets to eat.

PLANTS TO ATTRACT FRUIT-EATING BIRDS
Black currants and gooseberries (*Ribes* species)
Buckthorn (*Rhamnus californica*)
Elderberry (*Sambucus* species)
Oregon grape (*Mahonia aquifolium*)
Rowan (*Sorbus aucuparia*)
Wax myrtle (*Myrica californica*)
Wild grape (*Vitis californica*)

Gooseberry

Elderberry

Oregon grape

Rowan

Below: *The small berries of the black currant* (Ribes nigrum) *are popular with birds, such as thrushes, as well as people.*

Below: *Flocks of cedar waxwings* (Bombycilla cedrorum) *may appear in fall or winter to strip a backyard bush of berries.*

ATTRACTING OMNIVOROUS BIRDS

The need to survive has driven many resident backyard birds to adopt an omnivorous diet, which lets them exploit various foods as they become available. This is a highly successful strategy, and the chief reason behind the success of many species in colonizing our towns and backyards.

Birds that eat anything digestible/edible are known as omnivores. This is not to say that an omnivorous bird will eat any item of food that is put in front of it, and in most cases omnivores have specific feeding needs that may vary seasonally or in response to local variations in their habitat. In fact, the vast majority of birds tend to be somewhat omnivorous, although this tendency is usually most pronounced when their normal food source is in short supply.

Being an omnivore is usually the most successful survival strategy in rapidly changing environments, or in places subject to extreme seasonal variation. It is also noteworthy that many larger birds are omnivores because their body size makes specialization difficult unless their habitat—and, therefore, food supply—is very consistent all year round.

In time, successful omnivores can become very numerous. Members of the crow family, such as magpies and jays, will eat smaller birds and immature chicks, among other foods. This results in an unusually high number of these large birds.

Above: *Jays and other corvids have a very varied diet, eating insects, meat, fruit, seeds, and songbird eggs and nestlings.*

HABITAT PREFERENCES
The changing seasons bring times of alternate plenty and shortage for birds with highly specialized diets. Eating many different foods is usually a much more

Above: *Towhees, such as this spotted towhee, feed on seeds, insects, acorns, and berries, mostly finding food on the ground.*

successful strategy. Because omnivores will eat both plant and animal matter, they survive well in many environments and often prove highly adaptable. Species such as gulls have no problem adapting to living near humans and have recently started scavenging in landfill sites and city streets. This should not be so surprising because modern cities are similar in many ways to tall, rocky cliffs, and as gulls often nest or roost on top of tall buildings, where they are safe from predators, it is only natural that they should feed nearby.

As habitats change, creatures that best adapt to them tend to prosper. Urban bird populations have changed over time, and pigeons have now reached epidemic proportions in many cities. Surprisingly, backyard birds are now often urban in their distribution, with higher densities in towns than in the surrounding countryside. The most common species of these urbanized populations are often omnivores, and the backyard is an ideal habitat.

FEEDING STRATEGIES
Being omnivorous has obvious advantages, but various foods often require adaptations to the digestive system. Some omnivorous

---

OMNIVORES

Typical species Corvids, including jays, crows, and magpies, and also thrushes, finches, starlings, and gulls.

Backyard benefits Omnivores can be a mixed blessing in backyards, particularly if you have a vegetable plot. On the other hand, their varied diet includes many backyard pests.

Resident species Resident omnivores often face a bleak prospect during winter. Food shortages, exacerbated by resident competitors and incoming winter migrants, means that there is a naturally high mortality rate.

Migratory species The vast majority of omnivorous birds are able to avoid the necessity of migrating vast distances,

but some, including members of the crow family, travel short distances to escape harsh winter weather, and often take up temporary residence in backyards at this time.

Natural diet Many omnivores have set patterns regarding exactly what and when they will eat. These species are often insect eaters in the summer months, for example, before their digestive tracts adapt for their winter diet of berries and seeds.

Supplementary diet Omnivores should be provided with a varied diet. Numerous mixes exist, and the best idea is to provide a full range of food types, including grain, small seeds, suet, fruit, and even some live food.

**PLANTS TO ATTRACT
NECTAR FEEDERS**
California fuchsia (*Epilobium* species)
Currants and gooseberries (*Ribes* species)
Honeysuckle (*Lonicera* species)
Manzanita (*Arctostaphylos* species)
Monkeyflower (*Mimulus* species)
Penstemon (*Penstemon* species)
Sage (*Salvia* species)

Honeysuckle

Monkeyflower

Penstemon

Sage

species lengthen their digestive tracts in winter to get more out of relatively poor-quality food. This lets them be mostly vegetarian in winter, switching to an insectivorous diet in summer.

The beaks of omnivorous birds are usually relatively long and unspecialized, however, this can vary considerably according to their history. For example, in some parts of Europe, there are now

Below: *Ivy* (Hedera helix) *berries are eaten by many species, including pigeons, doves, jays, thrushes, and waxwings.*

populations of feral ring-necked parakeets derived from escaped cage birds. These birds are much more omnivorous than the original wild populations in Africa and Asia that eat fruit, berries, nuts, and seeds, probably as a result of their foraging meat and bacon rinds from backyard bird tables. It is this ability to adapt and exploit unfamiliar food sources that differentiates omnivores from birds with restrictive diets.

MIGRATORY SPECIES
Omnivores, like most birds, will migrate if food becomes scarce. However, they rarely undertake the huge journeys characteristic of insectivores, with many species only traveling a few hundred miles. Even when omnivores do migrate, it is not always the whole population that does so. In fact, the most likely migrants in a normally resident bird population are invariably females and young. Many common species move from one area to another, while others simply move into towns from the countryside. Some species regarded as nonmigratory will sometimes fly long distances when faced with harsh winter conditions, but because these newcomers look just like the residents, their arrival often goes largely unnoticed.

Omnivores, such as some corvids and towhees, undertake short flights to warmer areas. For example, blue jays move from northern parts of their range in fall. Green-tailed towhees breed in mountainous parts of the southwest and move to lower elevations for winter. Some species change

Below: *Corvids, such as the black-billed magpie, are adaptable feeders. This has enabled them to become numerous.*

Above: *The sweet fruits of serviceberry* (Amelanchier) *mature in midsummer to be eaten by a wide variety of birds.*

their habits and distribution over the year, raising families and feeding in backyards during the spring and summer, where they can raise up to three broods. After the breeding season, they "feed up" for the coming winter, and often move out into the surrounding countryside to do so.

THREATS
Competition Omnivores are highly adaptable and able to exploit new situations and food sources, but this brings them into contact with new competitors. Some urban birds are highly aggressive and will often chase away newcomers.

Disease Any increase in population raises the chances of disease spread. Omnivorous birds often congregate where there is a food source, and disease becomes more prevalent than for birds following a more solitary life.

Habitat changes As changing habitats favor certain incoming species, others are less favored, and some omnivorous birds that were formerly common in cities are now scarce or absent, having been unable to adapt to modern city life.

Predation Like all birds, omnivores face predators in either backyards or their natural habitats, but they are usually numerous enough to cope with any losses. In backyards, cats are usually the main threat, although other birds (including birds of prey) can also take their toll.

PLANTING GUIDE FOR BIRDS

The species listed below are just a small selection of the many varieties that can be planted to attract birds. Your choice will depend on personal preference and on the space available, soil type, and the position, whether in sun or shade. A good rule is to choose the widest variety of plants possible.

TREES

The trees listed here provide food, such as fruits and insects, and also make good nesting sites for birds. If space allows, large trees, such as oaks and maples, will support a wealth of insect life.

Crab apple *Malus sylvestris*
Height: 35ft (10m). Spread: 35ft (10m). This small woodland tree grows in fertile, well-drained soil in backyards. It prefers full sun or partial shade. In late spring, this deciduous tree produces white flowers. In fall, it bears red fruit, which are eaten by birds, such as finches and thrushes. The cultivated apple *(Malus domestica)* is also highly attractive to birds.

False acacia (Black locust)
Robinia pseudoacacia
Height: 75ft (25m). Spread: 50ft (15m). This quick-growing tree is a native of North America. It needs a sunny position, and will grow in poor soil, but not waterlogged ground. Scented, drooping white flowers

Below: *Waxwings (Bombycillidae) are among the many birds that feast on rowan berries during fall.*

Above: *The crab apple* (Malus sylvestris) *is sometimes found growing wild in rows of hedges and along woodland edges.*

appear in late spring or early summer. This deciduous tree with dark-green leaves attracts seed eaters, such as finches.

Mountain ash (Rowan) *Sorbus aucuparia*
Height: 50ft (15m). Spread: 25ft (8m). This small deciduous tree has delicate, frondlike leaves. It requires light, moist soil, which can be acidic, and prefers full sun or partial shade. In fall, the rowan produces small scarlet berries, which provide food for many birds. The whitebeam *(Sorbus aria)* and wild servicetree *(S. torminalis)* are related trees.

Lodgepole pine *Pinus contorta*
Height: 50–80ft (15–25m).
The lodgepole pine is native to North America, as are the Monterey pine *(Pinus radiata)* and black pine *(P. nigra)*. These evergreen conifers have needlelike leaves and bear cones that ripen in their second year. All three prefer full sun and moist soil. The dense evergreen foliage provides shelter for nesting birds, while the cones provide food for seed eaters.

European bird cherry *Prunus padus*
Height: 50ft (15m). Spread: 35ft (10m). The European bird cherry is a small deciduous tree that produces white

Above: *The common oak is renowned for supporting larger numbers of invertebrates than any other tree.*

scented flowers in spring. Its black cherries are eaten by birds, such as finches, in fall. It prefers full sun and needs well-drained soil. Many *Prunus* species attract birds, including the wild black cherry *(P. serotina),* the chokecherry *(P. virginiana),* and the European plum *(P. domestica).*

English Oak *Quercus robur*
Height: 100–135ft (30–40m).
Spread: 85ft (25m).
This large deciduous tree is suited to only large backyards. It requires well-drained soil and is a slow grower. The oak supports a huge range of insects whose caterpillars provide food for nesting birds. It produces acorns in fall. Relatives include the fast-growing red oak *(Quercus rubra),* and live oaks, which have evergreen leaves.

Black maple *Acer nigrum*
Height: 65ft (20m). Spread: 25ft (8m). This native of North America is now grown in European backyards. The leaves of this deciduous tree turn bright orange in fall. It needs sun or partial shade and fertile, well-drained soil. Winged fruits and insects living on the tree provide food for birds. Relatives include the red maple *(A. rubrum),* the silver maple *(A. saccharinum),* and the sugar maple *(A. saccharum).*

SHRUBS

Seed-bearing shrubs will attract birds, such as sparrows, buntings, and finches, while berry bearers nourish thrushes, warblers, orioles, and vireos. Dense shrubs provide cover and safe sites for birds to nest.

Barberry *Berberis vulgaris*
Height: 6ft (2m). Spread: 10ft (3m).
This evergreen shrub bears scarlet berries that are eaten by many birds. Sharp spines make this a good hedging plant. It grows in sun or partial shade in most well-drained soils. The Japanese barberry *(Berberis thunbergii)* grows in similar conditions, but is deciduous, with leaves that turn orange in fall. This produces pale flowers in spring, followed by bright red berries in fall.

European cranberrybush (Guelder rose, Viburnum) *Viburnum opulus*
Height: 12ft (4m). Spread: 12ft (4m).
This deciduous shrub produces white flowers in spring and red berries in fall. It requires sun or semi-shade and well-drained soil. Relatives include laurustinus *(V. tinus),* which bears white flowers and black fruit. Blackhaw *(V. prunifolium)* is popular with birds, as are nannyberry *(V. lentago),* and arrowwood *(V. dentatum).*

Hawthorn *Crataegus monogyna*
Height: 30ft (9m). Spread: 8ft (2.4m).
This deciduous, spiny bush prefers sun but will tolerate shade. Its white blossoms are attractive in spring. The crimson berries are eaten by birds, such as titmice and thrushes, in fall. Dense foliage provides good cover for nesting birds.

Below: *Hawthorn is sometimes found growing wild in hedges. Many birds eat the berries, and wood pigeons eat the leaves.*

Above: *Warblers and titmice are among the species that harvest caterpillars and butterflies from butterflybush blooms.*

Firethorn *Pyracantha coccinea*
Height: 7ft (2m). Spread: 7ft (2m).
This evergreen shrub is sometimes grown as a hedge or along a wall. It grows in sun or partial shade and any well-drained soil. It has dark green leaves and produces white flowers and clusters of scarlet berries. The dense, spiny foliage provides safe nesting sites for birds, while thrushes, pigeons, and other species eat the berries.

Common elderberry (Black elderberry) *Sambucus nigra*
Height: 30ft (9m).
This deciduous shrub does well in partial shade. It provides good cover for nesting birds. The pale blossoms of early summer are followed by drooping clusters of small black berries, which attract birds. The American elderberry *(S. canadensis)* and red elderberry *(S. racemosa)* are also popular with many birds.

Cotoneaster *Cotoneaster microphyllus*
Height: 3ft 4in (1m). Spread: 7ft (2m).
This evergreen shrub has rigid, drooping branches. The dense foliage provides safe nesting sites for birds, while in fall, the berries are eaten by species such as thrushes. It prefers full sun. A relative known as rock or rock-spray *(C. horizontalis)* provides similar attractions for birds and will grow along walls, banks, or the ground.

Dogwood *Cornus sanguinea*
Height: 13ft (4m). Spread: 10ft (3m).
The bright red stems of this deciduous shrub provide color in winter. It needs sun

and grows well in chalky soil. The small black berries are eaten by birds in fall. Many *Cornus* species are attractive to birds, including Siberian dogwood *(C. sericea* L. ssp. *sericea)* and flowering dogwood *(C. florida),* a small tree.

Orange eye butterflybush *Buddleja davidii*
Height: 15ft (5m). Spread: 15ft (5m).
This sprawling deciduous shrub requires full sun and well-drained soil. In midsummer, it produces drooping spikes of scented lilac flowers that attract butterflies. In turn, the insect life attracts insect eaters, such as warblers. Buddleja can look untidy and should be pruned back severely in spring.

Serviceberry *Amelanchier lamarckii*
Height: 20ft (6m). Spread: 10ft (3m).
The green or tawny leaves of this deciduous shrub turn red or orange in fall, providing a blaze of color. It needs full sun or semi-shade and prefers slightly acidic soil. The berry clusters are eaten by many types of birds. Related species, such as the common serviceberry *(Amelanchier arborea)* and the Canadian serviceberry *(A. canadensis),* are also popular with birds.

Dog rose *Rosa canina*
Height: 10ft (3m).
This deciduous rambling shrub grows wild in some woods and rows of hedges. It prefers sun and fertile soil. The pale pink flowers open in summer, following by juicy red hips that are eaten by many birds. Many species of cultivated shrub roses, such as *Rosa rugosa,* also attract insects, insect eaters, and fruit-eating birds.

Below: *Dog rose flowers give off a delicate scent. Thrushes (Turdidae) are among the birds that eat the fruit.*

Above: *Woodbine blooms produce more scent toward evening. The fruit may be eaten by birds, such as house finches.*

Above: *Blackberry plants flourish on waste ground. The berries feed wood pigeons, crows, starlings, and finches.*

Above: *Virginia creeper is a highly ornamental climber, particularly in fall. It can be grown up buildings and walls.*

CREEPERS AND CLIMBERS

Leafy climbers offer sheltered nesting sites for birds. Some creepers and climbers provide foods, such as fall berries, nectar, or a wealth of insects, to eat.

Woodbine (Honeysuckle)
Lonicera periclymenum
Height: 23ft (7m).
This deciduous climber grows well up walls. It requires sun or partial shade and fertile, well-drained soil. The sweet-scented pink or yellow flowers attract insects and insect eaters, while some bird species, such as hummingbirds, sip the nectar. The red berries are enjoyed by warblers and finches.

Blackberry (Bramble) *Rubus fruticosus*
Height: 10ft (3m). Spread: 10ft (3m).
This prickly deciduous climber runs wild in hedges and on waste ground. It grows in either sun or partial shade. Small white flowers in summer are followed by black fruits that are enjoyed by birds and humans. Other *Rubus* species such as European dewberry *(R. caesius)* and cloudberry *(R. chamaemorus)* produce edible fruits.

Virginia creeper
Parthenocissus quinquefolia
Height: 50ft (15m) or more.
This fast-growing, deciduous climber clings to walls with its tendrils. Its foliage provides cover for nesting birds. The leaves turn crimson or purple in fall, when the plant also produces dark blue berries, which are eaten by crows and thrushes. This creeper grows best in sun or semi-shade in fertile, well-drained soil.

Grape vine *Vitis vinifera*
Height: 100ft (30m).
This woody, deciduous climber is grown for its juicy green or purple fruit, which is enjoyed by birds as well as humans. The fleshy fruit is used in wine-making. The vine's green, scented flowers open in early summer. It needs full sun or semi-shade and fertile, well-drained soil, and can be grown against walls and trellises.

Below: *The grape vine can be a useful screening plant when grown up a trellis. There are hundreds of varieties.*

HERBACEOUS PLANTS

Flowering plants provide food, such as seeds and insects and their caterpillars. Some attract slugs, snails, and other invertebrates, which also feed some types of birds. As with other types of plants, old-fashioned and native plants should predominate, but non-native species can play an important role, too.

Sunflower *Helianthus annuus*
Height: 10ft (3m). Spread: 2ft (60cm).
This native of North America grows wild on wasteland. A leggy annual, the long green stems bear single large, deep yellow flowers with massive seed heads.

Below: *Sunflowers are often seen growing as a crop. Many bird varieties, including this lesser goldfinch, enjoy eating the seeds.*

The seeds feed doves, nuthatches, crows, and other birds. The plant requires full sun and fertile, moist but well-drained soil. It may need to be staked when in bloom.

Michaelmas daisy *Aster novi-belgii*
Height: 3ft (90cm). Spread: 20in (50cm). This North American native grows wild on waste ground and damp sites. A tall perennial, it has branching stems and likes sun or partial shade and fertile, well-drained soil. Purple, daisylike flowers with yellow centers appear in fall. These attract insects, such as bees and butterflies. The seeds also provide food. Many other asters are also popular with birds.

Cornflower *Centaurea cyanus*
Height: 3ft (90cm). Spread: 1ft (30cm). This tall perennial has slim, gray-green leaves. It requires a sunny position and fertile, well-drained soil. The flowers appear in late fall—most commonly deep blue, but also pink, red, purple, or white. These attract insects, which feed birds. Cornflower seeds are eaten by titmice, finches, and members of the crow family.

Yarrow *Achillea millefolium*
Height: 2ft (60cm). Spread: 2ft (60cm). This perennial herb grows wild in hedges, grasslands, and meadows. With its delicate, frondlike leaves, it requires

Below: *Insect eaters feed on aphids attracted to the yarrow. Sparrows, finches, and titmice eat the seeds.*

full sun and moist, well-drained soil. It produces clusters of pale flowers in summer or fall. These attract insects, which provide food for birds, as do the yarrow's seeds.

Dill *Anethum graveolens*
Height: 3ft (90cm).
This slender plant is often found on waste ground. It prefers full sun and sandy soil. The seeds are used in cooking, so it makes a good herb garden plant. The tall stems support flattened clusters of yellow flowers in late summer. The seeds provide food for birds, while slugs attracted to dill plants feed some bird species, such as thrushes.

Marigold *Calendula officinalis*
Height: 2ft (60cm). Spread: 1ft (30cm). This quick-growing plant with light green, scented leaves is often found growing wild on waste ground. It requires a sunny position but will grow in most well-drained soils. Cultivated varieties bear long-lasting yellow or orange, daisylike blooms from spring to fall. The plant attracts insects and slugs, which provide a source of food for invertebrate-eating birds.

Foxglove *Digitalis purpurea*
Height: 3–5ft (1–1.5m). Spread: 2ft (60cm). This tall, upright plant may grow wild in woods and heathland. It grows best in semi-shade and needs moist, well-drained soil. In summer, the foxglove produces tall spikes of bell-shape flowers that may be purple, pink, or white. These attract bees, which provide food for insect eaters. The seeds also nourish birds.

Above: *The many varieties of marigold brighten backyards with their single- or double-headed flowers.*

Coreopsis (Largeflower tickseed)
Coreopsis grandiflora
Height: 1½–4 ft (45–120cm).
The many varieties of coreopsis produce bright yellow, daisylike flowers from early summer to fall. These long-lasting blooms provide color and attract insects, which in turn draw insect-eating birds. *Coreopsis* species require full sun and fertile, well-drained soil.

Below: *Foxglove flowers attract bumblebees, which are hunted by flycatchers. Some birds eat the seeds.*

MAKING BIRD FEEDERS, BIRDBATHS, AND NEST BOXES

Perhaps it is the opportunity to create a world in miniature, while simultaneously giving nature a helping hand, that has ensured the continued popularity of nest-box construction. Bird boxes and also feeders and birdbaths can be plain, pretty, or fanciful without affecting their primary function. Having satisfied the basic requirements, the finish is up to individual taste. The projects given here present a wide variety of ways to provide your local feathered community with food, drink, and nesting sites.

Left: *Although highly embellished, this house still retains its practical function, providing a safe, dry site for birds to nest.*

Above: *From rudimentary woodwork to more complex projects, bird-feeder construction can suit every skill level.*

Above: *Simple feeders, such as this one, look very attractive when filled with foods of different colors and textures.*

Above: *Even unoccupied nest boxes make charming decorative features that enhance many different backyard settings.*

BUILDING MATERIALS

Bird boxes, feeders, and birdbaths can be constructed using a wide variety of materials. Your garage will probably contain many suitable items, such as sticks, string, garden wire, paint, varnish, and scraps of wood. You may be able to improvise using materials not listed here.

ALUMINUM MESH
Useful for making bird feeders, this is available from hardware stores and some hobby suppliers. Birds can peck food through a coarse mesh, while a fine gauze can be used to line the bottom of a feeder to enable rain to drain away.

CLAY
A birdhouse molded from potter's clay will need to be fired in a kiln. Self-hardening clay does not need firing, and is available in various colors, including stone and terra cotta. You will need to varnish the clay to make it water-resistant.

COCONUT
Birds love fresh coconut, and when they have eaten the contents you can use the shells as parts of a birdhouse or fill them with a bird treat. Never put out dry, shredded coconut.

CORRUGATED ROOFING MATERIAL
Any scrap that you are able to purchase from a hardware store would be enough to cover a large birdhouse. You will need to buy special screws to attach it.

Below: *Paintbrushes will be useful for decorating projects. You will need medium-size brushes as well as very fine ones.*

Above: *Hanging basket liners can be purchased in various colors, including green, which blends with backyard settings.*

HANGING BASKET LINERS
Basket liners are available in a soft green with a texture that quite closely resembles moss. They can be cut to size and molded over chicken wire.

PAINT AND VARNISH
Use exterior-quality paint with a satin or matte finish. If you use latex paint, it will need to be protected with a varnish designed for exterior use, such as yacht varnish. For fine work, use craft enamels or artist's acrylics.

PAINTBRUSHES
You will need a range of small household paintbrushes, along with medium and fine artist's brushes for detailed decoration. Clean brushes in turpentine if you are using oil-base paints.

PALETTE
A white ceramic tile, or even an old plate, is useful for mixing paint colors.

STORE-BOUGHT BIRDHOUSES
As an alternative to making your own birdhouse, you can buy inexpensive ones from garden centers and customize them to suit the style of your backyard.

Above: *Shells provide a decorative finish to projects. Collect them responsibly— by recycling old necklaces, for example.*

ROOFING SLATES AND TILES
Beautiful old roofing slates and tiles can often be purchased from architectural salvage yards to make excellent weatherproof roofs for birdhouses.

SELF-ADHESIVE ROOF FLASHING
This material is tough and waterproof. It looks like lead and makes an invaluable covering for birdhouse roofs.

SHELLS
These make pretty decorations. You can buy them from craft stores or, better still, use an old shell necklace.

STICKS
Garden stakes are available in a range of colors. Thick stakes can be used to support some houses. Willow sticks can be used for weaving. These are available stripped or unstripped, and become very pliable once soaked. Straight hazel twigs can be gathered in the backyard or hedge.

STRING
Ordinary household string is useful for many projects, as well as for hanging up feeders. Green garden string and natural raffia make good binding materials, and

garden string has also usually been treated for outdoor use to help it last longer. Sea grass string is both strong and decorative.

WIRE

Chicken wire that is plastic-coated is both attractive and easy to work with, because it will not scratch your hands. Garden wire is also plastic-coated and comes in various gauges. Galvanized wire is useful for building and suspending birdhouses. Florist's wire is thinner and is good for binding.

WOOD

For long-lasting, weatherproof houses, use lumber that is at least ⅝ inch (15mm) thick. Planed pine is easily available in a wide range of widths. For outdoor use, treat it with preservative, or paint or varnish it. Tongue and groove or shiplap boards make attractive walls for larger birdhouses. Marine- or exterior-quality plywood is easy to cut with a fretsaw for decorative panels. A birdhouse made from a hollowed-out log looks good in natural surroundings.

Clockwise from top left: *Natural and planed wood, a store-bought birdhouse, natural and treated willow, aluminum mesh and wire sheets, galvanized and plastic-coated wire, a range of paints, paintbrushes, string, liner, roof slate, coconut, self-adhesive flashing, clay, sticks, and shells.*

BUILDING EQUIPMENT

No special equipment is needed for building bird boxes and feeders, and only basic carpentry skills will be required. Be careful when using new equipment; you might want to practice on a scrap first. Before cutting, always recheck against the template, or double-check your measurements.

ADHESIVES
Glue all joints in wooden birdhouses, using wood glue, before nailing or screwing them together. Masking tape can be useful for holding wood together while the glue is drying. Two-part epoxy resin glue makes a strong bond when you are joining disparate materials. Small stones or shells can be embedded in premixed tile cement for a decorative finish. Always use an exterior-grade glue, especially when you are working with white glue.

BROWN PAPER
Heavy craft paper makes a good protective covering for your work surface when painting or gluing. Old newspaper is also ideal as protective covering.

CRAFT KNIFE AND SCISSORS
Always use a sharp blade in a craft knife and protect the work surface with a cutting mat. When using self-adhesive flashing, cut with a sharp knife, rather than scissors.

DRILL AND BITS
A drill will be needed to make holes for screws and other attachments. Spade bits can be used to make entry holes up to 1 inch (2.5cm). Hole saws, which fit

Below: *Drill holes using a clamp to keep your work steady. If you use countersink screws, you will need a countersink bit.*

Above: *Glue can be spread using a gun, simple spatula, or small stick. Wipe off any excess glue before it dries.*

onto a drill, are available in a range of sizes and are ideal for cutting larger entry holes for birdhouses. You can also cut an entry hole using a fretsaw and jigsaw if a hole saw is not available.

GLOVES
Wear gardening gloves to protect yourself from scratches when you are handling, bending, or cutting wire. You can also wear

Below: *Pliers will be useful to bend and mold wire, and also to cut it. Protect your hands by wearing thick gloves.*

Above: *Hammer steadily and gently, being careful to keep your free hand well away from the hammer head.*

a pair of latex gloves to keep your hands clean whenever you are painting or varnishing, or using modeling clay.

HAMMER AND NAILS
Use galvanized nails or plated molding nails, which will not rust.

PENCIL AND RULERS
Use a sharp pencil and a ruler for accurate marking out of wood. Use a metal ruler when cutting with a craft knife.

PLIERS AND CUTTERS
General-purpose pliers and small, round-nose ones will be useful for working with wire. You will also need wire cutters. Lead flashing, for roofs, can be cut using tin snips.

SANDPAPER
Smooth the edges of the wood after cutting using medium-grade sandpaper wrapped around a wooden block. Roll a piece of sandpaper around your finger to smooth the edges of entry holes.

SAWS
Use a tenon saw for square cutting, unless you are making large cuts, where a panel saw is best. A jigsaw is ideal for curved shapes.

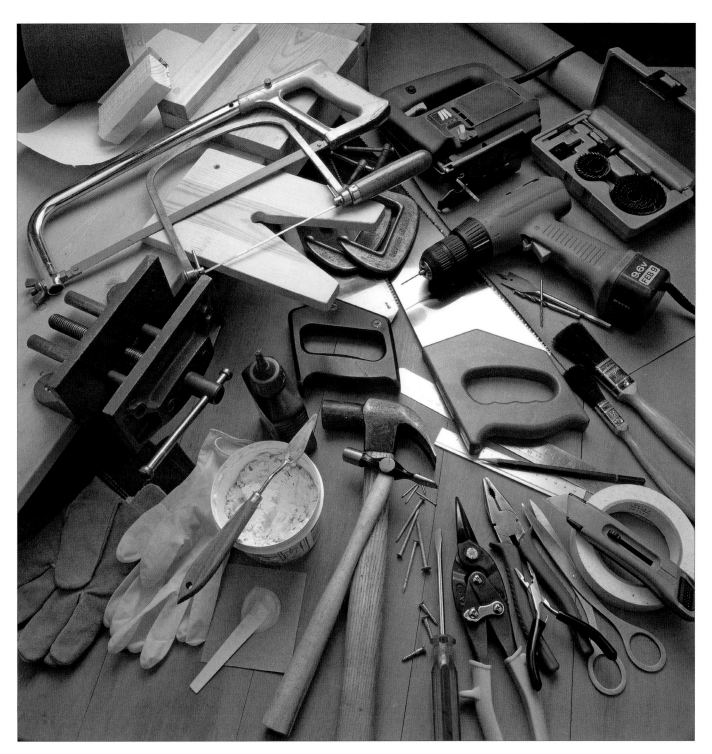

Use a fretsaw to cut small, intricate shapes; clamp the wood on a birdsmouth board, which supports the work but has a V notch for the saw blade, screwed to the workbench. Use a hacksaw to cut metal.

SCREWS AND SCREWDRIVER
Screws, not nails, should always be used to secure attachments in large, heavy structures. Buy Pozidriv screws for outdoor use, because these tend to be plated and, therefore, will be less inclined to rust.

VISE AND CLAMPS
A vise or adjustable workbench will be essential for holding wood steady when you are sawing it, and can also help when you are gluing. A bench hook will be helpful when you are cutting lumber with a tenon saw, because it is useful for cutting strips to length. You will need to clamp a coconut in a vise to saw it in half. Clamps of various sizes, and even clothespins can be useful for holding your work together while you are assembling it.

Clockwise from top left: *Sandpaper and wooden blocks, panel and tenon saw, drill kit and bits, brown paper, hacksaw, paintbrushes, pencil and ruler, craft knife and masking tape, scissors, pliers and cutters, screwdriver and screws, hammers and nails, epoxy resin glue, wood glue and spatula, latex and fabric gloves, and vise.*

BIRD FEEDERS AND BIRDBATHS

Many species of backyard birds have suffered quite serious declines in recent years. By providing food and water, you will help the local bird population to remain fit and healthy, so that the birds are more likely to breed successfully when the mating season comes around.

Even a well-stocked backyard can be an unforgiving place for birds as winter draws in. Late fall marks the time when many birds will visit your backyard, seeking extra supplies of food. However, feeding can be beneficial throughout the year, especially in springtime when parent birds must find food for their young. By supplementing bird diets with extra food, you are arguably maintaining a falsely high population of birds in your backyard, but this in turn helps some species to survive when their natural habitats have been reduced by human activities.

FEEDERS
Different species of birds have different feeding habits. Hanging food is ideal for titmice and chickadees, placed high enough up so that cats cannot reach

Above: *Feeders are available in a wide range of shapes and sizes, and make attractive additions to the backyard.*

Above: *In the wild, hummingbirds sip nectar from flowers. They visit backyards to drink sugary liquids from special feeders.*

the birds while feeding. If the food is too exposed, however, the birds may be in danger from falcons, unless there is nearby cover, such as trees and hedges. Trees, large shrubs, or even a dead branch firmly planted in the ground, can act as a support for feeders. Securely attach your feeders to the branches using thin, pliable wire.

PONDS AND BIRDBATHS
Birds need a constant supply of water for both bathing and drinking. It is essential for them to keep their feathers in good condition for insulation for long, bitter winter nights. Some birds, such as titmice, may drink more in winter because their seasonal diet of dry nuts is not sufficient to hydrate them. Seed eaters in general need plenty of water to compensate for the lack of moisture in their diet.

Ponds, of course, provide water all year round for bathing and drinking, and will also attract many other types of wildlife to your backyard. We are not all fortunate enough to have the space or facilities for ponds or larger water sources, but a birdbath is an attractive option, which will enhance your backyard as well as prove extremely useful to local birds.

DIFFERENT TYPES OF FEEDER
By using a range of bird feeders, you can provide a greater variety of food items. In so doing, you will increase the chances of more species visiting your backyard.

Bird feeder table
Tables are excellent for a wide range of small backyard birds and also for larger birds that perch or stand in order to feed. Food placed on the table sustains birds in the critical winter season, in spring when birds are nesting, and throughout the year.

Glass/plastic feeder
These types of feeders are usually filled with mixed seeds, which are made accessible to birds through a series of small hoppers in the sides.

Coconut shell
A coconut sliced in two is an excellent way of providing food for small, clinging birds; you can fill it with suet or seeds.

Squirrel-proof feeder
To discourage squirrels, make bird food inaccessible. This type of feeder has a cage to protect the seed.

Wire feeder
These are mostly for peanuts, and are useful because they prevent birds from choking on whole nuts.

Bird feeder table   Glass feeder   Coconut shell   Squirrel-proof feeder

to human visitors. You can also create your own birdbath by following some of the projects shown in this book.

Whatever birdbath you choose, make sure that it has either sloping sides or a ramp if the sides are steep, so that birds can easily walk in and out, and small animals do not become trapped. Do not forget to keep the birdbath clean and filled with fresh water, and crack any ice that forms on the surface in winter.

Left: *Like all birds, American robins benefit from a dip in a birdbath. Seed eaters in particular need plenty of drinking water.*

Below: *Pieces of broken crockery make a wonderful mosaic pattern. The sloping sides provide easy access to the water.*

A birdbath need not be an elaborate affair. A puddle is the simplest form of all. You can make a more permanent watering hole by scraping out a shallow puddle shape in a flower bed, lining it with plastic, and securing the plastic in place with stones. Another simple and unobtrusive option might be an inverted trashcan lid securely placed on bricks.

There are many commercially available birdbaths, which not only serve a useful purpose for birds but add a point of interest to any backyard. Fountains, or any form of dripping water, make ponds and baths more enticing to birds as well as appealing

Below: *A traditional stone birdbath makes an atmospheric addition to any backyard, as well as benefiting birds.*

NEST BOXES

In recent years, nest boxes have become a familiar sight in many backyards, chiefly because people like to see birds raising their young. Nest boxes have proved extremely valuable for a variety of birds because they provide alternative, artificial nesting sites for many species.

Before you erect a nest box, decide what type of bird you are trying to attract. Various species have different needs. Choosing the wrong type of box or putting it up in an inappropriate place may mean that it is not used. If a box is to be used immediately, it needs to be in place by the start of the breeding season, and that usually means late winter. However, there is never a wrong time of year to put up a box, and they often provide winter shelter. A box so used is more likely to be used again next season.

STORE-BOUGHT BOXES

There has been a rapid increase in the range of commercially produced bird boxes, and numerous designs are now available to suit a wide range of backyard birds, from owls and woodpeckers to swallows, bluebirds, wrens, sparrows, and titmice. Many specialty producers of bird boxes can be found on the Internet.

The best designs are usually solid and simple. In general, beware of fussy, overly ornate boxes, because they can be useless. If you are buying a box it needs to be waterproof, but must have a drainage

Below: *Some birds that nest in groups, such as these purple martins* (Progne subis), *will use communal nest boxes.*

Above: *The sight of a parent bird, such as this bluebird, feeding a brood of chicks in the backyard is wonderfully rewarding.*

hole in the bottom to let any water that blows or seeps in escape. If there is any standing water, it will make the box cold, might lead to disease, and will increase the chances of the box rotting. For the same reasons, make sure that the bottom of the box is inside the sides and not secured to the bottom, or water will seep straight into the bottom. The lid must fit tightly,

Above: *Doves roost in dovecotes with ledged entrances. However, in general, an outside ledge can attract predators.*

preferably with a hooked catch to prevent predators, such as squirrels or cats, from getting in and eating the chicks. Boxes with a perch under the entrance hole should be regarded with caution, because they can be used by predatory squirrels to stand on. Lastly, avoid using any boxes that have been heavily treated with preservative. The fumes will be off-putting to birds, and what is more, they could prove poisonous to the adults or chicks.

When you buy bird boxes, make sure that they are accompanied with instructions and other useful information regarding their positioning to maximize the chances of birds taking up residence. The best brands may also offer advice on how you can improve your backyard to suit particular species. Buying a bird box from a reputable supplier is probably the simplest (if most expensive) way to achieve success.

SECURING A BIRD BOX

It is not difficult to hang up a bird box, but choosing the right position is important. It must be attached securely so that it does not fall when occupied, particularly when well-grown nestlings become more active.

DIFFERENT TYPES OF NEST BOX

There is no standard design for a bird box. What birds really need is a secure and weatherproof home, safe from predators. However, do remember that different bird species have different preferences regarding the type and location of a box.

Enclosed box This style of nest box has a small, usually circular entrance hole. An enclosed box will suit many species, including chickadees, titmice, bluebirds, wrens, nuthatches, house finches, and woodpeckers. The size of the box and the size and shape of the entrance hole varies with the species you intend to attract. Small birds, such as titmice and chickadees, need relatively small boxes with round holes about 1⅛ inch (2.8cm) wide, while larger birds, such as woodpeckers and owls, need larger boxes with holes that are 2¼ inches (6cm) or more across.

Open-front box Some birds, including winter wrens, will use a nest box with a large, rectangular entrance hole for nesting. The opening width should be about 1½ inches (4cm) for wrens.

Nesting shelf Song sparrows, American robins, and phoebes will use a box with an entirely open front—also called a roosting box—for resting. Barn swallows, blue jays, and cardinals also roost in this style of box.

Duck box Usually large and square, these are attached to poles sunk in water to keep predators away. The rectangular entrance is reached via a ramplike ladder.

Communal box Birds such as purple martins, starlings, and house sparrows form communal nests. In the case of house sparrows, these are commonly sited under the eaves of houses. However, modern energy efficiency means that many former nest sites have been sealed off, and house sparrows often have difficulty in breeding. Communal nest boxes can help to boost numbers of these species.

Swallow nest cup Swallows may have difficulty finding nest sites, and the smooth walls of modern buildings often cause nests to fall, sometimes with the young inside. Near roads, vibration caused by heavy vehicles may also shake nests loose. Artificial nests, made of a wood and cement mix, are sometimes supplied attached to an artificial overhang ready for use.

Owl box These vary considerably in their design and are often more of a tube rather than a box. Smaller owl boxes are used by other large birds because they are often at least three times the size of a standard bird box. There are many designs, but all need a well-drained floor and easy access for cleaning at the end of the season, and are best placed in a large tree in the lower to mid canopy.

Enclosed box

Open-front box

Duck box

Communal box

Swallow nest cup

Owl box

Boxes can be hung at 6 feet (1.8m) above ground, but they can be placed higher than this, and a height of 12 feet (3.7m) or more will defeat many predators.

When positioning a bird box, make sure that it is protected from prevailing cold winds and hot sun, preferably giving it a shady aspect or wall that faces away from the strong midday or afternoon sun. Try to ensure that the birds have a fairly clear flight path to and from the nest, and try to angle the box slightly downward to help exclude rain. Remember that birds are often territorial and, in most cases, do not like being crowded together. Leave some space between the boxes unless providing for communal species, such as sparrows. There may be natural possibilities already in your backyard that, with a little thought,

can be turned into good nest sites. Birds may nest in an old shed that has had the door left purposely ajar, or set up home in a hole in the eaves of a house or outbuilding.

MAINTENANCE

Inspect the box in late summer or early fall, and remove any nest material or other debris. This helps reduce parasites. You can add some clean straw if you want small birds to use it over winter. In late winter, clear the box out again ready for the nesting season. Finally, provide nesting materials, such as string, cloth, wool, dried grass, and excess hair from your cat or dog.

Right: *If you find a nestling on the ground, leave it alone. The parents will not be far away, and may abandon it if you intervene.*

WIRE BIRD FEEDER

Small aluminum soda cans and aluminum mesh form the basis for these simple feeders, which, when filled with seeds or peanuts and hung from an old umbrella frame, will attract a range of species.

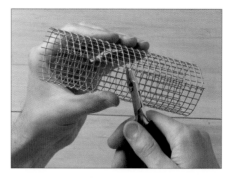

1 Cut a small aluminum soda can in half, then draw a decorative scalloped border around each half and cut out using scissors. Trim off any jagged edges.

2 Cut a rectangle of mesh to fit, rolled up, inside the can. Roll the mesh around a bottle. Join the edges by hooking the cut ends through and bending them with pliers.

3 Pierce a hole in the bottom of the can. Fit the mesh cylinder into the two halves of the can, then thread them onto galvanized wire. Twist the lower end of the wire into a flat coil so that the feeder cannot slide off.

4 Leave enough wire above the top so you can slide the top off for refilling, then allow an extra 3 inches (7.5cm). Cut the wire. Twist the end into a flat coil, then make a hook by bending the wire over a felt-tip pen.

YOU WILL NEED

small aluminum soda cans
old scissors, wire cutters
aluminum mesh
bottle with straight sides
small pliers, awl
galvanized wire
permanent felt-tip pen

TYPICAL FOOD

peanut hearts, sunflower seeds

TYPICAL VISITORS

titmice and chickadees
woodpeckers and finches

Above: *Woodpeckers are well-suited to taking nuts from wire feeders, with their long, straight bills and powerful claws.*

BOUNTY BOWER

In winter, the food you provide can make the difference between life and death for birds. Once you have started, continue to put food out each day, but for a real treat offer this gourmet selection.

1 Skewer an apple and thread it onto a long piece of garden wire. Wind the end around the bottom of the apple to prevent it from slipping off. Embed sunflower seeds into the flesh of the apple. You can adjust the quantities to suit the number of birds that call at your bower.

2 Screw metal eyelets into the bottom of a selection of pinecones. Thread them with string and tie the cones together in size order. Hang the string on an existing bower.

YOU WILL NEED
skewer
garden wire
wire cutters
metal eyelets
string
scissors
raffia
darning needle
strong thread
hacksaw
drill
unsalted, unroasted smooth peanut
    butter (from health-food stores)

TYPICAL FOOD
apple
millet bunches
whole coconut
peanuts in their shells
sunflower seeds
mixed birdseeds
thistle (niger)
pinecones

TYPICAL VISITORS
goldfinches and grosbeaks
titmice and chickadees
blue jays

3 Tie a selection of millet bunches with raffia. Using a darning needle and strong thread, thread unshelled peanuts to make long strings. Saw a coconut in half. Drill two holes near the edge of one half and thread a piece of wire through them. Twist the ends of the wire together.

4 When the seeds have been pecked out of the cones, you can revamp them by filling with unsalted, unroasted smooth peanut butter and dipping in small mixed seeds.

COCONUT FEEDER

A plastic tube, made from a recycled bottle, makes a practical seed dispenser. The coconut shell roof lifts off to the side, letting you refill the plastic tube as necessary. Titmice are particularly adept at using this kind of feeder and their acrobatics can be entertaining.

Above: *Finches, such as American goldfinches, grosbeaks, siskins, and this house finch (Carpodacus mexicanus), often visit feeders. Separate populations of house finches exist in eastern and western parts of the United States.*

YOU WILL NEED
2 coconuts
drill
hole saw
knife
hacksaw
1½-inch (4cm)-diameter plastic
    bottle with straight sides
scissors
florist's wire
twigs
small pliers
string
bead

TYPICAL FOOD
sunflower seeds
mixed seeds or thistle

TYPICAL VISITORS
finches
sparrows
redpolls
titmice

1 Drill two holes in the top of each coconut and drain the milk. Cut two 2-inch (5cm) holes from one on opposite sides and a third at the top. Remove the flesh with a knife.

3 Beneath each large side hole in the first coconut, drill two tiny holes on either side. These will be used for holding the perches. Drill two additional holes on each side for attaching the roof.

5 Attach a perch beneath each side hole by threading florist's wire through the small drilled holes and around a twig, twisting it to form a cross over the center. Using small pliers, twist the ends of the wire together inside the coconut to secure it.

2 Saw the second coconut in half. Remove the flesh from one half to form the roof of the feeder. Make a small hole in the top and two holes on each side near the rim.

4 Remove the top and bottom of a plastic bottle to make a tube. Cut two semicircles at the bottom on opposite sides to let seeds spill out. Place the tube in the first coconut through the large hole at the top.

6 Attach the roof to the base by threading string through the side holes in the coconuts. Tie a bead to a doubled piece of string to act as an anchor, and thread the string through the central hole of the roof for hanging the feeder.

BOTTLE FEEDER

This elegant and practical seed feeder keeps the contents dry. You will be able to regulate the flow of seeds by adjusting the height of the bottle, but do not forget to cover the opening while you insert the filled bottle into the frame to avoid spilling any seeds.

Above: *Sparrows, such as song sparrows, are among the most common visitors to seed feeders. In recent years, some types of sparrows have declined, but putting out seeds for them can help reverse the trend.*

YOU WILL NEED
bottle
pierced galvanized metal L-shape
  bracket
hacksaw (if needed)
galvanized wire
pliers
5-inch (12.5cm) pie pan with
  removable base
aluminum gauze
old scissors
epoxy resin glue
florist's wire

TYPICAL FOOD
black sunflower seeds
striped sunflower seeds
mixed seeds

TYPICAL VISITORS
titmice
sparrows
juncos
goldfinches
siskins

1 Measure your chosen bottle against the metal bracket and, if the bracket is too long, cut off the excess metal using a hacksaw. However, it does not matter if a little of the bracket shows above the top.

3 Place the bottle in position on the bracket and wrap the wire around it, forming a crisscross shape. Secure the wire by threading it through a hole on the bracket at the back.

5 Take the bottle out of the wire frame and set it aside. Remove the base of the pie pan and use it as a template to cut out a circular piece of aluminum gauze. Glue the gauze into the base of the pie pan.

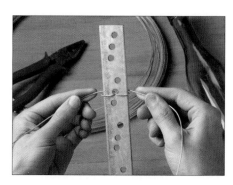

2 Cut a piece of wire long enough to wrap around the bottle in a crisscross fashion. Thread both ends of the wire through an appropriate hole positioned near the top of the bracket.

4 Repeat the process at the neck of the bottle, so that the bottle is held in place by two sections of crossed wire. Twist the ends of the wire together at the back of the bracket using a pair of pliers.

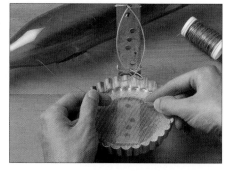

6 Using florist's wire, attach the pan to the bracket by wiring through the aluminum gauze. Add the bottle. The gap between the bottle neck and the pan should be wide enough to let seeds trickle through.

RUSTIC BIRD TABLE

A basic table is one of the simplest ways of dispensing food to birds. One of the advantages is that it can take many different kinds of food. You can make this attractive table simply from two pieces of rough lumber, nailed together with wood strips to strengthen the structure. The lip around the edge stops nuts and seeds from rolling off. String is tied to a hook in each corner so that the table can be hung in a tree. You could also hang a fat ball from where the strings meet.

Above: *Flocks of purple finches* (Carpodacus purpureus) *forage at bird tables in winter. These finches are especially fond of sunflower seeds.*

YOU WILL NEED

rough lumber, two ½ x 5 x 10-inch
    (1 x 13 x 25cm) lengths
wood strips, two 1 x 1 x 10-inch
    (2.5 x 2.5 x 25cm) lengths and
    four ½ x 2 x 11-inch (1 x 5 x 28cm)
    lengths
nails
hammer
wood preservative
paintbrush
4 brass hooks
2 yards (2m) sisal string
scissors

TYPICAL FOOD

varied, including seeds, bread

TYPICAL VISITORS

finches and cardinals
sparrows and juncos
titmice

1 Join together the two pieces of rough lumber by positioning them side by side and placing the two 10-inch (25cm)-long strips across the wood, one at each end. Nail the strips securely in place to make the bottom.

2 Nail the four 11-inch (28cm)-long wood strips around the edges of the flat side of the table, creating a lip of at least 1 inch (2.5cm) to ensure the food is not spilled.

3 Lightly paint all the surfaces of the table with wood preservative and let dry.

4 Screw a brass hook into each corner of the table to attach the string.

5 Cut the sisal string into four equal lengths and tie a small loop in one end of each piece. Attach each loop to a hook, then gather up the strings above the table and tie in a loop for hanging.

KITCHEN BIRD TABLE

This original bird table uses cooking and cleaning equipment in ingenious ways, and makes an offbeat sculpture at the same time. The strainers let rain drain away, and the finial is the head of a balloon whisk, into which a fat ball can be inserted.

1 Clamp the strainer handle under a wooden block and bend it 90 degrees. Then bend it farther by hand to fit around the broom handle. Repeat the same process with the other strainers.

2 Nail a piece of scrap wood to the bottom of the broom handle and firmly anchor this in the bucket using large beach pebbles.

3 Position the strainers along the length of the broom handle and hold each one in place by threading a wooden spoon into the bent handle. Once you are happy with the arrangement, sand grooves into the broom handle for the spoons to fit into.

YOU WILL NEED
clamps
metal strainers
wooden block
scrap wood
protective gloves
broom handle
nails
hammer
galvanized bucket
beach pebbles
wooden spoons
sandpaper
balloon whisk
hacksaw or wire cutters
galvanized wire

TYPICAL FOOD
fat ball
sunflower seeds
mixed seeds
peanut hearts
leftovers and kitchen scraps

TYPICAL VISITORS
thrushes and bluebirds
cardinals
blue jays
sparrows
chickadees

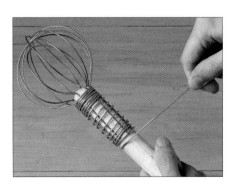

4 Using either a hacksaw or wire cutters, remove the handle of a balloon whisk and attach it to the top of the broom handle using a length of galvanized wire. This provides a holder for a fat ball.

PALLADIAN BIRD TABLE

This classical-style feeding table looks elegant and impressive but is actually relatively simple to make. It will not only attract birds that enjoy eating seeds, fat, and scraps, but will also beautify any backyard setting. It can be mounted on a pole, hung from a branch, or secured to a wall using a large bracket.

Above: *Virginian cardinals* (Cardinalis cardinalis), *are among the species attracted to bird tables holding seeds and scraps.*

YOU WILL NEED
½-inch (12mm) medium-density
    fiberboard (MDF) or exterior-grade
    plywood (for the base)
¼-inch (6mm) medium-density
    fiberboard (MDF) or exterior-grade
    plywood
ruler, pencil
saw
glue gun and glue sticks
8 threaded knobs, 1¼ inch (30mm)
    diameter x ¾ inch (20mm) deep
4 dowels, ⅝ x 4¾ inches (16 x 120mm)
drill and ⅛-inch (3mm) bit
exterior-grade filler
fine-grade sandpaper
medium paintbrush
off-white latex paint
exterior-grade varnish

TYPICAL FOOD
varied, including seeds, fat, scraps

TYPICAL VISITORS
titmice and chickadees
finches and cardinals

1 Mark and cut out all the pieces, following the template given at the back of the book. Assemble the base and steps with wood glue. You can apply hot glue using a glue gun if you possess one.

3 Glue each half of the roof onto the top of the gable triangles. Make sure each roof half overlaps the ceiling by the same amount at the sides and each end.

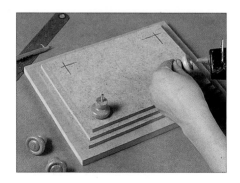

5 Glue the threaded cupboard knobs in position at each corner mark on the base and the ceiling. Let dry thoroughly. Meanwhile, drill each end of the dowel columns to accommodate the protruding thread of the knobs.

2 Mark the positions of the columns at each corner of the top step and on the underside of the ceiling. Glue the main gable triangles in place on each end of the ceiling piece.

4 Let stand long enough for the roof glue to dry thoroughly. Next, glue the decorative gable triangle in place centrally on the face of the front gable.

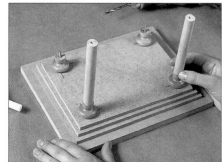

6 Apply glue to each thread and assemble the dowels between the base and the roof. Fill any gaps with exterior-grade filler. Rub down with fine-grade sandpaper and paint with off-white latex paint, followed by several coats of exterior-grade varnish.

SEASHORE BIRD TABLE

The pretty decorative details and distressed paintwork of this bird table are reminiscent of seashore architecture. You can use plain dowels—or a broom handle—to make the supports for the roof, or recycle the turned legs from an old piece of furniture.

Above: *European starlings (Sturnus vulgaris) have spread across North America since being introduced from the Old World.*

YOU WILL NEED
¾-inch (2cm) pine board
pencil, ruler
jigsaw or scroll saw
drill
wood glue
4 screws
screwdriver
fretsaw
4 dowels, ¾ x 8 inches (2 x 20cm)
⅛-inch (4mm) plywood
sandpaper
plated molding nails
hammer
watercolor paints
paintbrushes
petroleum jelly
white latex paint
blowtorch
satin yacht varnish
water bowl

TYPICAL FOOD
varied, including kitchen scraps

TYPICAL VISITORS
starlings
mockingbirds
sparrows and juncos
finches and thrushes

1 Using the templates, mark out the base, roof base, and roof ends on pine board. Cut out using a jigsaw. Drill a ¾-inch (2cm) hole in each corner of the two bases. Glue and screw the roof ends to the roof base.

3 From the ⅛-inch (4mm) plywood, cut five strips 1 inch (2.5cm) wide for each roof end panel. Cut seven 1-inch (2.5cm) strips for each side of the roof. Cut out the scalloped edging pieces, four strips for the eaves, and two lozenges for the finials. Sand surfaces.

5 Paint the bird table with a diluted mixture of cobalt blue and burnt umber watercolor paint. Let dry, then smear on a thin layer of petroleum jelly with your fingers. Apply white latex paint and dry it with a blowtorch to make the paint crack.

2 In the base, drill a starter hole for the fretsaw. Cut out a 3-inch (7.5cm)-diameter hole, 2 inches (5cm) in from one short side. Glue the four doweling supports in place on the frame and base. Let dry overnight.

4 Glue the plywood strips across the roof ends and nail in place with the nails. Attach the roof slats along the sides of the roof, and the scalloped edges all around the roof edge and the base. A piece of cardboard can hold the nails steady while hammering.

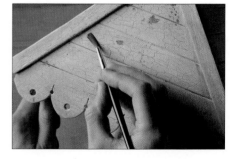

6 To age the paintwork, apply a diluted, equal mixture of yellow ocher and burnt sienna watercolor. Let dry, then finish with a coat of satin yacht varnish. Attach to a store-bought stand and place a water bowl on the table.

BAMBOO BIRD TABLE

It is a real treat to watch birds feeding, and seeing them at close range from the comfort of your armchair is even better. This bamboo structure is designed to hang on a wall from two cup hooks. Position it near a window so that you can see the birds easily.

Above: *Northern mockingbirds* (Mimus polyglottos) *visit urban and rural backyards in most of the United States. They can mimic the songs of many other birds.*

YOU WILL NEED
tenon saw
lumber scrap
pencil
ruler
drill
bamboo stakes
clips
garden string
scissors
scrap roofing material
baking pan
2 clothespins
wire whisk

TYPICAL FOOD
fat ball
peanuts in their shells
sunflower seeds
bread crumbs, kitchen scraps
cracked corn

TYPICAL VISITORS
titmice and chickadees
finches and juncos
jays and mockingbirds

1 Mark a 4½ x 6¼-inch (12 x 16cm) rectangle on the lumber scrap and cut it out. Drill a hole in each corner and push in four 3-foot (90cm) stakes. Cut two short lengths of cane and clip them diagonally at the top to hold the uprights in place.

3 Tie on the roof supports on each side, again using the templates given at the back of the book as a guide. Use garden string or twine to tie the supports.

5 To attach the roof, drill four holes in the roofing sheet. Unclip the top diagonals and push the roof down over the uprights until it is resting on the roof supports. Tie on the long top diagonals.

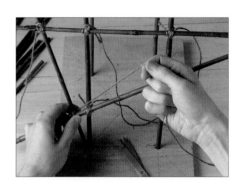

2 Using the templates at the back of the book as a guide, tie on the horizontal stakes using garden string. These will hold the baking pan firmly on each side. Add two diagonal canes on each side as shown to reinforce the structure.

4 Join the two sides of the structure, first attaching the bottom diagonal canes, then with two pieces running straight across at the level of the feeding tray.

6 Snip off the long ends of the string and attach the feeding tray with two clothespins. Use the top long diagonals to hang food from, such as a whisk as a fat ball holder, or nuts.

RUSTIC FEEDERS

These two feeders in different styles originate from the same basic store-bought model. One has been sanded and given a driftwood-style paint effect, while the other has been camouflaged beneath found objects, including a rusty metal sheet and a short length of plasterer's angle bead.

Above: *The American goldfinch* (Carduelis tristis) *is sometimes called the "wild canary" after the male's bright yellow plumage.*

YOU WILL NEED
2 store-bought wooden bird feeders
light gray latex paint
medium paintbrushes
sandpaper
clear glue, sand
stub wire
pencil
corks or dowel
natural twine
shells, twigs, or moss
craft knife
thick florist's wire
protective gloves
sheet of old tin metal
tin snips or saw
glue gun and glue sticks
plasterer's angle bead
black spray paint

TYPICAL FOOD
peanut hearts, sunflower seeds

TYPICAL VISITORS
woodpeckers
titmice and finches

1 Paint the first feeder and let it dry. Rub down with sandpaper to give the surface a weathered, driftwood effect. Apply clear glue to the roof and sprinkle sand over it. Twist lengths of stub wire around a pencil and weave natural twine through them to imitate coils of rope.

2 Add natural objects found either in the countryside or on the seashore, such as shells, twigs, and moss, to decorate and personalize the feeder. Shells can be attached with glue. Use pieces of cork or dowel to seal the feed chambers, and tie a loop of florist's wire to suspend the house.

3 For the second feeder, wearing protective gloves, snip pieces of old tin metal to make a roof. Remove all sharp edges and glue in place. Glue moss around the base.

4 Make the roof ridge from plasterer's angle bead sprayed with black paint. Glue it firmly to the house. Plug the feed holes with corks or dowel and suspend with wire as before.

Left and right: *Two very different results can be achieved using the same basic store-bought feeder. You can experiment with different materials and applications to create your own designs. You can be quite creative with the choice of found objects you use to give your personalized feeder a flavor of whatever is in its immediate environment. This will help it to harmonize with the backyard setting. Or you can use materials such as shells, collected while on vacation, to produce a delightful memento.*

GLASS GAZEBO FEEDER

Constructed from recycled tin cans and small pieces of glass, this converted lantern makes a highly attractive feeder, which will shine, jewel-like, from among the surrounding dark foliage.

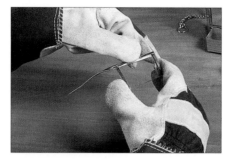

1 This lantern required extra glass to be installed. If this is the case, measure the areas needed and reduce all measurements by ¼ inch (6mm) to allow for the metal border around each panel. Using a china marker, mark the measurements on the glass, then cut out by running a glass cutter in a single pass along a ruler, while pressing firmly. Tap along the score line to break the glass. Wear protective gloves when handling glass.

2 Still wearing gloves, cut ⅜-inch (9mm) strips of metal from a used tin can using tin snips. Wrap a strip of metal around each edge of each glass panel. Trim, then smear a small amount of soldering flux onto the adjoining surfaces of each corner joint.

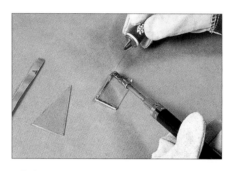

3 Solder the corner joints of each panel. Heat up a joint using a soldering iron and apply solder until it flows between the surfaces to be joined. Remove the heat source. The solder will set in seconds, but the metal will remain hot for some time.

YOU WILL NEED
glass lantern
tape measure (optional)
thin glass (optional)
china marker (optional)
try square (optional)
glass cutter (optional)
ruler
protective gloves
shiny tin can (not aluminum),
    washed and dried
tin snips
flux and soldering iron
solder
fine wire mesh

TYPICAL FOOD
peanut hearts
black sunflower seeds
striped sunflower seeds

TYPICAL VISITORS
titmice
sparrows and juncos
finches, siskins, redpolls
blue jays

4 Measure openings for the hoppers and fold sections of metal, using a try square or ruler to keep the folds straight. Solder the meeting points of each hopper. Cut a base from fine wire mesh, then solder the base, panels, and hoppers in place.

WOVEN WILLOW FEEDER

*Made from the supple branches of unstripped willow, this woven basket feeder will look very picturesque
in the backyard. It can be used to dispense foods such as peanuts. The conical roof is packed with
moss. As well as adding weight, this will provide valuable nesting material for breeding birds.*

YOU WILL NEED

about 150 willow sticks, soaked
knife or bodkin
clothespin
pruning shears, awl (optional)
pencil or pen, string
6 long strands ivy, moss
glycerin (optional)
garden twine

TYPICAL FOOD

peanut hearts or seeds

TYPICAL VISITORS

warblers and buntings
jays and finches

Left: *Blue jays* (Cyanocitta cristata)
*sometimes gather in small flocks outside
the breeding season.*

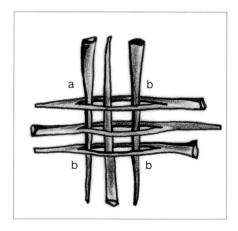

1 Trim six soaked willow sticks to a length
of 9 inches (23cm) from the butt (thick) end.
Pierce the center of three of these rods
using a knife or bodkin and push the other
three willow sticks through them to form
a cross. The willow sticks should then be
arranged with the butt ends pointing in
alternate directions. Push the rods together.

2 The cross you have made will form the center of the base of the
feeder. Insert the tips of two long willow sticks into the slits to
the left of the short rods and hold them in place by gripping the
slit rods. Take one long willow stick in front of the three uprights,
and behind the next three rods. Take the second willow stick
behind the first three rods and in front of the next three, crossing
its partner at (b). Continue this weave for two complete rounds.
Pry the rods apart to form the spokes of a wheel and continue
weaving. Try to keep your weaving as tight as possible.

3 Continue to weave the base of the feeder basket, adding new
weavers either butt to butt or alternatively tip to tip. The new one
is placed to the left of, and under, the old end, which should finish
resting on a bottom rod, while the new weaver carries on over it.
Join both new weavers at the same time, on neighboring bottom
rods. Continue with your weaving until the base of the basket
measures about 7 inches (18cm), finishing with tips. Temporarily
secure the ends with a clothespin and then trim the bottom rods
flush with the weaving.

  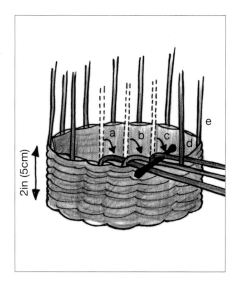

4 Having finished the base, you can now start to fashion the uprights that will support the cone-shape roof of the bird feeder. Start by selecting 12 new willow sticks. Trim the butt ends of the rods by slicing down the back of each one with a sharp knife to make a thin wedge shape. Insert each new willow stick to the left of a bottom rod. You may need to loosen the weave first, using a bodkin or awl, before you can fit in the new rod if you have woven the base very tightly.

5 Using your thumbnail or the blade of a knife, make an indentation in each of the new willow sticks where they join the base, then gently bend each one up to form the uprights and temporarily tie them all together at the top with string. You can now start to make the sides of the basket. Begin by inserting three new willow sticks, tip end first, to lie to the right of three consecutive uprights. Take the left-hand weaver in front of two uprights, behind the third and out to the front again.

6 Repeat with the second and third rods. Continue this pattern, pushing the weavers down, until the sides of the basket measure 2 inches (5cm). Join in new weavers butt to butt or tip to tip, laying the three new rods to the right of the three old rods. To finish the basket, make a kink in each upright over a pencil or pen about twice the diameter of the rod. Bend the first rod (a) behind the second (b) and around to the front. Bend (b) over and behind (c), then bend (c) over and behind (d) and around to the front.

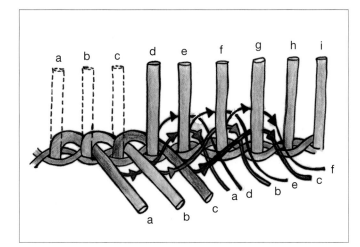 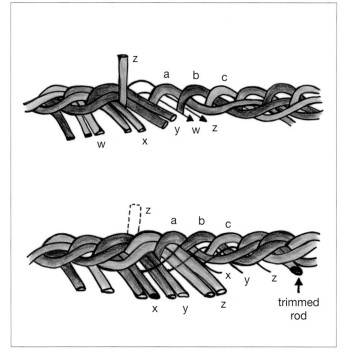

7 To finish off the border: rod (a) travels in front of (c) and (d) and behind (e) and lies in front. Rod (d) bends down and lies beside and to the right of (a). Rod (b) travels in front of (d) and (e) and behind (f) and lies in front. Rod (e) bends over and lies beside and to the right of (b). Rod (c) travels in front of (e) and (f) and behind (g) and lies to the front. Rod (f) lies down beside and to the right of (c). There are now 3 pairs of rods (ad), (be), and (cf). Continue the work, always weaving with three pairs of rods until the end of the border. Always start with the far left pair of rods (ad) but use the right-hand rod (d), (e), and (f) and make each rod do the same journey (in front of two uprights, behind one) and pull down the next upright (g), (h), and (i), until there is only one upright left.

8 To finish the border, starting with the far left pair as before, each right-hand rod goes in front of two rods (which are not now upright) and behind the third, coming out through the original "arches" made with a, b, and c. Pull all the rods well down into place, lying tightly together. Trim the ends neatly all around the basket.

9 To make the frame for the roof, select 12 rods and trim them to 12 inches (30cm). Tie them securely together, 2 inches (5cm) from the tips, using ivy. The ivy can be stripped of its leaves, or preserve the leaves by soaking them in glycerin, diluted half and half with water, for several days. Bend a willow stick into a circle a little larger than the basket. To secure the rods for the roof to the circular frame, take two long ivy stems, stripped of leaves, and tie them to the left of an upright. Wind one length around the upright above the frame and the other around the upright below the frame. Take both pieces around the frame to cross between the first and second uprights, then around the frame to the second upright. Repeat the pattern.

10 Weave the roof using the same pattern as for the sides of the basket, using two sets of three rods, then change to a pairing weave, going in front of one upright and behind the next. Near the top, use a single rod weaving in and out, and go as high as you can. Next, stuff the roof with moss.

11 To hold the moss in place, tie garden twine across the bottom of the roof, connecting each upright with the ones on the opposite side to make a star pattern. Cut four rods 8 inches (20cm) long and trim both ends of each into flat wedges. Push them, equally spaced, into the weave of the roof and into corresponding positions in the basket, using a bodkin to open the weave if necessary.

COPPER BIRDBATH

You will have hours of pleasure watching many different species of birds drinking from or preening and cleaning in this beautiful yet eminently practical beaten copper birdbath.

1 Using a china marker and a piece of looped string, mark a 17¾-inch (45cm) circle on the copper sheet.

2 Wearing protective gloves, cut out the circle with a pair of tin snips. Carefully smooth any sharp edges using a file.

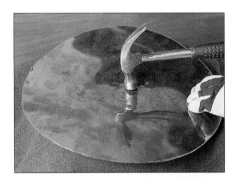

3 Put the copper on a blanket and hammer it lightly from the center. Spread the dips out to the rim. Repeat, starting from the center each time, to get the required shape.

4 Continue hammering until you have a shallow dish shape that will let birds enter and leave the water without difficulty. To make the perch, cut 1 yard (1m) of copper wire, loop, and hold the ends in a vise. Insert a cup hook into the chuck of a hand drill or slow-speed power drill. Put the cup hook through the loop. Run the drill to twist the wire. Drill three ⅛-inch (3mm) holes around the rim of the bath.

YOU WILL NEED
china marker
string
copper sheet, 20 SWG (0.9mm)
protective gloves
tin snips
file
blanket or carpet square
hammer
13 feet (4m) medium copper wire
cup hook
drill and ⅛-inch (3mm) bit

TYPICAL VISITORS
titmice
finches and siskins
sparrows

5 Bend a knot into one end of each of three 1-yard (1m) lengths of wire. Thread the wires through the holes from beneath the birdbath. Slip the twisted wire over two of the straight wires to form a perch, and hang in a suitable position.

6 Maintain a constant supply of fresh drinking water all year round to help ensure the health of your local bird population. Once the birds have got used to this new feature, many different varieties will visit to bathe and drink.

CHROME BIRDBATH

The gently sloping sides of a trashcan lid will let smaller birds paddle, while larger birds can have a good splash in the middle without emptying the water. A night-light attached under the bath will prevent the water from freezing over on winter days.

1 Using a hacksaw, saw across the middle of the trashcan lid handle. Bend back both sides of the severed handle using pliers.

2 Wearing protective gloves, remove the handle from the cheese grater using pliers. Once you have managed to detach one side of the handle from the securing rivet, the other will work free more easily.

YOU WILL NEED
hacksaw
galvanized trashcan lid
pliers
protective gloves
cylindrical metal cheese grater
round fence post to suit size of grater
galvanized nails, hammer
night-light

TYPICAL VISITORS
sparrows and towhees
thrushes and robins
thrashers and catbirds
finches
redpolls and siskins

3 Push the narrow end of the cheese grater onto the post and secure it with nails through the holes left by the handle rivets.

Above: *Dark-eyed juncos* (Junco hyemalis) *are among the most frequent visitors to birdbaths, splashing to wet their feathers.*

4 Squeeze the two sides of the lid handle together to insert them into the wide end of the grater. Place a night-light inside the grater. This can then be lit, with care, to provide an interesting feature and prevent the water from freezing on cold days.

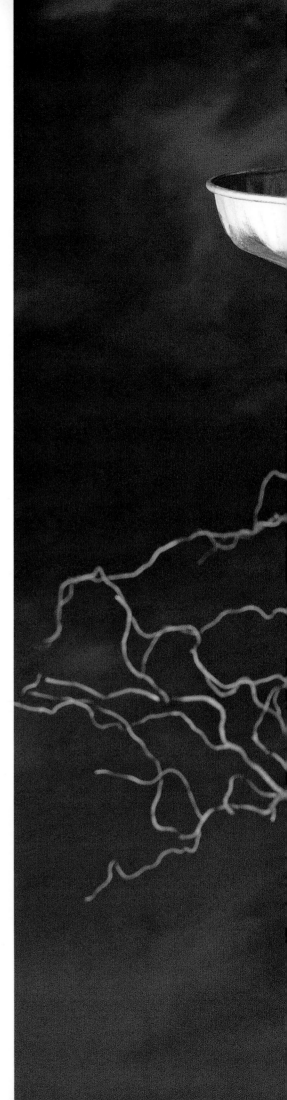

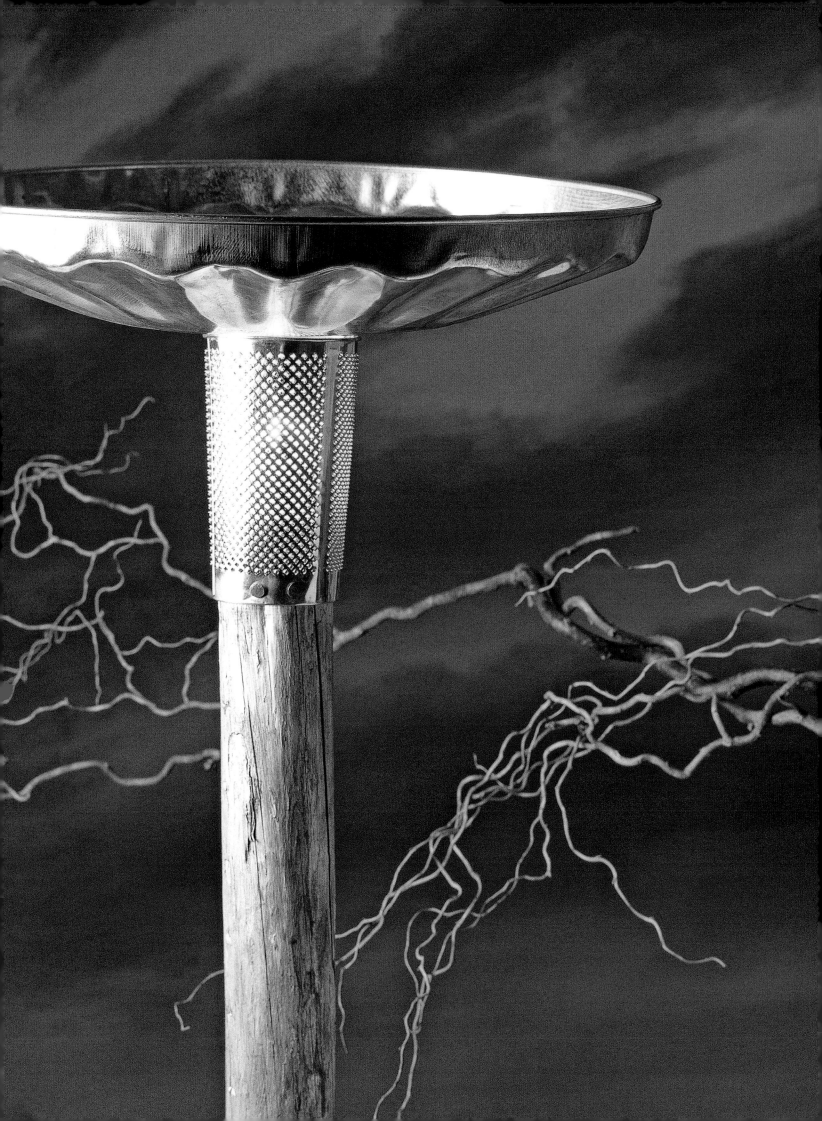

NESTING MATERIALS DISPENSER

This sculptural container will not only look elegant in your backyard but will encourage birds to build their nests nearby. At the start of the breeding season, keep the dispenser filled up with materials, such as scraps of wool, fur, fabric, straw, feathers, and even hair, all of which will be most welcome to backyard birds.

Above: *Northern orioles* (Icterus galbula) *gather plant fibers, bark, and twine to weave a well-constructed hanging nest. This individual has a length of twine in its beak. Most birds build the basic nest structure using tough plant fibers, such as twigs, leaves, and dry grass. The interior is lined with soft, warm materials, such as moss, hair, and feathers. By providing nesting materials, you will give birds a helping hand to raise their young.*

YOU WILL NEED
chicken wire, approximately
   10 inches (25cm) wide
protective gloves
wire cutters
small pliers
thin and thick garden wire
plastic picnic plate
awl
coffee can lid
epoxy resin glue
large wooden bead

TYPICAL VISITORS
finches
warblers and orioles
sparrows and juncos
titmice and chickadees

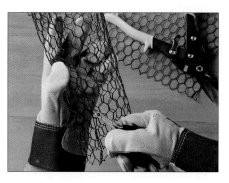

1 Cut a rectangular piece of chicken wire and roll it into a cylinder. Join the wire along the edges by carefully twisting the cut ends together. Using a pair of pliers, pull the bottom of the cylinder to draw the wires together into a tight roll.

3 Splay out the rim of the container at the top. Bind the bottom with thin green garden wire. Secure both ends of the wire.

5 Make holes to match the positions of the wires around the edge of a plastic plate, using a heated awl. Thread the plate, upside down, onto the wires. Glue a coffee can lid to the plate to make a container for food or water.

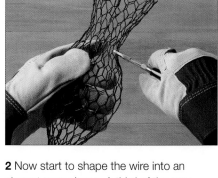

2 Now start to shape the wire into an elegant vase shape. A third of the way from the top, form a neck by squeezing the wires together with the pliers. To create the belly of the container, pull the holes open farther to fatten out the shape.

4 Attach four lengths of thicker wire, evenly spaced, around the rim of the container. Loop them through and secure the ends.

6 Connect the four wires to a single wire threaded with a large bead. Twist the wires neatly into position. Now you are ready to hang the dispenser from a tree or large shrub, so that nesting birds can pluck the contents at will.

ENCLOSED NEST BOX

This box will attract birds to nest in your backyard. The small, round entrance hole will suit wrens, titmice, bluebirds, and other species. Having nested once, birds can return year after year.

1 The lumber used in nest boxes should preferably be of hardwood, such as oak. Softer woods, such as pine, can also be used, but will start to rot more quickly. Whatever wood you use will last longer if you give the finished box a coat of exterior-grade varnish.

2 Measure the dimensions on the lumber, referring to the template at the back of the book, and mark them clearly using a pencil and carpenter's square. Always double-check your measurements before cutting. Mark the names of each section in pencil.

YOU WILL NEED

length of lumber, ½ x 6 x 56¾ inches
    (1 x 15 x 142cm)
pencil
ruler
carpenter's square
saw
sandpaper
screws
screwdriver
drill with 1¼-inch (3cm) drill bit
rubber strip (for hinge)
varnish
paintbrush

TYPICAL INHABITANTS

titmice and chickadees
nuthatches
wrens
house finches
house sparrows

3 Cut the pieces using a sharp carpentry saw and put them to one side. Sand off any splintered edges to the wood.

4 Carefully screw the sections together. Do not use nails, because these can cause the wood to split and let water into the box.

5 On the front face of the box, make a hole with a large drill bit. Attach the roof, using the rubber strip as a hinge. Varnish and hang the box in the backyard, choosing a suitable spot out of direct sun and high enough to be out of reach of predators.

ROOST AND WREN BOX

Not all of the birds that nest in your backyard will like boxes with small entrance holes. A box with a large rectangular hole will attract winter wrens for nesting. Other species, including American robins, phoebes, blue jays, sparrows, and swallows, may use an open-front box as a nest or roost.

Opposite page: *A box with a large, rectangular entrance hole as shown will attract winter wrens as a nest site. Eastern phoebes* (Sayornis phoebe), *above, will nest in a similar box with an entirely open front. Eastern phoebes nest throughout the east of the Rockies and overwinter in some southern states. These birds will nest on buildings and bridges with ledges and can be tame when breeding. An entirely open-faced box can also attract cardinals, blue jays, barn swallows, and song sparrows as a nest or roost.*

YOU WILL NEED
length of lumber, 5⁄8 x 6 x 44½ inches
    (15 x 152 x 1129mm)
wood glue
hammer
nails or panel nails
pencil
strip of burlap or rubber (for hinge)
varnish, paintbrush

TYPICAL INHABITANTS
wrens
American robins, phoebes, blue jays,
    and some sparrows and swallows;
    these will also roost in a similar
    box with an entirely open front

1 Cut out the lumber using the template given in the back of the book. Arrange the pieces of wood in position to make sure that they all fit properly.

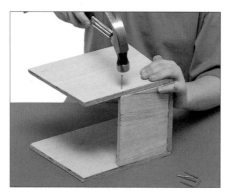

3 Glue on the other side and nail all the pieces together. Place the box on the rear board, and draw around it in pencil.

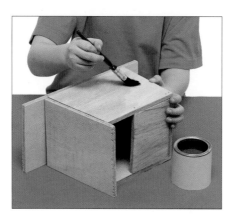

5 The box will last longer if you give it a coat of exterior-grade varnish both inside and out. Let the box stand overnight so the varnish dries thoroughly.

2 Glue the low front of the box to the base. Give the glue a little time to dry. Now add one of the side pieces of the box. Align it carefully and glue it in place.

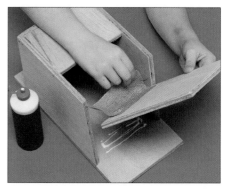

4 Using your pencil guidelines, nail the rear to the box. Add the roof by gluing and nailing on the burlap hinge.

6 Nail the box to a tree or post, about 7 feet (2m) from the ground. Face the box away from any direct sunlight, because this could harm young birds.

CUSTOMIZED NEST BOX

Store-bought nest boxes are available in every shape and size. An inexpensive birdhouse can be transformed with a splash of paint and a few decorative touches. The Shaker-style paintwork on this birdhouse uses leftover paint, the finial is cut from scrap lumber, and the perch is an apple-tree twig.

Above: *Great crested flycatchers (Myiarchus crinitus) of eastern woodlands nest in tree cavities or bird boxes with a small entrance hole. The nest is lined with string, rags, and frequently snakeskins. The female lays 5–6 pale, brown-spotted eggs. Like other tyrant flycatchers (Tyrannidae), it mostly catches flying insects. This species is bold and noisy.*

YOU WILL NEED

store-bought nest box with
   2 holes
latex paint in 2 contrasting colors
paintbrush
permanent felt-tip pen
decorative finial cut from a piece
   of scrap pine
white glue
apple-tree twig

TYPICAL INHABITANTS

titmice and chickadees
crested flycatcher
nuthatches
house sparrows
woodpeckers and pigeons; these will
   nest in a larger box of this type

1 Paint the box with the main color of latex paint and set it aside to dry. Draw the door and heart motifs using the permanent felt-tip pen.

2 Fill in the design and the finial with the contrasting color of latex paint and let dry completely. Glue the finial in place at the front of the roof ridge using white glue.

3 Apply a little glue to the apple-tree twig and gently push it into position in the small hole beneath the main entrance hole. Let the glue dry before hanging the box up.

DECORATED BIRDHOUSES

Inexpensive store-bought plain boxes can be customized to suit your taste. Paint makes for the simplest transformations—an alpine chalet and a Shaker-style dwelling are pictured here. You can also create a leafy hideaway using fabric shapes. Paint each house with primer and let dry before you begin.

YOU WILL NEED
store-bought birdhouses
paintbrushes
primer and latex paints
matte varnish and brush
pencil, paper, and scissors
self-adhesive roof flashing
waterproof green canvas
staple gun
waterproofing wax (optional)

TYPICAL INHABITANTS
titmice and chickadees

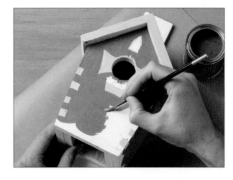

1 To create an alpine chalet, draw the design on the box. Paint the roof, shutters, and other details in pale blue. When this is dry, paint the walls of the house rust red.

2 Add details on the gable, shutters, and stonework in white and gray. Paint flowers, grass, and leaves along the front and sides in yellow and green. Varnish when dry.

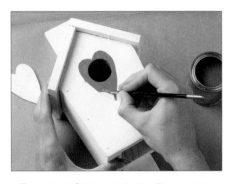

1 To make a Shaker-style dwelling, cut a heart out of paper and position it over the entry hole. Draw around it in pencil and paint the heart rust red.

2 Paint the walls in duck-egg blue using a larger paintbrush. When this layer is dry, paint on little starbursts in rust red using a very fine artist's brush.

3 Cut a piece of roof flashing to fit the birdhouse roof. Cover the roof, folding the edges under the eaves. Protect the paintwork with matte varnish.

1 To make a leafy hideaway, paint the birdhouse a color complementary to your green canvas, such as mid-blue, and let dry. Cut the canvas into 1½-inch (4cm) bands and scallop one edge. Staple the bands onto the house, starting at the base and letting the scallops overhang.

2 Staple more canvas bands around the front and sides, with each layer overlapping the last. When you reach the entry hole, snip the top of the canvas and glue it down inside. Staple on the next band, then trim back the central scallop to form a few small fronds above the entry hole.

3 Overlay strips on the side of the roof. Cut the top strip double the width, with a scalloped edge along both sides, so that it fits over the roof ridge. Finally, staple bands along the gable ends. Spray the finished house with waterproofing wax, if not using a waterproof fabric.

LAVENDER HIDEAWAY

This hand-painted project takes only a short time to make using a store-bought birdhouse. Even the heaviest shower will pour freely off the lead roof, leaving the occupants warm and dry inside.

1 Paint the birdhouse with lilac paint and let it dry. Sketch out the decorative design using a pencil. Fill in the sketch using acrylic or watercolor paints. When the paint is dry, cover the whole house with several coats of exterior-grade matte varnish.

2 Make a paper pattern to fit the roof, using the template at the back of the book as a guide. Allow ½ inch (12mm) extra for turning under each side and the rear, and 1¼ inches (32mm) extra for the scallops.

YOU WILL NEED
store-bought birdhouse
lilac latex paint
medium and fine paintbrushes
pencil
acrylic or watercolor paints
exterior-grade matte varnish
paper, scissors
protective gloves
thin sheet lead
tin snips or craft knife
soft hammer or wooden mallet

TYPICAL INHABITANTS
titmice and chickadees
wrens and nuthatches
bluebirds and house sparrows

3 Transfer the design onto a piece of thin sheet lead and cut it out using tin snips or a craft knife. Wear protective gloves or wash your hands thoroughly afterward.

Above: *Chestnut-backed chickadees* (Poecile rufescens) *are hole nesters and are well suited to this box.*

4 Hold the lead roof in place and mold to shape by tapping the lead with a soft hammer or wooden mallet until the correct fit is achieved. Turn the ½-inch (12mm) allowance under at the back and at the eaves to secure the roof in place.

FOLK-ART TITMOUSE BOX

This box is simple to make, but with its traditional weathered look, it makes the perfect springtime retreat for titmice and other hole nesters, such as nuthatches, wrens, and bluebirds. Mounted on a post in a quiet position, it should be safe from prowling predators, such as cats.

1 Mark and cut the basic house on MDF or plywood following the template at the back of the book. Mark a vertical line on the front panel. Mark a horizontal line across at the base of the triangle. Where the two lines cross, draw a $1\frac{1}{4}$-inch (32mm) circle, using a compass. Cut out the hole by first drilling a pilot hole, then enlarging it with a keyhole saw. Assemble the front, back, sides, base, and the smaller roof piece of the house using white glue and panel nails hammered down flush with the surface of the wood.

YOU WILL NEED

$\frac{1}{4}$-inch (6mm) medium-density
  fiberboard (MDF) or exterior-grade
  plywood
small piece of lumber (for base)
saw
compass
drill, keyhole saw
white glue
panel nails and hammer
latex paint: blue-gray and white
medium paintbrush
medium-grade sandpaper
protective gloves
lead sheet, tin snips
staple gun and staples
copper wire and wire cutters

TYPICAL INHABITANTS

titmice and chickadees
nuthatches

2 Paint the whole house, including the loose roof piece, with blue-gray latex paint. When dry, paint the walls of the house white. When these are dry (about 2–3 hours), distress the surfaces by rubbing with medium-grade sandpaper until the blue-gray paint shows through.

3 Wearing protective gloves, cut a strip of lead the depth of the roof by 2 inches (5cm) wide, using tin snips. Staple this to the loose roof half. Position the roof halves together, bend the lead to fit, and staple through the lead into the secured roof half.

4 Drill two small holes just below and to either side of the entrance hole. Bend a piece of copper wire into a flattened loop slightly wider than the distance between the holes. Pass the two ends of the wire through the holes and turn them down just inside the box to hold the perch in place.

Above: *Titmice (Paridae) nest in tree holes and bird boxes. They line their nests with warm materials, such as moss and leaves.*

Above: *This titmouse box can be adapted with different embellishments. It can be attached to a pole or hung from a tree.*

ROCK-A-BYE BIRDIE BOX

This box constructed from plywood is made to suit small, acrobatic birds, such as wrens, nuthatches, and titmice. The removable roof is covered with flashing to repel rainwater. The box hangs on stout string, although if you have a problem with predators, it would be safer to use greased wire.

Above: *Carolina wrens will nest in tree stumps, walls, mailboxes, and birdhouses. These birds of thickets do not migrate.*

YOU WILL NEED
paper
pencil
scissors
¼-inch (6mm) plywood
drill
sandpaper
fretsaw
birdsmouth board or clamp
¼ x ¾-inch (6 x 18mm) half-round
    molding
tenon saw
wood glue
panel nails
hammer
scrap wood
varnish
paintbrush
self-adhesive roof flashing
knife
cutting mat
string or wire

TYPICAL INHABITANTS
titmice and chickadees
wrens

1 Copy the templates at the back of the book, cut out, and use to mark out the shapes for the base and roof on thin plywood. Drill an entry hole in one side of the top and sand the edges.

3 Glue and then nail the lengths of molding around the base, with the flat side facing outward. You will find the easiest way of working is to start with the central strip and then work out.

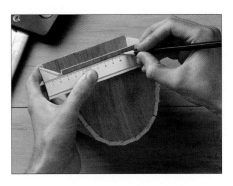

5 Mark a line around the base, about ¼ inch (6mm) below the top edge of the sides, and trim back the molding to this level to allow the roof to overlap the base. Apply a coat of varnish to the box.

2 Cut out the plywood shapes, using a fretsaw and birdsmouth board or clamp. Next, cut the half-round molding into 4-inch (10cm) lengths to make the base, and 6-inch (15cm) lengths to make the roof.

4 Make a simple template to the width of the box from a piece of scrap wood and use it to space the sides of the roof. Attach the roof slats as before, allowing for an overlap on each side.

6 Cut a strip of 6-inch (15cm)-wide roof flashing, long enough to cover the roof, and smooth it over the molding strips. Hammer the surface if you prefer. Attach a length of string for hanging.

SLATE-ROOF COTTAGE

As long as a birdhouse is weatherproof and sited in a safe, sheltered position, its external appearance will not affect the inhabitants. This sturdy-looking house, which will suit chickadees, nuthatches, or house finches, is actually made of wood faced with air-drying clay and roofed with slate.

Above: *The house finch (Carpodacus mexicanus) is common in cities in eastern parts of the United States and the arid west.*

YOU WILL NEED
pencil
ruler
¾-inch (2cm) pine board
tenon saw
drill
wood glue
nails, hammer
enamel paints
paintbrushes
paper
scissors
terra-cotta air-drying clay
board
rolling pin
knife
epoxy resin glue
blunt-end modeling tool
acrylic paints
satin exterior varnish
varnish brush
slate
face mask
hacksaw

TYPICAL INHABITANTS
house finches and nuthatches
titmice and chickadees

1 Using the templates at the back of the book, cut out the birdhouse pieces from the board. Drill an entry hole in one side only. Glue and nail the box together. Draw, then paint, the door and window on the front.

3 Cover the whole of the front of the house with a layer of epoxy resin glue, but be careful to avoid the painted door and window. Now carefully lay the clay over the front. You may need to adjust it slightly to fit it in the exact position.

5 Paint over some of the bricks using acrylic paints to imitate the varied colors of real brickwork. Let it dry, and then coat with a satin exterior varnish.

2 Make paper patterns of the sides and front. Cut out the entry hole, front door, and window. Roll out the clay to a depth of ⅜ inch (8mm) thick. Lay the patterns on the clay and cut around them.

4 Inscribe the fancy brickwork around the window and door using a blunt-end modeling tool, then use a ruler to press in horizontal lines as a guide for the standard brickwork. Inscribe the brickwork with the modeling tool. Repeat on the side walls.

6 Cut a piece of slate to size, wearing a face mask. It helps to saw through each side edge before cutting across. Drill four holes for nails, and nail the roof to the sides.

RIDGE TILE RETREAT

This elegant birdhouse is divided into two. With an entry hole at each end, it is made to suit birds, such as purple martins, which live in colonies. An old ridge tile makes an excellent roof.

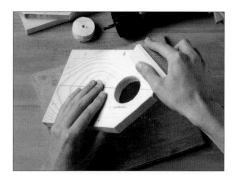

1 Using the templates at the back of the book, mark and cut out the components for the birdhouse, adapting the pitch of the roof to fit your tile. Drill an entry hole in each end.

2 Sand all the surfaces. Glue and then nail the floor to the sides. Next measure and mark the center line of the box and glue the dividing wall in position.

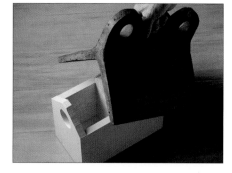

3 Glue and nail each gable end piece to the sides. Paint the outside of the birdhouse and let it dry thoroughly.

4 Place the ridge tile in position on top of the birdhouse. This house can be erected in a tree or placed 15–20 feet (4.5–6m) off the ground in a quiet location.

YOU WILL NEED
pencil, ruler
¾-inch (2cm) pine board
tenon saw
drill
hole saw
sandpaper
wood glue
galvanized nails
hammer
paint
paintbrush
ridge tile

TYPICAL INHABITANTS
purple martins
starlings

Below: *Purple martins nest in colonies in woodland, farmland, and urban areas. Early settlers hung up gourds for them to nest in.*

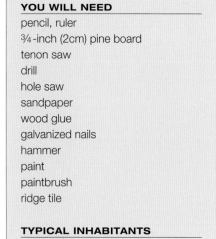

SWIFT NURSERY

Swifts build their nests in tall chimneys, under the eaves of houses, or in hollow trees. Although they will sometimes take to boxes with front-facing access holes, an entrance hole underneath is better, because it prevents house sparrows and starlings from taking over the box.

Above: *Swifts* (Apodidae) *spend their daylight hours on the wing, hunting flying insects. The chimney swift* (Chaetura pelagica) *is so-called because it likes to nest in colonies in chimneys.*

YOU WILL NEED
pencil, ruler
carpenter's square
¾-inch (2cm) pine board
tenon saw
¾-inch (2cm) square pine strip
paper
fretsaw
birdsmouth board or clamp
hammer, panel nails
wood glue
tongue-and-groove board
drill
sandpaper
latex paint in cream and black
paintbrush
self-adhesive roof flashing
scissors
varnish

TYPICAL INHABITANTS
swifts

1 Using the templates at the back of the book, mark and cut out all the pieces for the box, except the front, from pine board. Cut lengths of wood strips for the front. Cut a paper pattern for the entry hole at one end of the base and cut it out with a fretsaw.

2 Glue and nail the base to the back of the box. Glue and nail the ends in place and add the top wood strip. Cut the tongue-and-groove board into 6-inch (15cm) lengths. Glue and nail to the front of the box at the wood strip and the edge of the base.

3 Let the glue dry. Then drill a ⅝-inch (15mm) hole at each joint, placing a piece of scrap lumber behind the tongue-and-groove to prevent it from splitting. Now trim the lower edge of each board to form a chevron shape. Drill two holes in the back of the box for attaching to a wall. Sand and paint the box, then let dry. Paint the outside with varnish to protect the wood.

4 Cut two wood strips for the roof, using the template at the back. Mark positions for the strips on the underside of the roof using the box as a guide. Secure the strips with short nails. Paint the underside black. Cover the top of the roof with strips of self-adhesive flashing and fit the roof onto the box. Overlap the last strip of flashing to the back of the box. Hang the box onto a wall.

POST BOX

A thick wooden stake can be hollowed out and turned into an unusual nest box for small birds, such as titmice and nuthatches. The box can be sited on its own or form part of a backyard fence. The cover of roof flashing protects the box from the elements and also helps prevent the wood from splitting.

Above: *White-breasted nuthatches (Sitta carolinensis) build their nests in tree cavities and in birdhouses. The nest, usually made of twigs and grass, is lined with hair and feathers. In winter, they commonly visit backyard bird tables to take peanut picks, sunflowers, suet, and mixed seeds.*

YOU WILL NEED

drill and 1-inch (25mm) bit
fence post of 4-inch (10cm) diameter
chisel
mallet
self-adhesive roof flashing
craft knife
cutting mat
protective gloves
lead flashing
compass
pencil
ruler
scrap wood
vise
pliers
nails
hammer

TYPICAL INHABITANTS

titmice and chickadees
wrens
nuthatches

1 Using a 1-inch (25mm) bit, drill an entry hole into the side of the post 2 inches (5cm) from the end, then drill out the end to a depth of about 6 inches (15cm).

3 Cover the end of the post with self-adhesive roof flashing. Pierce the flashing in the center of the entry hole and cut back to the edges. Turn back the flashing inside the hole, but be careful not to significantly reduce the size of the entry hole that the birds will use.

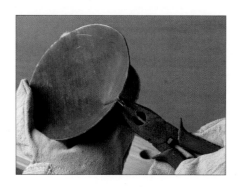

5 Wearing gloves, bend the lead into a cone shape. Then join the seam by squeezing the edges together with pliers. Flatten the seam against the cone.

2 Use a chisel and mallet to remove the waste wood left in the end of the post after drilling. Work to create a roughly circular cavity at least 6 inches (15cm) deep.

4 Wearing protective gloves, cut out a circle of lead flashing for the lid and remove one-quarter of the circle, using the template at the back of the book. Clamp the lead between two pieces of scrap wood and fold one cut edge at 90 degrees. Fold the second edge over twice at 90 degrees, as shown.

6 Attach the roof to the post using two nails, but leave one not fully nailed in, so that it can be removed to gain access to the box when you need to clean it out.

CLAY POT ROOST

For this project you will need access to a kiln (perhaps through a local education center or school), but you do not need to be skilled in pottery. Cut the entry hole to suit your choice of potential resident, and site the pot in a sheltered position, out of reach of predators.

Above: *European starlings (Sturnus vulgaris) are gregarious birds that feed and root in flocks. These birds are well adapted to living alongside people and are a common sight in cities as well as on farmland. They like to roost on buildings, but their droppings can create mess.*

YOU WILL NEED

paper
pencil
scissors
latex gloves
terra-cotta clay
rolling pin
craft knife
length of 4-inch (10cm)-diameter
　　plastic plumbing pipe
round cutter
awl
fresh leaves, to decorate
kiln

TYPICAL INHABITANTS

wrens
titmice and chickadees
feral pigeons
starlings
crested flycatchers
house sparrows

1 From the paper, cut a 4½-inch (12cm) circle, a 4½ x 6½-inch (12 x 17cm) rectangle, and a 15-inch (38cm) semicircle. Roll out the clay to ⅜ inch (8mm) thick and cut out the shapes. Cover the pipe in paper and roll the rectangle of clay around it.

3 Keeping the pipe inside the clay cylinder, attach the circular base, smoothing the edges together. Press fresh leaves into the cylinder to decorate. Remove the pipe.

5 Mold a small bird from leftover clay to decorate the top of the lid. Model the wings separately and then moisten them before pressing them on to the body. Draw the feathers and eyes using an awl.

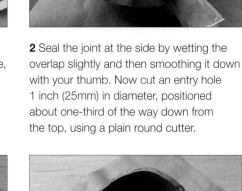

2 Seal the joint at the side by wetting the overlap slightly and then smoothing it down with your thumb. Now cut an entry hole 1 inch (25mm) in diameter, positioned about one-third of the way down from the top, using a plain round cutter.

4 To make the lid of the roost, curl the semicircle of clay into a cone shape. Join the edges as before by moistening and then smoothing them with your fingers.

6 Attach the bird by smoothing a little clay over the bottom of the bird and the top of the lid. Wrap in plastic and allow to dry slowly. When completely dry, fire the base and the lid separately in a kiln.

SEASHORE NEST BOX

Inspired by early twentieth-century seashore architecture, this pretty box is designed for hole nesters, such as titmice, nuthatches, and bluebirds. Fretwork is satisfying to make, but it requires practice and patience. However, your efforts will be rewarded once you see your creation hanging in the backyard.

Above: *Titmice resemble chickadees but are a little larger, with a distinct crest. This is a tufted titmouse* (Baeolophus bicolor).

1 Using the templates at the back of the book, mark and cut out the base, back, sides, and lid from ¾-inch (2cm) pine. Cut the notches in the side pieces. Plane the edges of the base and lid to line up with the sides. Cut a length of dowel for the perch.

2 Mark out the back plate, front, circular frame for the entry hole, and the decorative panel for the lid front on ⅛-inch (4mm) plywood; cut out using a fretsaw and birds-mouth board. Cut out a 1-inch (2.5cm) entry hole in the front panel. Sand the surfaces.

YOU WILL NEED
ruler, pencil
jigsaw
¾-inch (2cm) pine board
tenon saw
plane
⅜-inch (8mm) dowel
⅛-inch (4mm) plywood
fretsaw
birdsmouth board or clamp
drill
sandpaper
wood glue
plated molding nails
hammer, nails
watercolor paints in cobalt blue,
    burnt umber, turquoise, yellow
    ocher, burnt sienna
paintbrushes
petroleum jelly
2 butterfly hinges, with screws
tourmaline antiquing medium
white latex paint
blowtorch
satin yacht varnish
screwdriver and screws

TYPICAL INHABITANTS
titmice and nuthatches
bluebirds
tree swallows

3 Glue the sides, base, and back support together and secure with molding nails. Glue and nail the fretwork panel to the front edge of the lid. Drill a hole for the perch below the entry hole, and glue into place, then glue and nail the front to the sides.

4 Paint the box with a diluted mixture of cobalt blue and burnt umber watercolor paint, in equal proportions. Let dry, then smear on a thin layer of petroleum jelly with your fingers. To age the hinges, paint with tourmaline antiquing medium.

5 Treating one surface at a time, apply a coat of white latex paint and dry it with a blowtorch to make the paint crack. Add a little turquoise and yellow ocher watercolor to the latex to make green for the entry hole frame and backboard.

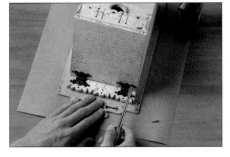

6 Glue and nail the back panel onto the box. To age the paintwork, apply a diluted mixture of yellow ocher and burnt sienna watercolor until you achieve the desired effect. Let dry, then finish with varnish. Screw on the hinges to attach the lid.

DUCK HOUSE

You do not need a very large pond to provide a home for ducks, such as mallards. If possible, the house should be positioned on an island or raft to provide protection from predators. The ramp for this desirable house has horizontal struts to make sure the occupants do not slip. Post caps on each leg will protect the lumber on dry land. If it is to stand in water, use lumber pressure-treated with preservative.

YOU WILL NEED

¾-inch (2cm) pine board
1¾-inch (45mm) square pine strip
¾ x 1¾-inch (20 x 45mm) pine strip
rabbeted shiplap boards
pencil
ruler
carpenter's square
tenon saw
jigsaw
sandpaper
wood glue
nails
hammer
exterior paint
paintbrush
corrugated roofing sheet
Styrofoam filler
roofing screws and cups
screwdriver
lumber decking or treated lumber
large, flat work surface

TYPICAL INHABITANTS

ducks, including mallards and
   shovelers

Left: *Mallards (Anas platyrhynchos) are among the most widespread and familiar ducks in North America. These waterbirds sometimes nest in backyards near lakes or rivers that contain thick vegetation to provide cover for the nest site. The appearance of the male differs markedly through the year. In the breeding season, the handsome green head, white collar, and brown chest distinguish him from the female. In late summer, he molts into a dull plumage, which closely resembles the female's in its drab hues.*

Left: *Northern shovelers (Anas clypeata) have a broad bill that enables them to feed more easily in shallow water. They typically swim with their bill open and trailing through the water to catch invertebrates, although they also forage both by upending themselves and catching insects on reeds. These ducks choose wet ground, often some distance from open water, as a nesting site. Like the young of other waterfowl, the young birds take to the water soon after hatching.*

1 Mark out and cut out all the components for the duck house using the templates given at the back of the book. Carefully cut out the curved roof pine strips and then the arched opening using a jigsaw. Sand all the edges smooth.

2 On a large, flat work surface, lay out two of the legs parallel to one another. Position the cross rail on top of the legs, using the carpenter's square to make sure all three parts are at right angles to one another. Now attach the cross rail using wood glue and nails.

3 Turn the leg assembly over and attach the first curved roof pine lath. Repeat the process with the other two legs.

4 Connect the front and back with the two lower cross rails. These are nailed to the inner side of the legs.

5 Nail and glue the upper side rails at both sides. These rails are attached to the outside of the legs. This completes the basic framework of the duck house.

6 Shiplap the back and sides of the house, starting at the top. Glue and nail the top piece in place, but do not drive the nails in fully. Only do so after the lower piece has been glued and nailed in place.

7 Shiplap the front in the same way, securing the door sides first. Make sure that you align the door sides carefully to give a straight, clean line when the duck house is assembled.

8 Finish off the house walls by attaching the four corner pieces. Paint the house inside and out, and let it dry. Put in the floor, which rests in place on the cross rails.

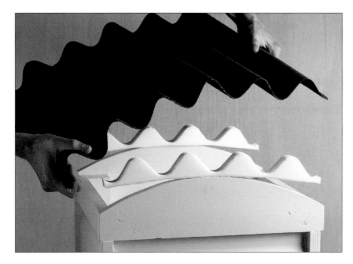

9 Cut a piece of roofing sheet to the measurements given at the back of the book, and cut two strips of Styrofoam filler to fit the arched front and back walls. Position the roof, locating it centrally.

10 Attach the roof to the front and back walls of the house, using special roofing screws and cups to secure it.

11 Make a simple ramp by joining two planks of lumber decking with cross pieces. Nail an extra cross piece to the back of the ramp at the top to hook over the pine strip under the door.

RUSTIC CABIN

This charming cabin is constructed around a basic box with a sloping roof. Faced with "logs," it will harmonize well with any backyard setting, offering a nursery for hole-nesting birds.

YOU WILL NEED
¼-inch (6mm) medium-density fiberboard (MDF) or exterior-grade plywood
ruler, pencil
hammer, nails
saw
twigs and branches
axe or small-scale log splitter
glue gun and glue sticks
dark gray latex paint
medium paintbrush
drill
keyhole saw
½ x 4-inch (12 x 100mm) carriage bolt
moss or moss-covered branch

TYPICAL INHABITANTS
wrens
titmice and chickadees

1 Mark and cut out the basic house in MDF or plywood following the template at the back of the book. Make "logs" from small branches by splitting the branches lengthwise so there is a flat side for sticking to the box and a rounded surface with bark for the outside.

2 Assemble the basic box with glue and nails. Paint it with dark gray latex paint, so that any small gaps between the logs will not show when they are attached.

3 Glue the logs to the front. To make the entry hole, cut through the logs and the box below using a drill and then a keyhole saw.

4 Cut a ½-inch (12mm) hole in the roof at the front corner and insert a carriage bolt for the "chimney." Continue to attach logs to the rest of the house, shaping them to fit and making the roof logs overlap the walls slightly as a protection against rain. Neaten the corners of the walls by trimming each log end with a saw. Glue a piece of moss or mossy branch to the opening as a perch.

Left: *Carolina chickadees (Parus carolinensis) nest in tree stumps or birdhouses. These little birds are regular visitors to bird feeders. In winter, they forage in mixed flocks with other small birds.*

WREN'S LOG CABIN

Designed for nesting wrens, which like open-front boxes, this log cabin-effect box can also provide a roost for songbirds, such as robins and phoebes. To suit wrens, position it low down in a well-hidden site, preferably surrounded by thorny shrubbery, and well away from any other birdhouses.

Above: *Winter wrens (Troglodytes troglodytes) are easily overlooked because of their tiny size and skulking habits. However, their song is surprisingly loud. They also produce a ticking sound. These little birds breed from March to July, constructing a domed structure in thick vegetation, where the female lays 5–8 eggs. The young hatch after 16–17 days and take a similar time to fledge.*

YOU WILL NEED
sticks—newly cut hazelwood from coppiced woodland is best, because the coppiced stems can be cut to length to produce short, strong, straight sticks
ruler, pencil
tenon saw
bench hook
hammer
short, fine nails or sturdy panel nails
4-inch (10cm) square plastic tray
piece of sod
knife

TYPICAL INHABITANTS
wrens
robins, swallows and sparrows; these may use this box as a roost

1 Select evenly sized, straight sticks and cut them to length, using a tenon saw and bench hook. You will need 4 sturdy uprights 6 inches (15cm) long, 10 sticks to make the base 4¾ inches (12cm) long, and about 50 sticks for the sides, 4 inches (10cm) long.

3 Attach the two sides by nailing more small sticks across the back. You may need to brace the structure. Work from bottom to top, hammering nails into the uprights at an angle to keep the structure strong.

5 Build up the top of the box by adding two more of the shorter sticks to each side, on top of the existing pieces. Gently nail the new sticks on top of the walls.

2 Construct the first side by nailing 4-inch (10cm) lengths to two of the uprights. Use short, fine nails or sturdy panel nails. Nail on the two end sticks first to make a rectangle, then fill in with other sticks. Repeat to make the other side.

4 Turn the box over. Attach one stick at the top of the front, then leave a gap of about 2 inches (5cm) for the entrance hole before completing the rest of the front. Use the 4¾-inch (12cm) sticks to make the base.

6 Fit the tray into the top so that it rests on the uprights, or so that the lip rests on top of the walls. Cut a piece of sod to fit and place it in the tray to make the roof.

THATCHED BIRDHOUSE

As long as the basic box requirements are fulfilled, the finish is up to you. Made for hole nesters, such as bluebirds, swallows, and titmice, this box should be sited somewhere quiet, so that the birds are not disturbed while nesting. Leave the house out during winter for use as a snug roost.

Above: *Eastern bluebirds benefit from the provision of nest boxes because starlings and sparrows can take over their nest sites.*

YOU WILL NEED

pencil, ruler
carpenter's square
¼-inch (6mm) medium-density
   fiberboard (MDF)
tenon saw
drill
wood glue
masking tape
small metal eyelet and hook
craft knife
cutting mat
metal ruler
self-adhesive roof flashing
premixed tile cement
palette knife
aquarium gravel
sisal hanging-basket liner
white glue
paintbrush
raffia
large-eyed needle
clothespins
diluted brown watercolor paint
matte varnish
varnish brush

TYPICAL INHABITANTS

bluebirds
titmice and chickadees

1 Following the templates at the back of the book, mark and cut out the component parts from MDF. Drill an entry hole in the front wall and, if required, drill a small hole in the back wall for hanging.

2 Glue the base and walls together and then hold the structure in position with masking tape until the glue is dry. Screw in an eyelet ½ inch (1cm) from the top back corner of the right-hand wall.

3 Cut a strip of roof flashing 5 inches (13cm) wide to the length of the roof ridge. Position the two roof pieces side by side, leaving enough of a gap to let the roof hinge open. Remove the backing and cover the ridge with the flashing.

4 Working on a small area at a time, spread premixed tile cement over the house walls. Embed aquarium gravel firmly into the cement, choosing darker stones to outline the entrance hole. Cover the walls of the house completely.

5 Coat the sisal with diluted white glue and let dry. Cut a rectangle 5½ x 11 inches (14 x 28cm) for the thatch, and a strip 3 x 6 inches (7.5 x 15cm) for the ridge. Stitch two rows of large cross-stitch in raffia along the sides of this strip, then glue and stitch it across the thatch.

6 Glue the thatch to the roof. Secure it with clothespins until dry. Screw in the hook at the back of the roof, then glue the other side of the roof to the walls, securing it with masking tape until dry. Wash the cement with brown watercolor and, when dry, give it a coat of varnish.

NESTY NOOK

This cosy home to suit hole nesters, such as wrens and nuthatches, is formed from plastic-coated chicken wire covered with moss. To suit wrens, place the nest in a hidden position, low down in thick undergrowth. To suit nuthatches, the nest should be placed in a tree.

Above: *Red-breasted nuthatches (Sitta canadensis) usually nest in cavities in pine trees. They smear the nest entrance with pitch to discourage predators. The female lays 5–6 eggs inside. In winter, the birds forage widely. They feed mainly on pine seeds, but will also visit bird tables to take suet and seeds. In summer, their diet includes insects and wood-boring grubs.*

YOU WILL NEED
chicken wire
wire cutters
large leaves
sisal hanging-basket liner
scissors
pliers
hairnet
moss
sea grass string
garden wire

TYPICAL INHABITANTS
nuthatches
wrens
titmice and chickadees
sparrows
woodpeckers; these will use a nest
   with slightly larger dimensions,
   placed in a high position in a tree

1 Cut a square of chicken wire measuring about 12 inches (30cm). Line it with large leaves. Cut a square of hanging basket liner made of sisal to the same size and lay it down on top of the leaves.

2 Fold the four corners into the center and join the sides by twisting the ends of the wires together. Leave the center open. Tuck in the wire ends to ensure that there are no sharp parts poking out to harm the bird.

3 Pull at the wire structure from the front and back to "puff" it out and create a larger space inside for the bird to nest.

4 Carefully stretch a hairnet over the whole nest structure. Be careful to keep the entrance hole clear.

5 Stuff moss evenly between the nest and the hairnet to cover the chicken wire completely. Work on one part at a time until you are satisfied with the look of the whole.

6 To define the entry hole, form a ring of sea grass string and secure it by twisting garden wire around it. Wire it into position around the hole.

SCALLOP SHELTER

This little nest designed for swallows and martins is made of papier-mâché. It is easily replaced each season, although the chicken wire container will last longer. Attach it to the wall with two cup hooks, in a dry place under the eaves. The scallop shell is purely decorative.

Above: *Barn swallows* (Hirundo rustica) *originally nested on rocky ledges, but now they mostly nest under the eaves of buildings, using mud for the nest itself. They are found in most parts of the world.*

YOU WILL NEED
newspaper
bowl of water
plastic bowl
wallpaper paste
brush
scissors
corrugated cardboard
pencil
masking tape
acrylic paints
paintbrush
chicken wire
protective gloves
wire cutters
small pliers
drill
scallop shell
florist's wire

TYPICAL INHABITANTS
swallows
martins
titmice

1 To make the papier-mâché, tear a newspaper into small squares and soak it in water. Cover one half of a plastic bowl with a layer of wet, unpasted pieces of paper. The pieces should slightly overlap.

3 When the papier-mâché is completely dry, remove it from the plastic bowl and trim the rough edges to make a neat half-bowl shape. Now cut out a semicircle of corrugated cardboard, which will form the backing for the nest.

5 Paint the nest in variegated muddy tones. Cut a piece of chicken wire using wire cutters. Wrap it around the nest and join the wire ends together at the sides.

2 Brush paste liberally over the first layer and add more pieces, pasting each layer, until you have built up about six layers. Let it dry out completely in a warm place.

4 Attach the cardboard to the papier-mâché bowl shape using masking tape, then reinforce the structure by adding a few layers of pasted paper over the back and edges. Let the nest stand in a warm place to dry out thoroughly.

6 Squeeze the chicken wire with the pliers to shape it to the form. Drill two small holes in the top of the scallop shell and one at the bottom, and wire it onto the frame.

WILLOW STICK NEST

Half-coconuts are just the right shape and size to make snug nests for small birds. Two halves are wedged into a bunch of willow sticks, and a woven sea grass wall completes the nest.

1 Soak the willow sticks overnight to make them pliable. Wedge them around a stick using a napkin ring. Saw a coconut in half and scrape out the contents. Using raffia, tie the willow sticks together at the top.

2 Insert the coconut halves. Starting by the rim of the lower half, weave sea grass string around the sticks for three rounds.

3 Create a gap by doubling the string back on itself and changing the direction of the weaving for about four rounds.

YOU WILL NEED
about 15 willow sticks
straight stick or bamboo pole
wooden napkin ring
coconut
saw
knife
raffia
sea grass string
scissors
TYPICAL INHABITANTS
wrens
titmice and chickadees

4 Complete the weaving with three more rounds. Wedge the top of the coconut into position above the weaving and secure it by retying the sticks at the top if necessary.

Left: *Acrobatic black-capped chickadees* (Parus atricapillus) *construct cup-shaped nests of plant fibers, moss, fur, and feathers. They also use artificial nests, such as these.*

HOLLOW LOG NEST BOX

Choose an appealing log for this nest box. Depending on its size, you can adapt it to suit the type of bird you want to attract, from titmice to woodpeckers. Mossy logs look beautiful, as do chunks of silver birch. Avoid pieces of wood with knots or branches, because they are difficult to split neatly.

Above: *Place the nest box high in a tree to attract woodpeckers, such as this northern flicker (Colaptes auratus). These birds use their short, stiff tails to balance upright on the trunk while they extract grubs from beneath the bark. They usually nest in tree holes excavated with their sharp beaks.*

YOU WILL NEED
2 logs
pencil
ruler
straight-edge chisel
mallet
drill
saw
hammer
nails
garden wire
scissors
pliers

TYPICAL INHABITANTS
woodpeckers
starlings
titmice and wrens

1 Mark out a square on the end of one log. Use a mallet and straight-edge chisel to split off the first side, making sure that you work evenly along the line.

2 Repeat this process to remove all four sides of the square. Drill an entrance hole through one of the sides, making a sizable hole if you want to attract woodpeckers.

3 Saw a ¾-inch (20mm) slice off one end of the center of the log to form the base.

4 Using the base piece, reassemble the log by nailing the four sides together.

5 Wrap a length of garden wire around the top of the box, twist the ends to tighten it, and hold the sides securely together.

6 Split the second log to make a roof for the nest box. Attach it using one long nail, so that the roof can easily swivel open.

NEST-IN-A-BOOT

An old boot provides the basis for this original nest box. It is filled halfway with gravel to stabilize it, and a small basket makes a perfect foundation for the nest itself. Try to find an interesting seed pod or other natural decoration for the roof. The birds will not need the little ladder, but children will love it.

Above: *Boreal chickadees of northern conifer forests usually nest close to the ground in natural cavities. The nest is lined with moss and feathers. These birds are less tame than black-capped chickadees.*

YOU WILL NEED
rubber boot
scissors
gravel
small round basket
awl
string
small sticks
epoxy resin glue
wooden curtain ring
protective gloves
chicken wire
wire cutters
small pliers
sisal hanging-basket liner
large-eyed needle
raffia
interesting seed pod
garden wire

TYPICAL INHABITANTS
titmice and chickadees
wrens
starlings; these may use this nest
    if made with a larger entry hole

1 Cut down the boot to a suitable size and cut out a small entry hole toward the top. Fill the bottom of the boot with gravel, then wedge a small round basket into position below the entry hole.

3 To make the roof, cut a semicircular piece of chicken wire, using wire cutters and wearing protective gloves. Curve the wire to form a cone. Join the sides by twisting the ends of the wire together using pliers.

5 Sew cross-stitches along the joint using string and a large-eyed needle. Now cross-stitch around the bottom with raffia. Insert the seed pod decoration into the point of the roof and glue in place.

2 Make two small holes below the entry hole to either side. Thread a long piece of string through these and tie on little sticks to form a ladder. Glue on a wooden curtain ring over the entry hole as reinforcement.

4 Wrap a piece of the sisal hanging-basket liner around the cone of chicken wire, pressing the wire rim firmly into the matting. Turn in the edges of both the matting and the chicken wire.

6 Make four pairs of holes, evenly spaced around the rim of the boot. Attach the roof to the boot using four lengths of garden wire and twist the wires together. Snip off any excess wire.

DOVECOTE

This beautiful structure will make a comfortable roost for up to half a dozen doves, but it could be adapted to accommodate more birds by increasing the number of tiers. The dovecote is probably best sited on the side of a building, but it can also be mounted on a stout post.

Above: *Mourning doves* (Zenaida macroura) *are common in both cities and rural areas throughout the United States. The scientific name* macroura *means "long-tailed."*

YOU WILL NEED
pencil, ruler
carpenter's square
½-inch (12mm) and ¼-inch (6mm) plywood
jigsaw
¾-inch (20mm) pine board
tenon saw
¾ x 1¾-inch (2 x 4.5cm) pine strip
sandpaper
wood glue
nails
hammer
drill
screws
screwdriver
paint
paintbrush
self-adhesive roof flashing
craft knife and cutting mat
metal ruler

TYPICAL INHABITANTS
pigeons
doves

1 Using the template at the back, mark and cut out the backboard from ½-inch (12mm) plywood with a jigsaw. Cut the roof shapes and arches from ¼-inch (6mm) plywood.

3 Join the sides and center by gluing and nailing on the front pine wood strips. Fit the back wood strips into the notches cut in the center piece. Attach by nailing in the center of the wood strip and at each end.

5 Cover the small roof sections with self-adhesive roof flashing. Cover the main roof with horizontal strips of flashing. Start from the bottom of the roof and overlap each section, letting some overlap on the final piece to attach to the backboard.

2 Mark and cut out all the pine lumber parts from ¾-inch (20mm)-thick planks, using the templates provided. The sides and center need wide boards. Sand all the surfaces.

4 Drill pilot holes for the screws in the backboard. Attach the backboard to the frame using glue and screws. Paint the frame and the arched fronts and let dry. Attach the fronts using glue and nails.

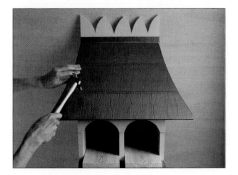

6 Using nails, assemble the last parts in the following order: first the small roof sections; then the floors; then the main roof. Attach the dovecote to a wall by screwing through the backboard from the inside. Be careful doing this, because the structure is heavy.

CLAPBOARD HOUSE

This smart-looking New England-style house is suitable for hole nesters, such as tree swallows, bluebirds, and titmice. It provides a decorative feature to any backyard, as well as a nest site for birds.

Above: *Tree swallows* (Tachycineta bicolor) *nest in tree holes but will use enclosed nest boxes. The nest is lined with feathers. The female lays 4–6 eggs. These birds over-winter in various parts of the United States.*

YOU WILL NEED
¼-inch (6mm) medium-density
    fiberboard (MDF) or plywood
pencil, ruler
saw
white glue
hammer, panel nails
birch veneer
colored woodstain
craft knife
1/16 x ¾-inch (1.5 x 19mm) balsa
    wood strips
compass
latex paint: off-white, dark brown,
    and brilliant white
medium and fine paintbrushes
exterior-grade varnish
drill with ⅛-inch (3mm) bit
2 x 2-inch (50 x 50mm) wooden post
screwdriver
3-inch (75mm) screw, plus smaller
    screws

TYPICAL INHABITANTS
titmice
tree swallows
bluebirds

1 Mark and cut out the basic house onto MDF or plywood following the template at the back of the book. Assemble using glue and panel nails. Mark a sheet of veneer into ¾ x 1½-inch (19 x 38mm) shingles and rub randomly with woodstain. Cut out the shingles with a craft knife. Glue them in overlapping rows to the roof of the house.

2 Cut balsa wood strips to length to use as clapboarding. Glue in position. Set the compass to transfer the cutting angles or make paper templates to show the shapes to be cut. Paint the clapboarding with off-white latex and dark brown windows. Paint window frames and doors using a fine brush and white latex paint. Varnish.

3 Cut a 5 x 8-inch (12.5 x 20cm) base from plywood. Drill pilot holes at each corner and in the center. Fasten to the top of the post with a central 3-inch (75mm) screw. Screw through the corners into the house.

DIRECTORY OF BACKYARD BIRDS

Many people derive pleasure from watching backyard birds. This pastime can be enjoyed without special equipment, but binoculars and a sketch pad, notebook, or similar items can add to your understanding. To help identify the birds that visit your backyard, the following pages present illustrations and in-depth profiles of 80 of the most commonly sighted American species, giving details of distribution, size, habitat, nests, eggs, and food, along with descriptions of songs and behavior. The order here reflects the standard order used in bird classification.

Left: *Woodpeckers, such as this pileated woodpecker* (Dryocopus pileatus), *appear in backyards containing mature trees or located near woodlands.*

Above: *Hummingbirds, such as this broad-billed variety, can be enticed to backyards by feeders containing sweet liquid.*

Above: *Northern cardinals are among the most colorful birds that visit backyards. They accept a variety of bird table offerings.*

Above: *Like other members of the crow family, blue jays* (Cyanocitta cristata) *are highly intelligent backyard birds.*

AQUATIC BIRDS

Coots, moorhens, and rails belong to the group of crakes. These water-loving birds can often be seen out in the open, but when frightened they usually scuttle to the safety of dense vegetation by the water. Ducks are freshwater birds whose appearance and distribution can differ markedly through the year.

AMERICAN COOT

Fulica americana

American coots may set up home by large ponds and lakes in parks and backyards. They can become tame when supplied with bread. The cock and hen look similar, but can be distinguished by their different calls. These coots have proved to be highly adaptable, to the extent that their numbers appear to have increased overall in recent years. They rapidly colonize new areas of suitable habitat, although populations can be adversely affected by very cold springtime weather, which makes food harder to find. They often migrate south in large numbers to avoid the worst of the winter weather.

Identification
Predominantly slate gray, more blackish on the head. White undertail coverts. Bill is whitish, with red near the tip, enlarging into a broad shield with red at the top. Sexes are alike, although hens are often significantly smaller. Young birds are predominantly brown, with duller bills.

Distribution From Alaska southward across much of North America through Central America and the Caribbean into parts of Colombia in South America.
Size 17in (43cm).
Habitat Permanent areas of wetland, including coastal inlets in winter.
Nest Floating heap of dead aquatic vegetation.
Eggs 3–12, buff with dense, fine blackish spotting.
Food Aquatic vegetation.

MOORHEN

Common moorhen *Gallinula chloropus*

Even a relatively small pond can attract moorhens, and they may nest in backyards with dense vegetation near the pond. Although usually found in areas of fresh water, they are occasionally seen in brackish areas. Their long toes enable them to walk over aquatic vegetation. These birds feed on the water or on land. Their diet varies according to the season, although seeds of various types make up the bulk of their food. Moorhens are less wary than most rails or crakes, swimming in open water. If danger threatens, they will either dive or swim underwater. They are adept divers, remaining submerged by grasping onto underwater vegetation with their bills. In public parks, moorhens can become tame, darting in to obtain food provided for ducks. During the breeding season, pairs of moorhens set up and defend territories and perform complex courtship rituals.

Identification
Slate gray head, back, and underparts. Grayish black wings. A prominent white line runs down the sides of the body. The area under the tail is white and has a black central stripe. Greenish yellow legs have a small red area at the top. The bill is red, apart from a yellow tip. Sexes are alike.

Distribution South from the Great Lakes to much of the eastern USA. Also Florida, the Gulf Coast, and California, and through Central America. Common in much of South America except northeast and south.
Size 12in (30cm).
Habitat Ponds and other areas of water edged by dense vegetation.
Nest Domed structure hidden in reeds.
Eggs 4–7, buffish with dark markings.
Food Omnivorous.

MALLARD

Anas platyrhynchos

Distribution Occurs throughout much of North America, although is more scarce in the far north of Canada. Also found in Mexico.
Size 24in (60cm).
Habitat Open areas of water.
Nest Scrape lined with down feathers.
Eggs 7–16, buff to grayish green.
Food Plant matter and some invertebrates.

These ducks are a common sight by rivers and canals in towns and cities. They are also seen in backyards with or near ponds and streams, where they may nest in dense cover. They may gather in large flocks, especially outside the breeding season, but are most evident in the spring, when groups of unpaired males chase potential mates. The nest is often built close to water, usually hidden under vegetation, especially in urban areas. These birds feed both on water, upending themselves or dabbling at the surface, and on land.

Identification
Cock in breeding plumage has metallic green head with a white ring around the neck. Chest is brownish with gray underparts, and blackish area surrounds the vent. Bluish speculum in the wing, most evident in flight, bordered by black-and-white stripes. Hen is brownish buff overall with darker patterning, and displays same wing markings as drake. Hen's bill is orange, whereas that of male in eclipse plumage is yellow, with a rufous tinge to the breast.

BLUE-WINGED TEAL

Anas discors

Distribution Breeds in south Alaska, Newfoundland, and central USA. Winters along Pacific and Atlantic coasts. Also present in Caribbean and Central America, with range extending to northern part of South America, even as far as Chile.
Size 16in (41cm).
Habitat Marshes and shallow lakes.
Nest Down-lined scrape.
Eggs 6–15, grayish green to buff.
Food Plants, invertebrates.

Blue-winged teal are a common sight on ponds and other wetlands in low marshy areas right across central North America. They return to their northern breeding grounds in May, with pairs nesting on their own and choosing sites concealed in vegetation. The eggs take nearly four weeks to hatch, with the young being unable to fly for a further five weeks or so. These teal feed on aquatic snails, crustaceans, and virtually any plant matter by dabbling, upending themselves rather than diving for food. They are long-distance travelers. Their regular migratory routes take them over land to South America rather than across the Gulf of Mexico. Strong and fast in flight, they are sometimes found well outside their usual range, including on Hawaii and the Galapagos Islands. They also regularly cross the Atlantic to reach the UK, Europe, and as far south as northwest Africa.

Identification
Blue upperwing coverts with a green speculum. Drake has a white area around base of bill, and a grayish head with darker crown. Underparts red-brown with black speckles. White areas on sides, black rump. Male in eclipse similar to female. Duck brownish, with whitish area at base of bill. Young have spotted underparts.

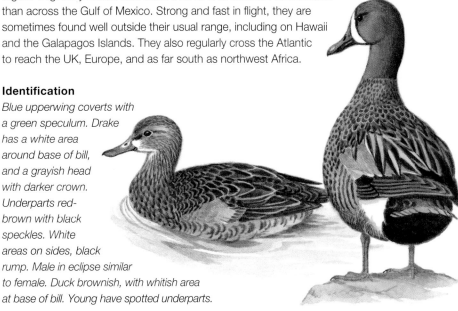

FALCONS AND OWLS

Agile aerial predators, falcons are opportunistic hunters that rely on strength and speed to overcome their prey, which often includes smaller birds. The diet of most owls includes rodents. It is possible to determine their exact diet by examining their pellets, which are the indigestible remains of their prey.

AMERICAN KESTREL

Falco sparverius

The smallest North American falcon, the American kestrel can easily be overlooked unless it is hovering conspicuously by a roadside. Keen eyesight allows it to see a mouse from up to 90 feet (30m) away. It dives down quickly to seize the unsuspecting quarry in its sharp talons. After making a kill, the kestrel flies up to a convenient perch with its meal, or back to the nest if it has young. In urban backyards, house sparrows and other small birds fall prey to these falcons. In summer, insects such as grasshoppers can play a vital part in nourishing a growing brood. The vast range of these kestrels shows them to be adaptable feeders.

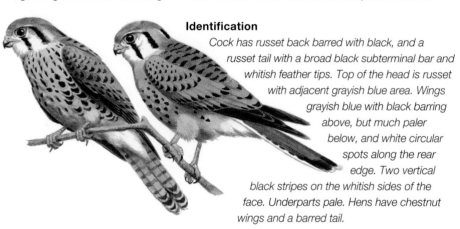

Identification

Cock has russet back barred with black, and a russet tail with a broad black subterminal bar and whitish feather tips. Top of the head is russet with adjacent grayish blue area. Wings grayish blue with black barring above, but much paler below, and white circular spots along the rear edge. Two vertical black stripes on the whitish sides of the face. Underparts pale. Hens have chestnut wings and a barred tail.

Distribution Range extends over virtually all of the Americas, from Alaska in the north to Tierra del Fuego at the southern tip of South America.
Size 10½in (27cm).
Habitat Open countryside, farmland, and urban areas.
Nest Typically in a hollow tree.
Eggs 3–7, white with brown blotching.
Food Insects and small vertebrates.

PRAIRIE FALCON

Falco mexicanus

Prairie falcons are opportunistic hunters, a key factor in their spread across much of North America. Their diet consists mainly of small birds, including backyard species, and also rodents. In dry areas, they take numbers of reptiles, including lizards, snakes, and tortoises. Prairie falcons prefer to catch their prey at or just above ground level, but also harry smaller birds in flight. Breeding occurs from March to July, depending on latitude. With woodland becoming scarce, these falcons have adapted to using cliff faces, laying on the rock rather than building a nest, although pairs may take over nests abandoned by other large birds.

Identification

This falcon has a brown crown, with white streaking running around each side of the head above the eyes. White area behind each eye, and a dark streak running from below each eye onto the cheeks. Dark brown ear coverts, with a brown-and-white spotted neck and underparts. Bill pale yellow, darker at its tip. Legs and feet yellow. Sexes are alike. The young birds have grayish legs and feet, with long flight feathers extending back almost as far as the tail feathers.

Distribution British Columbia eastward through Canada around the southern part of Hudson Bay to Newfoundland, and through western USA to northern parts of Mexico and east via Texas along the Gulf coast to Florida.
Size 20in (51cm).
Habitat Prairies and plains.
Nest Often lays on a cliff ledge.
Eggs 4–5, whitish, marked with brownish blotches.
Food Meat eater.

EASTERN SCREECH OWL

Otus asio

Distribution Eastern North America, from eastern Montana and the Great Lakes down via the Gulf states to northeastern Mexico.
Size 8½ in (22cm).
Habitat Variable, from forests to suburban areas and parks.
Nest In a hollow tree or nest box.
Eggs 2–8, white.
Food Small mammals and invertebrates.

Lightly wooded areas, including backyards, are favored by these birds of prey. In true owl fashion, eastern screech owls hunt at night, and despite their size are able to take relatively large quarry, including adult rats. They are opportunists, catching anything from earthworms to snakes and even moths, which can be seized in flight. In urban areas, they are even known to plunge into backyard ponds at night, seizing unwary fish near the surface. The shape of their wings means that virtually no sound betrays their presence until after they have launched their deadly strike. As with other owls, the study of the pellets regurgitated after meals has allowed ornithologists to confirm their feeding habits. In the breeding season, these owls lay up to eight eggs in a tree hole or nest box. They will harry intruders, including humans, if they feel the nest is threatened. The red and gray morphs of these owls are equally common, sometimes even cropping up in the same nest. Habitat appears to play no part in determining coloration.

Identification

Red and gray color morphs occur, also brownish intermediates. Widely spaced crossbarring on underparts matches spacing of vertical stripes on a whitish ground. Yellowish green base to the bill. Prominent ear tufts may be raised or lowered. Lines of white spots with black edging extend diagonally across top of wings. Sexes alike.

BARN OWL

Tyto alba

Distribution Ranges from southern British Columbia across to New England and southward through Central America into South America. Also occurs in western Europe, Africa, and the Middle East.
Size 15in (39cm).
Habitat Prefers relatively open countryside, including farmland.
Nest Hollow tree or inside a building.
Eggs 4–7, white.
Food Voles, amphibians, insects.

Barn owls seek out dark environments in which to roost, using buildings for this purpose in some areas. They are sometimes seen in rural backyards near open country, or swooping low over farmland. Some individuals choose to pursue bats in areas where these are common. Male barn owls often utter harsh screeches when in flight, which serve as territorial markers, while females make a distinctive snoring sound to request food at the nest. These owls pair for life, which can be more than 20 years, and will sometimes nest in large, oblong boxes placed in outhouses. Barn owls have adapted to hunting along roadsides, but here they risk being hit by vehicles.

Identification

This owl is very pale in color, with a whitish, heart-shaped face and underparts. Top of the head and wings are grayish, with spots evident. Eyes are black. Males are often paler than females.

WOODPECKERS

Few groups of birds are more closely associated with woodlands than woodpeckers. They are well-equipped to thrive in these surroundings, using their powerful bills to obtain food and also carve nest holes. However, not all are exclusively arboreal, because some species find food in the air or on the ground.

RED-BELLIED WOODPECKER

Melanerpes carolinus

Red-bellied woodpeckers have a diet that changes through the year. Over the summer, invertebrates form a high percentage of their diet. They also prey on vertebrates, including the nestlings of other species. In fall, fruits of various kinds figure more prominently. During winter, they feed largely on nuts and seeds, including from backyard feeders, although cocks still search for insects. These woodpeckers prefer to feed off the ground, and are most likely to be sighted in deciduous trees, particularly oaks. Pairs nest through much of the summer, often raising two or even three broods of chicks. The breeding chamber is usually larger than that used for roosting.

Identification

Cocks have a red top to their head, extending to the back of the neck, whereas in hens only the nape is red. Black-and-white barring extends over the back and wings, and to the central tail feathers. Underparts are grayish white, with reddish suffusion to center of abdomen.

Distribution Eastern North America, from Ontario southward via South Dakota and southern Minnesota as far as central Texas and Florida.
Size 9½ in (24cm).
Habitat Open woodland, parks, and suburban areas.
Nest Tree hollow.
Eggs 3–8, white.
Food Omnivorous.

GILA WOODPECKER

Melanerpes uropygialis

Distribution Ranges from southwestern USA to Sonora. Other races occur in Baja California.
Size 9½ in (24cm).
Habitat Scrubland and woods, extending into urban areas.
Nest Tree hollow.
Eggs 3–6, white.
Food Invertebrates, seeds, and fruits.

Gila woodpeckers are naturally bold, which means that they readily feed on backyard bird tables, driving off other species, such as starlings, which may otherwise monopolize this food. These woodpeckers are noisy, conspicuous, and also aggressive by nature, particularly when close to the nest site, which may be located in a tree. Alternatively, because they occur in arid areas, it may be sited in the less conventional surroundings of a tall cactus, as high as 23 feet (7m) off the ground. This affords good protection from predators, but can only be occupied once the hole has dried up thoroughly and is not leaking sap. The breeding period is usually between April and June, although a pair may sometimes nest again in July. Once fledged, the young remain with their parents until the adults begin nesting again.

Identification

This species has a pale grayish head and underparts, with a slightly whiter area above the bill and barring on the flanks. Black-and-white barring also extends down over the back and wings, and onto the tail feathers, too. Cocks can be distinguished by the small red cap of plumage on the top of their head.

DOWNY WOODPECKER

Picoides pubescens

Distribution Ranges widely across much of the wooded region of North America, from southeastern Alaska to Newfoundland, and south to Florida.
Size 6½ in (17cm).
Habitat Forests, orchards, parks, and backyards.
Nest Tree hollow.
Eggs 3–6, white.
Food Mainly invertebrates.

Downy woodpeckers are relatively common and can be found in a variety of habitats. These small woodpeckers are relatively tame, and it is possible to attract them to backyard feeding stations by offering suet, particularly in the wintertime when other foods are likely to be scarce. They feed largely on wood-boring insects, but are usually forced to seek out plant matter, such as nuts, through the winter. The breeding period varies across their extensive range, being later in the north, where egg laying is unlikely to occur before May. Unusually for a woodpecker, the nest site is chosen by the female, and is almost invariably sited in a dead tree. At this time, their distinctive drumming sounds can be heard echoing through the forest, as they tap on branches within their territory to keep in touch. Nesting duties are evenly shared, with pairs subsequently splitting up over the winter period to seek food and roost in tree hollows on their own.

Identification
Black on the head and ear coverts, plus a mustachial stripe with intervening white areas. Back and underparts are also white. There is a band of scalloped white markings in the vicinity of the shoulder, with spots on the black wings and inner tail feathers. Cocks have a bright red area at the back of the head.

RED-HEADED WOODPECKER

Melanerpes erythrocephalus

Distribution Canada and the USA, from Manitoba and southern Ontario in the north southward as far as Florida and the Gulf Coast.
Size 9½ in (24cm).
Habitat Open woodland, farmland, country roads, golf courses.
Nest Hole in a tree or fence post.
Eggs 4–10, white.
Food Plant matter, including nuts and acorns, invertebrates, rodents, and occasionally eggs and nestlings.

Red-headed woodpeckers sometimes appear in backyards near farmland or close to orchards with dying trees, containing plentiful dead wood. They eat a wide range of plant and animal foods, with their diet being influenced by the season. They are unusual in that they hunt not only by clambering over the bark of trees, but also by hawking insects in flight. They will even swoop down onto the ground and hop along there seeking prey. These woodpeckers will raid the nests of other birds, seizing both eggs and chicks, and they also catch mice. In northern parts of their range, they often migrate southward during the cold months of the year, seeking plentiful supplies of acorns and beech nuts when other foods are scarce. They also lay down stores of food, concealing nuts, acorns, and large insects in cavities or hiding them under the bark, and returning to eat them later. European starlings occasionally evict these birds from their nest holes, chiseled out of rotten wood in a tree.

Identification
This species has scarlet plumage covering the head, bordered by a narrow band of black feathering. White underparts, bluish black coloration on the back and tail. Prominent white patch on the wings, which are otherwise bluish black. Sexes are alike. Young birds are much browner overall, including the head.

DOVES AND PIGEONS

The characteristic dumpy appearance of doves and pigeons, along with their relatively subdued coloration, makes them easy to identify. There is actually no strict zoological distinction between these two groups, although the term "pigeon" is usually applied to larger species.

WHITE-WINGED DOVE

Mesquite dove *Zenaida asiatica*

Flocks of white-winged doves often congregate in crop-growing areas around harvest time, foraging on the ground for cultivated grains. They are very adaptable by nature and can also be found in habitats ranging from semidesert to mangrove swamps. They are attracted to backyards by sunflower and other seeds placed on bird tables. During the breeding season in the USA, pairs of white-winged doves from eastern areas breed in large colonies, while those occurring farther west tend to nest individually. Subsequently, many head south for winter, with birds from Texas flying as far as Costa Rica. Although they are often hunted for game, white-winged doves are still common in most areas, and the species is currently expanding its distribution in parts of the Caribbean.

Identification
So-called because of the evident white area on the leading edge of the wings when folded. Wings and tail feathers otherwise mainly brownish, with an adjacent grayer band. The head, neck, and upper chest have a pinker tinge. Prominent area of bare blue skin around the eyes. Hens are duller, with less iridescence on the neck.

Distribution Range extends across southern USA and Mexico, except for the southeast, southward as far as Costa Rica and Panama. Also present in the Caribbean.
Size 12in (30cm).
Habitat Relatively open areas, including farmland, parks, also rural and urban backyards.
Nest Loose platform of twigs.
Eggs 2, creamy buff.
Food Various seeds and grains.

MOURNING DOVE

Carolina dove *Zenaida macroura*

These doves are so-called because of the plaintive, mournful sound of their calls. Their scientific name *macroura* means "long-tailed." They have benefited from the provision of bird tables, particularly in the northern part of their range, and often visit rural and urban gardens for food, such as seeds and millet. Their powerful wings and sleek shape help these doves to fly long distances on migration, and northerly populations overwinter in Central America. In southern USA, such as Florida, mourning doves are resident throughout the year. They prefer to look for food on the ground if not feeding on a bird table, and groups often wander across fields in search of seeds and other edible items. Mourning doves are now recorded overwintering farther north than they did in the past, partly as a result of more feeding opportunities from backyard bird tables.

Identification
Some variation in appearance through these doves' wide range, with cocks displaying pinkish buff coloration on the face, extending to underparts, with a dark streak just above the neck. Upper surfaces of wings and tail are brown, with several large dark spots evident on the wings. Hens duller and browner overall.

Distribution Extensive range across much of North America, from southern Canada southward across the USA through Central America to Costa Rica and Panama, but distribution is affected by the season. Also occurs on the Greater Antilles in the Caribbean.
Size 13in (34cm).
Habitat Lightly wooded areas.
Nest Loose pile of twigs.
Eggs 2, white.
Food Seeds and some invertebrates.

INCA DOVE

Columbina inca; previously Scardafella inca

Distribution Southwestern USA south as far as Costa Rica. Range is extending north and south.
Size 8½ in (22cm).
Habitat Open areas, including fields, parks, and backyards.
Nest Fragile platform of twigs and other vegetation.
Eggs 2, white.
Food Seeds, fruits, berries.

Inca doves are typically encountered in relatively open countryside, but can also be seen in urban backyards throughout the year. The population is largely sedentary through its range, although sometimes these doves may be seen north of their breeding range in the USA, which extends across Oklahoma, Arkansas, and Nebraska. They were first recorded there around 1870. Too small to be hunted as game, these doves are relatively tame and will nest in urban backyards. Like many doves, pairs will breed two or three times in rapid succession when conditions are favorable, but their limited nest-building skills means that some nests will collapse, resulting in the loss of both eggs and chicks. A well-concealed site in vegetation is usually chosen, with both birds sharing incubation duties; the cock normally sits by day, while the hen takes over in late afternoon. The young grow rapidly and may leave the nest when only 12 days old, although they will not be able to fly strongly at this age.

Identification

Brownish upperparts, with a pinker tinge to underside. Black scalloping on both wings and body. Finer scalloping on the head, which is grayer. Tail is relatively long and tapering. Rufous underwing coverts seen in flight, with a rufous bar evident when wings are closed. Hens are similar, but underparts less strongly suffused with pink.

FERAL PIGEON (ROCK DOVE)

Columba livia

Distribution Much of North America except the far north, through Central America and across most of South America, except for central Amazonia and extreme southern tip; also occurs in the Caribbean.
Size 14in (35cm).
Habitat Narrow ledges of city buildings.
Nest Loose pile of twigs.
Eggs 2, white.
Food Prefers seeds, but highly adaptable.

These birds are not native to the Americas, but were introduced from Europe, where they evolved from rock doves. This helps to explain why they often nest on narrow ledges high above sidewalks, just as their ancestors still do on windswept cliffs. Feral pigeons are common city birds, scavenging from leftovers and having virtually no fear of people. Large flocks of feral pigeons can cause serious damage to buildings, with their droppings and also by pecking away at the mortar, which provides calcium.

Identification

This species has a dark, bluish gray head with slight green iridescence on the neck. Light gray wings with two black bars on each wing. Feral pigeons often have longer wings than their ancestors, rock doves. Reddish purple coloration evident on the sides of the upper chest. The remainder of plumage is gray, with a black band at the tip of the tail. Various color morphs exist, typically displaying orangish red or white areas of plumage. The sexes are alike.

HUMMINGBIRDS AND BLUEBIRDS

Feeding either from flowers or special feeders in backyards, hummingbirds are one of the unique sights of the Americas. These birds are fascinating as they hover while feeding, showing their remarkable aerial ability. Bluebirds are also welcome visitors to backyards, with their bright colors and melodious songs.

RUBY-THROATED HUMMINGBIRD

Archilochus colubris

Identification

Metallic, greenish bronze upperparts. Has a large, glossy red area of plumage under the throat. The remainder of the underparts are whitish. Hens are similar in appearance, but they have a dusky white area on their throat instead of the glossy red patch of the cocks.

The small size of these hummingbirds is no barrier to their flying long distances back and forth to their wintering grounds. Cock birds usually arrive back in their breeding areas about a week before the hens are seen in May. Temperate areas hold insufficient plant nectar to sustain them through the winter. These hummingbirds are relatively unspecialized in their feeding habits, feeding from over 30 different types of plants. They are attracted to tubular red flowers and also to feeders filled with sweet liquid. Hens build their nest alone, binding it with the silk threads of spiderwebs.

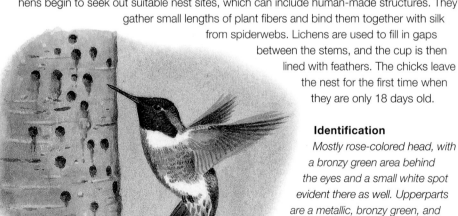

Distribution Breeds in eastern North America, moving south to Florida, Texas, and as far as Panama for winter. Sometimes seen in the Caribbean.
Size 3½ in (9cm).
Habitat Lightly wooded areas with flowering plants, suburban backyards.
Nest Cup built in trees bound with spiders' silk.
Eggs 2, white.
Food Nectar, pollen, sap, and invertebrates.

ANNA'S HUMMINGBIRD

Calypte anna

These hummingbirds are a familiar sight in backyards west of the Sierras, where they sip nectar from flowers and also from artificial feeders. They are sometimes seen feeding at holes in tree bark drilled by sapsuckers (*Sphyrapicus* species), which results in nutrient-rich sap oozing. At the outset of the breeding season, males become very territorial. Soon after, hens begin to seek out suitable nest sites, which can include human-made structures. They gather small lengths of plant fibers and bind them together with silk from spiderwebs. Lichens are used to fill in gaps between the stems, and the cup is then lined with feathers. The chicks leave the nest for the first time when they are only 18 days old.

Identification

Mostly rose-colored head, with a bronzy green area behind the eyes and a small white spot evident there as well. Upperparts are a metallic, bronzy green, and underparts are green and whitish. Hens lack the rose-colored plumage on the head, and have a brownish throat.

Distribution Western USA, from California and offshore islands southeast to Arizona; may move to southern Oregon during the winter. Sometimes even recorded in Alaska.
Size 4in (10cm).
Habitat Generally woodland areas with flowers, backyards.
Nest Cup bound in spiders' silk.
Eggs 2, white.
Food Nectar, pollen, sap, and invertebrates.

MOUNTAIN BLUEBIRD

Sialia currucoides

Distribution Breeds from southern Alaska southward through western North America, wintering as far south as northern Mexico.
Size 7in (18cm).
Habitat Open countryside, including parkland, backyards.
Nest Concealed cup-shaped structure.
Eggs 4–8, whitish to pale blue.
Food Invertebrates and berries.

The beautiful song of the mountain bluebird can be heard just before dawn, leading the Navajo people to describe them as "heralds of the rising sun." Almost immediately, when the sun appears, they become quiet again. These bluebirds breed in high mountain meadows. Pairs seek shelter when they are nesting, building in hollow trees, small caves, or even on cliff faces, although they will also adopt birdhouses. Invertebrates are an important source of food. However, late frosts can adversely affect the insect population, reducing the likelihood of breeding success if food is scarce when the chicks hatch. The young normally leave the nest at three weeks old, and the adult pair may rear another family before the end of summer. In fall, they leave mountain areas and descend to lower grasslands. During winter, berries feature more prominently in their diet, with the birds venturing regularly to feed on fruit, raisins, and peanut hearts from bird tables.

Identification
The cock is blue overall, being a deeper sky blue shade on the upperparts. The bill and legs are black. Hens are brownish gray, with white on the abdomen, and whitish scalloping seen on wings. These birds may have a reddish orange suffusion to the breast after the fall molt.

EASTERN BLUEBIRD

Sialia sialis

Distribution Occurs east of the Rockies from southern Canada to the Gulf states and Arizona, extending as far south as Nicaragua. Migrates south from northern areas for winter, being found no farther north than southern parts of New England and southern Michigan at this stage.
Size 7in (18cm).
Habitat Open woodland, farmland with scattered trees, orchards.
Nest Cup shape of grass.
Eggs 4–6, pale blue.
Food Invertebrates, including caterpillars, small vertebrates, fruit.

A member of the thrush family, this is the only bluebird seen east of the Great Plains, where it inhabits lightly wooded areas and agricultural land. Only the male is brightly colored, with a brilliant blue head and back and rusty red throat and breast. The female's colors are much more subdued, although still with some blue on the wings. The eastern bluebird's diet varies with the seasons. It feeds on invertebrates, particularly insects and caterpillars, in the spring and summer, and mainly on fruit in fall and winter. However, it is an opportunistic feeder, also taking small lizards and shrews. This bluebird is a partial migrant, with northerly populations moving south for winter in small groups or flocks of up to 100 birds. With its bright colors, this is a backyard favorite, which produces a soft, melodious song in flight, and whose return in spring is eagerly awaited by bird lovers. Eastern bluebirds nest in tree holes, fence posts, and also in nest boxes. In recent years, their numbers have declined, possibly partly due to competition for nest sites from introduced house sparrows and European starlings. The erection of nest boxes will, therefore, help to support the species.

Identification
Male has bright blue head, wings, and tail, offset by rusty red feathering on the throat and breast, becoming whiter on the abdomen. Hens are duller, with grayish blue upperparts, dull orange on the underparts, and pale blue on the wings. Young birds are brown and speckled with areas of whitish and some blue plumage. When perching, this species has a hunched appearance and often a drooping beak.

KINGBIRDS, LARKS, AND SWALLOWS

Many New World insect hunters undertake long migrations in the course of a year. Although the focus is often on birds from cool northern latitudes flying south for winter, many birds of the southern hemisphere also move north before the southern winter. Horned larks undertake migrations within North America.

TROPICAL KINGBIRD

Olive-backed kingbird *Tyrannus melancholicus*

This mainly South and Central American species is sometimes seen north of the Mexican border in the USA. Pairs have been recorded breeding in parts of Arizona, while some prefer to overwinter in the relatively mild climate of California. Here, they may be seen in backyards, hunting for invertebrates in characteristic fashion, swooping down to catch them in flight. Tropical kingbirds are usually most conspicuous toward dusk, as they hawk night-flying insects. These birds are very agile on the wing, able to drop almost vertically onto a branch from above. Pairs usually build their nests high up, out on a tree limb where they will be relatively safe from predators. The olive plumage on their back may help to conceal their presence when viewed from above during the nesting period. Incubation is carried out by the female alone, with the young fledging after approximately two weeks.

Identification

Grayish head with a blackish eye stripe, whiter on cheeks and throat. Grayish green on the back extends onto the chest, with rest of underparts yellow. Wings dark with scalloping on the shoulders. Coverts of the underwings are yellow.

Distribution Typically ranges from the extreme south of the USA and Mexico to Argentina, extending west of the Andes to Peru. Also occurs on Trinidad.
Size 9½in (24cm).
Habitat Trees, often close to water.
Nest Cup shape, made of vegetation.
Eggs 3–5, pinkish buff with darker markings.
Food Invertebrates.

HORNED LARK

Eremophila alpestris

This is the only true member of the lark family occurring naturally in the Americas. The horned lark is primarily a terrestrial species, walking rather than hopping on the ground. If disturbed, it will dart off a short distance before dropping down again. It favors open country where there is little cover. Pairs start nesting early, with hens incubating eggs in February in the northern USA. This can be hazardous if the weather turns bad, because the nest may be buried by snow. Horned larks are prolific breeders, however, and soon start again, with pairs producing up to 15 chicks in a good year. They are most likely to appear in backyards in fall, when they roam the countryside in large flocks, searching for food.

Identification

Characteristic narrow, raised black feathers on the sides of the head create the impression of horns. Facial color varies among races, from white to yellow, with variable black markings here. Prominent black stripe across the chest. Underparts whitish with dark flecking on the flanks. Wings a variable brown. Bill and legs blackish. Hens duller with indistinct horns.

Distribution Breeds as far north as Alaska and the Canadian Arctic, southward through much of the USA as far as Mexico. This species occasionally ranges down to northern Colombia in South America.
Size 7in (18cm).
Habitat Fairly arid country.
Nest Scrape on the ground.
Eggs 2–5, grayish white with brown markings.
Food Seeds and invertebrates.

BANK SWALLOW

Sand martin or African sand martin *Riparia riparia*

Distribution Throughout North America, except in the more arid regions of southwestern USA. Winters in South America.
Size 4in (11cm).
Habitat Open country, close to water.
Nest Holes in sandbanks.
Eggs 3–4, white.
Food Flying invertebrates.

In the summer months, bank swallows sometimes appear in backyards with large ponds. They are usually observed relatively close to lakes and other stretches of water, often swooping down to catch invertebrates near the surface. They are likely to be nesting in colonies nearby, in tunnels that they excavate on suitable sandy banks. These can extend back for up to 3 feet (1m), with the nesting chamber lined with grass, seaweed, or similar material. The eggs are laid on top of a soft bed of feathers. When the young birds leave the nest, they stay in groups with other chicks until their parents return to feed them, typically bringing about 60 invertebrates back on each visit.

Parents recognize their offspring by their distinctive calls. If danger threatens, the repetitive alarm calls of the adult bank swallows cause the young to rush back to the protection of the nest.

Identification
Mainly brown, with white plumage on the throat, separated from the white underparts by a brown band across the breast. Long flight feathers. Small black bill. Sexes alike. Immature bank swallows have shorter flight feathers and are browner than the adults.

NORTHERN ROUGH-WINGED SWALLOW

Stelgidopteryx serripennis

Distribution Breeds from southern Alaska and Canada southward through British Columbia, the southern prairies of Canada, and across virtually the entire USA to southern California and the Gulf Coast. Migrates to Central America, down as far as Panama.
Size 5in (13cm).
Habitat Open country.
Nest In existing burrows along riverbanks.
Eggs 4–8, white.
Food Invertebrates.

These swallows take their name from the tiny hooks on the feather vane of the outermost primary feather on each wing, near the shaft. These can only be seen with magnification; their purpose is unknown. Although they range over a wide area, northern rough-winged swallows are likely to be seen in backyards close to lakes and other wetlands, where they hawk insects, such as midges, on the wing. They also hunt prey, such as caterpillars and spiders, near the ground. Often seen in groups, they sometimes roost communally in holes to conserve warmth in cold weather. Pairs of these swallows start to nest in May and adopt a variety of existing cavities as nest sites, rarely excavating their own burrows. The nest chamber is lined with available materials, from seaweed to pine needles.

Identification
Mainly brown, darker on head and wings, with long, broad flight feathers. Tail brown, underparts whitish. Thin, narrow bill. Sexes are alike. Young birds have a cinnamon tone to the upperparts.

SWIFTS AND SWALLOWS

This group of birds spend much of their lives in flight. They undertake long journeys, moving south at the onset of winter, and returning to breed the following spring. Pairs frequently return to the same nest site they occupied previously—a remarkable feat of navigation after a journey covering thousands of miles.

CHIMNEY SWIFT

Chaetura pelagica

Chimney swifts have long wings and actively fly rather than glide, flapping their wings fast to stay airborne. When seen up close, their square-shape tails have spines at their tips. Dependent on flying insects for food, they are forced to head south for the winter, returning north to their breeding grounds in March and April. Just prior to migration, thousands may congregate at favored roosts. Their habits have changed following the spread of cities. Instead of the hollow trees that they would formerly have used for roosting, they have switched to using chimneys, barns, and similar sites, even breeding in these surroundings.

Identification
Dark brown overall, with a paler area around the throat. Stocky body with short tail feathers and long wings. Usually seen in flight from beneath, often at a great height as they soar high. Sexes are similar.

Distribution Range extends through eastern North America. Migrates through Central America on its way to and from its South American winter quarters in Peru and northern Chile.
Size 5in (13cm).
Habitat Urban and agricultural areas.
Nest Twigs held together with saliva.
Eggs 2–7, white.
Food Flying insects.

CLIFF SWALLOW

Petrochelidon pyrrhonota

The cliff swallow has adjusted its habits to benefit from the spread of urbanization in its North American breeding grounds. In the past, these swallows built their nests on cliff faces, as their name suggests, but now pairs will breed in barns, bridges, and similar structures. They will also use dry, hollowed gourds placed in suitable sites in backyards as artificial nests. These swallows may also nest in large colonies. The mud that forms the nest is scooped up in the swallow's bill, and, unlike in related species, is the only building material. The interior is lined with vegetation. Pairs typically take five days to build the nest. In fall, the swallows head south for winter, although a few fly no farther than Panama. Their return is greeted as a sign of spring.

Identification
Pale forehead, with blue top to the head, which is encircled with chestnut. Blackish area at base of throat. Upper chest and rump orangish brown, underparts otherwise whitish, with dark edging to undertail coverts. Back and wings dark, streaked with white. Young have blackish heads.

Distribution North America and Mexico, except northern Alaska and the far northeast. Migrates via Central America to southern Brazil, Paraguay, parts of Argentina, and even Chile.
Size 5½in (14cm).
Habitat Open areas near buildings.
Nest Gourd-shape structure of mud.
Eggs 3–6, white with brown speckles.
Food Invertebrates.

TREE SWALLOW

White-bellied swallow *Tachycineta bicolor*

Distribution North-central Alaska to Newfoundland south of Hudson Bay, south to northern Louisiana and Mississippi. Winters from southern California east to the south of Virginia and down through Central America to Panama. Also in the Caribbean.
Size 5in (12.5cm).
Habitat Breeds in wooded terrain.
Nest Tree cavity.
Eggs 3–8, white.
Food Invertebrates, some berries.

These swallows may be seen in huge flocks migrating to and from their breeding grounds. Nesting starts in early May in the far north of their range, with males laying claim to suitable tree holes. Nest sites are sometimes fought over, with rivals occasionally being killed in such encounters. The incidence of these disputes can be reduced by the provision of alternative sites in the form of nest boxes in backyards. Females may also battle to obtain a mate, sometimes even driving out a sitting resident. The hen is responsible for collecting the material for the nest, which is usually made up of dry grass and pine needles, with the eggs being laid on top of a bed of feathers. Studies have revealed that during the nearly three-week period in which they remain in the nest, the nestlings are fed about every three minutes. Success is, therefore, dependent on a good summer, and in bad weather, when invertebrates are scarce, fewer than one chick in four will survive through to fledging. Bayberry shrubs in backyards help to sustain them in winter.

Identification
Predominantly metallic, bluish green head, extending down over the back, shoulder area, and rump, while the wings and tail are blackish. Develops a less bluish hue after the breeding season. The remainder of the body is white. Sexes alike. Young birds have brown upperparts and often display a grayish band over the chest.

BARN SWALLOW

Hirundo rustica

Distribution Breeds from Alaska eastward across Canada and southward throughout the USA except the far south. Eurasian populations overwinter in Africa.
Size 7½in (19cm).
Habitat Open country, close to water, also farmland and suburban areas.
Nest Made of mud, built off the ground.
Eggs 4–5, white with reddish and gray spotting.
Food Flying insects.

These swallows undertake long migrations, with North American populations flying south as far as Argentina for winter. Their return to their northern breeding grounds is a welcome sign of spring. Cock birds arrive back before their partners and jealously guard the site from would-be rivals. Cocks fight with surprising ferocity if one of the birds does not back down. Although swallows sometimes use traditional nesting sites, such as caves or hollow trees, they now commonly build their nests inside buildings, such as barns, choosing a site close to the eaves. It can take as many as 1,000 trips to collect damp mud, carried back in the bill, to complete a new nest. They may also use artificial cup-shaped nests.

Identification
Chestnut forehead and throat, with dark blue head and back, and a narrow dark blue band across the chest. Wings are blackish. Underparts white. Long streamers on the tail feathers make the tail appear deeply forked. The sexes are alike.

CROW FAMILY

Studies suggest that corvids rank among the most intelligent of birds. Many display an instinctive desire to hoard food, such as acorns, to help sustain them through the winter. Their plumage is often mainly black, sometimes with gray and white areas. Corvids are generally noisy and aggressive by nature.

AMERICAN CROW

Common crow *Corvus brachyrhynchos*

Few birds have more highly developed communication skills than these crows. It is almost impossible to approach them without being noticed, because even when feeding they have sentinels keeping a lookout for danger. They are heavily persecuted in farming areas, due to the damage they can inflict on crops; however, the benefit they bring to farmers and gardeners in foraging for harmful invertebrates is often overlooked. American crows are highly adaptable birds, just as likely to be encountered in suburban backyards as in open countryside. Noisy by nature, they tend to be much less vocal in the vicinity of their nests, which are sited in tall trees, often in public parks. The height at which they build—60 feet (20m) or more off the ground—keeps them safe from most predators.

Identification
Jet black plumage, with dark eyes and a large black bill. Sexes are alike. Calls help to distinguish this species from other crows, while the fan-shape appearance of the tail in flight distinguishes them from ravens.

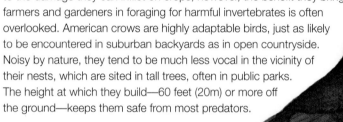

Distribution Occurs across much of North America, from British Columbia to Newfoundland and south to Baja California, Colorado, and central Texas.
Size 17½ in (45cm).
Habitat Ranges widely, including into suburban areas.
Nest Platform of sticks.
Eggs 3–7, greenish with brown blotches.
Food Omnivorous.

BLACK-BILLED MAGPIE

Pica hudsonia

Distinguishable from its European relative by its calls rather than its appearance, the black-billed magpie is a common sight through much of its range. These members of the crow family are agile on the ground, holding their tail feathers up as they hop along. They are often blamed for the decline of songbirds because of their habit of raiding nests, taking both eggs and young chicks. They will also chase other birds, particularly gulls, to make them drop their food. Bold and garrulous by nature, a pair of black-billed magpies create a commotion if their nest is threatened by a predator, such as a cat. Their calls draw other magpies, who then join in harrying the feline. Their nest is a large structure, with a protective dome of twigs.

Identification
Black head, upper breast, back, rump, and tail, with a broad white patch around the abdomen. When folded, wings have a broad white stripe and dark blue areas below. Black plumage may have a green gloss. The sexes are alike, but the cock frequently has a longer tail.

Distribution Western North America, extending from Alaska eastward to Ontario down to northeastern parts of California and northern New Mexico.
Size 19in (48cm).
Habitat Trees with surrounding open areas, grasslands, by streams.
Nest Dome-shape stick pile.
Eggs 2–8, bluish green with darker markings.
Food Omnivorous.

STELLER'S JAY

Cyanocitta stelleri

Distribution The largest distribution of all North American jays, extending from Alaska south through Central America as far as Nicaragua.
Size 12½in (32cm).
Habitat Woodland and forest.
Nest Mound of twigs.
Eggs 2–6, greenish or bluish with brown spotting.
Food Omnivorous.

A common jay in and west of the Rockies, Steller's jay ranges over a vast area, and has proved to be a highly adaptable species. In backyards where birds are supplied with food, and places such as at picnic sites in the Rocky Mountains in Colorado, these jays have become tame, accepting food from humans. Elsewhere, they are much shyer. They eat a varied diet; where food is likely to be hard to find because of snow in winter, they forage for acorns in fall, which are then stored for later use. Like many other corvids, they sometimes raid songbirds' nests to take eggs or chicks. They also eat insects and even frogs. Family groups may remain together over the winter in northern areas, with the young leaving in spring when the adult pair start to nest again. Mud is often used like cement to anchor the bulky nest of twigs together.

Identification
Dark, grayish blue head and back, with tall, dark, prominent crest. Blue underparts. Tail and wings are blue with black barring. North American populations have darker coloration and more prominent crests than those occurring farther south, which have a much bluer appearance overall. The sexes are alike.

BLUE JAY

Cyanocitta cristata

Distribution Occurs extensively in eastern North America from southern Canada south to Florida and northeastern Texas, although southerly populations tend to be smaller.
Size 12in (30cm).
Habitat Oak and pine woodlands, parks, and backyards.
Nest Cup shape of twigs and moss.
Eggs 4–5, greenish with brown spots.
Food Seeds, grain, invertebrates, fruit, berries, scraps.

This handsome bird is widespread throughout eastern North America, where in many areas it is the only jay. Both males and females have bright blue upperparts with a conspicuous head crest, black-and-white barring on the wings, and black barring on the tail. Blue jays are omnivores, feeding on a variety of foods, including seeds, grain, berries, small invertebrates, and scraps. They bury seeds and acorns. They are equally adaptable when it comes to living alongside humans, moving into parks and backyards, where they are usually seen alone or in pairs. Blue jays sometimes make themselves unpopular by chasing smaller birds away from feeders. However, their reputation as raptors of songbird eggs and chicks is largely undeserved. These jays are partial migrants, with northern populations moving south to escape harsh winters in loose flocks of up to 50 birds. Blue jays pair for life. Both sexes help to build an untidy nest of twigs in the fork of a tree or large shrub, and rear the single brood. Calls include a raucous scream, which these birds use to drive away predators, such as hawks and owls.

Identification
Blue head with prominent crest. White areas on the face edged by black feathering, which extends around the neck. Wings are blue, with distinctive white markings that are conspicuous in flight. Black barring extends from the flight feathers to the tail. Underparts off-white. Bill, legs, and eyes black. The sexes are alike.

TITS, TITMICE, AND CHICKADEES

These small birds are most likely to be seen in backyards during winter, when the absence of leaves makes them more conspicuous. They often visit bird tables and feeders during cold weather. They are very resourceful, displaying acrobatic skills as they dart about and hang upside down to feed.

TUFTED TITMOUSE

Baeolophus bicolor

This is the largest member of the tit family in North America. It is conspicuous, thanks to its noisy nature. The vocal range of male tufted titmice is especially varied, with individuals able to sing more than 15 different song patterns. Hens also sing, but not to the same extent, and mainly in spring and early summer. The range of these titmice has increased northward, largely because bird-table offerings provide them food throughout the year. In the south, they have been recorded as hybridizing with black-crested titmice *(B. atricristatus)* in central parts of Texas. The resulting offspring have grayish crests and a pale orange band above the bill. Despite their small size, these titmice are determined visitors to bird tables, driving off much larger species.

Identification

Characteristic black band immediately above the bill, with gray crest and crown. Cheeks and underparts are whitish, with pale reddish orange flanks. Sexes alike. Young birds are duller overall.

Left: *The nest cup is lined with soft material. These small birds can be fierce in defending their nests.*

Distribution Range extends across eastern North America, from southern Ontario south to the Gulf of Mexico, although not present in southern Florida. Range appears to be expanding in some areas of Canada.
Size 6in (15cm).
Habitat Light, deciduous woodland.
Nest Small tree holes and nest boxes.
Eggs 3–8, creamy white with brown spots.
Food Invertebrates in summer; seeds during winter.

CAROLINA CHICKADEE

Parus carolinensis

A regular visitor to bird tables in eastern states, Carolina chickadees can become very tame when supplied with food, such as sunflower seeds, suet, and peanut butter. This species is very closely related to the black-capped chickadee *(P. atricapillus),* which occurs farther north, and it is not unknown for the birds to hybridize where they overlap. Studies of their song patterns have revealed that the Carolina chickadee has a four-note call, whereas the black-capped type has a two-note whistle. Although pairs have their own territories during summer, Carolina chickadees form larger groups in the winter months. During cold weather, they spend much longer periods roosting in tree hollows to conserve their body heat, sometimes remaining there for up to 15 hours per day. This is also the time of year when chickadees are most likely to be seen visiting bird tables in search of food.

Identification

Black area extends to back of the head, with black under the bill broadening across the throat. White on the sides of the face. Underparts are whitish with a slightly orange cast. Wings and tail are primarily grayish olive. Sexes are alike.

Distribution Range extends from northeastern USA southward to Texas and northern Florida. Occasionally recorded in Ontario, Canada.
Size 5in (12cm).
Habitat Light, broad-leaved woodland.
Nest In small holes in trees, also uses nest boxes.
Eggs 3–9, white with reddish brown spots.
Food Invertebrates and seeds.

BUSHTIT

Psaltriparus minimus

Distribution Range extends from British Columbia in Canada south and eastward through the USA to parts of Mexico and Guatemala in Central America.
Size 4½ in (11cm).
Habitat Scrubland, open woodlands, suburbs, backyards.
Nest Pendulous mass.
Eggs 5–13, white.
Food Mainly invertebrates. Also berries.

Bushtits are the smallest species of North American tit. These lively birds forage in groups of up to 40 individuals, their movements helping to disturb insects and spiders that might otherwise remain hidden. Bushtits will comb plants in this way, which makes them welcome by gardeners, because they can devour unwanted infestations of pests rapidly. They are very agile birds, able to hang upside down from a branch or feeder when seeking food, and also have a bold nature, so it is often possible to observe them at relatively close quarters. There is a consistent difference in eye coloration between the sexes: the irises of cocks are invariably brown, whereas those of hens may vary from white through to yellow. Remarkably, this change may become apparent within a few days of the young birds fledging, although both sexes have dark eyes at first. Nesting pairs of these tits are surprisingly tolerant of others of their own kind, to the extent that they may allow them to roost in their nest. Flocks subsequently reform once the breeding season has ended.

Identification
Three groupings exist. Those from northern areas have brownish ear coverts, a brown cap, and gray upperparts, with paler, whitish underparts. Hens have grayer throats. Gray coloration extends onto the cap in the lead-colored variety. In the Central American black-eared form, cock birds have black areas on the sides of the face.

PLAIN TITMOUSE

Oak titmouse *Baeolophus inornatus;* previously *Parus inornatus*

Distribution This species' range covers much of western parts of the USA, extending down to Baja California and other parts of northwestern Mexico.
Size 5in (13cm).
Habitat Areas of oak woodland, also pinyon-juniper woodlands.
Nest Old woodpecker holes, also birdhouses.
Eggs 3–9, white.
Food Invertebrates, buds, and berries.

Until recently, the plain or oak titmouse was considered one species with the juniper timouse. Since 1996, the two have been classed separately because of differences in their songs and preferred habitat. The dull coloration of this titmouse helps it to blend in with its wooded habitat. Pairs maintain distinct territories throughout the year, and form lifelong bonds. If one bird dies, the surviving individual may mate with a new partner. Plain titmice breed only once during the year, with the young being driven away by their parents when about seven weeks old, and forced to seek their own territories. When feeding, these titmice will often comb branches in search of insects. During winter, acorns feature prominently in their diet—they can open these easily with their stout bill. They are also more frequent visitors to bird feeders in winter, taking food, such as sunflower seeds, cracked corn, suet, and baked goods. They will pick up edible items from the ground and convey them to a more secluded location to be eaten. At night, plain titmice will seek out suitable roosting holes, with pairs using separate locations, although they sometimes prefer a well-hidden perch. They will also roost in nest boxes.

Identification
Differences in depth of coloration and bill size occur through its range. Grayish brown overall, with a small crest at the back of the head. Underparts are a purer shade of gray than the back. Sexes alike. Formerly classified with the juniper titmouse (B. ridgwayi) *as one species.*

NUTHATCHES, KINGLETS, AND WRENS

Insects provide nuthatches, kinglets, and wrens with much of their diet, while some also eat other foods, for example, nuts in the case of nuthatches. These insect hunters use various techniques to feed. Nuthatches and kinglets comb the bark and foliage of trees, while wrens mainly hunt on the ground.

RED-BREASTED NUTHATCH

Sitta canadensis

Lively and active by nature, red-breasted nuthatches are well-adapted to an arboreal lifestyle. Their small size and compact shape enable them to climb up and down tree trunks with ease, their strong toes and claws providing sufficient anchorage for them to descend headfirst. They are adept at pulling insects out from under the bark, and move along narrow branches to pluck invertebrates off leaves. The seeds of conifers help to sustain them through winter, when invertebrates are scarce. At this time, they also take seeds, suet, and wheat from bird tables. These birds have an unusual method of deterring predators from the nest hole by smearing it with pine oil. This helps to obscure their scent, but their plumage becomes heavily stained as they pass in and out of the nest.

Identification

Black cap across the top of the head, with a black line running through the eyes, separated by an intervening white stripe. White on the cheeks too. Back, wings, and tail bluish gray, with rust-colored underparts. Short, narrow blackish bill, paler below, with black legs and feet. Hens have duller plumage on the head and paler underparts. Young birds are similar to hens.

Distribution Breeding range extends right across Canada from southeastern Alaska to Newfoundland. Winters across much of the USA, sometimes as far south as northern Florida, the Gulf coast, and Mexico.
Size 4½in (11.5cm).
Habitat Coniferous and oak woodlands.
Nest Tree hollows.
Eggs 4–8, white with reddish brown speckling.
Food Invertebrates and pine nuts.

RUBY-CROWNED KINGLET

Regulus calendula

These small warblers breed in the taiga forest in the far north of North America. They often search for food by hovering around the branches, darting down to seize caterpillars, and are able to balance right at the tips of branches thanks to their small size. It is not always easy to recognize the distinctive ruby red crown of the cock bird, because this feathering may be obscured. Ruby-crowned kinglets are very active birds, constantly on the move, and frequently flick their wings, as if they are startled and about to take off. The nest is located close to the end of a branch of a spruce tree or similar conifer, where the young will be fairly safe from predators. After the breeding season, these small birds travel southward, arriving at their wintering grounds in September. In northern states, they are very rare in winter, but are familiar residents in the south, visiting backyards for peanut picks, fruit, and baked goods.

Identification

Olive-brown upperparts with a paler, whitish area encircling the eyes. Throat area pale gray, becoming yellowish on the underparts. Wings dark, with prominent white band at the top and across the wings of the cock bird. Ruby red patch of feathering on top of the crown. Hens lack this color, and have more dusky stripes across the wings. Young have more brownish upperparts.

Distribution From Alaska, across Canada south of Hudson Bay to Newfoundland, south to the Great Lakes and New England. Overwinters from southern USA south through Central America as far as Guatemala.
Size 4¼in (11cm).
Habitat Forests and woodland.
Nest Woven from plant matter.
Eggs 5–10, creamy with fine darker speckling.
Food Insects and other invertebrates.

Distribution Occurs in western North America. Breeding range extends to British Columbia; wanders widely outside the breeding period. Separate populations in parts of Mexico, Guatemala, Honduras, Nicaragua, and northwestern Costa Rica.
Size 5½ in (14cm).
Habitat Rocky and arid areas.
Nest Made of vegetation.
Eggs 4–10, white with reddish brown speckling.
Food Insects and other invertebrates.

ROCK WREN

Salpinctes obsoletus

As its name suggests, this wren is mainly found in rocky terrain, although it may appear at picnic sites and in backyards in this habitat. Rock wrens are lively and easy to observe because they are naturally tame and conspicuous, moving from boulder to boulder in search of invertebrates. If danger threatens, they slip away. Their relatively loud song is especially evident during the breeding period. These wrens seek out small crevices in rocks as nest sites, creating a snug lining. They often build the nest on a bed of small stones that they collect themselves, for reasons that are unclear, but may have to do with nest sanitation. They gather a wide variety of material to incorporate into the nest site, ranging from rabbit bones to small pieces of rusty metal. Six subspecies of this wren have been identified, although one of these, the San Benedicto rock wren *(S. o. exsul),* from an island on Mexico's west coast, was wiped out by a volcanic explosion there in 1952.

Identification
This species has dark, grayish brown upperparts with black streaky markings. Chestnut brown rump, underparts whitish gray with fine dark streaking on the breast. Narrow, pointed grayish bill. Sexes alike. Young birds duller. Extent of black barring differs between races.

CACTUS WREN

Campylorhynchus brunneicapillus

Distribution Occurs in southwestern USA from California southward as far as central Mexico.
Size 8½ in (22cm).
Habitat Arid areas and desert.
Nest Large structure made of vegetation, often located in cacti.
Eggs 4–7, creamy white with spots.
Food Invertebrates.

Right: *Cactus wrens build their nests in cacti, with sharp spines guarding the site.*

Cactus wrens inhabit thickets in arid country, where they may appear in backyards. This surprisingly large wren is often seen near cacti. It builds a bulky nest of dried grass within the protective spines of cacti or in thornbushes. The nest interior is lined with fur or feathers; the entrance is to one side. Nests near the ground are concealed so they are less apparent to predators. The calls of the cactus wren have a monotonous tone, consisting simply of the sound "chut" uttered repeatedly. The cactus wren does not raise its tail vertically in true wren fashion, but holds it horizontally. These birds prefer to remain near the ground, flying low and hunting for invertebrates lurking there.

Identification
This larger wren may be identified by its white, dark-spotted underparts. Brown area on the top of the head extends over the nape, with a white stripe passing through the eye, and white streaking on the back. Prominent black spotting on the breast, becoming more streaked on the pale underparts. Barring is apparent on the wings and tail. The sexes are alike.

BACKYARD WRENS

These small, rather stumpy birds are often found in residential areas, especially the aptly named house wren, which has one of the widest distributions of all American birds. Other wrens have more localized distributions, benefiting from bird-feeder offerings to sustain themselves during cold winter months.

HOUSE WREN

Troglodytes aedon

The house wren is a nondescript bird, but its lively, jerky movements make it instantly recognizable. These wrens often visit backyards, usually being seen among dense vegetation because they are instinctively reluctant to leave cover for long. Although wrens are small in size, they can be determined and belligerent, especially in defense of a chosen nest site, such as a woodpecker hole in a tree, and are able to force the hole maker to go elsewhere. They will also take occupancy of a birdhouse, particularly when sited in a corner of a backyard where they feel secure. The pair collect a jumble of moss and small twigs to line the interior, adding feathers to make a soft pad for their eggs. House wrens are prolific breeders, frequently producing two broods of chicks during the season.

Identification
Brown upperparts, with black barring evident on the wings and tail. Underparts lighter brown, with whitish throat area. Generally indistinct pale eyebrow stripes. Narrow, relatively short bill. Sexes are alike. Young birds have a rufous rump and are a darker shade of buff on the underparts.

Distribution Present across much of North America except the far north, extending down through Mexico and right across South America.
Size 5in (12cm).
Habitat Dense vegetation in parks and backyards.
Nest Pile of twigs and sticks.
Eggs 5–9, white with brown spotting.
Food Invertebrates.

CAROLINA WREN

Thryothorus ludovicianus

Carolina wrens are relatively easy birds to identify, due partly to their extensive white facial markings. They move with the same jerky movements as other wrens, frequenting dense areas of vegetation in backyards through which they can move inconspicuously. Carolina wrens are also noisy birds, with a song that is surprisingly loud for a bird of their size. It is uttered throughout the year, rather than just at the start of the breeding season, and sounds in part like the word "wheateater," repeated constantly. Unfortunately, young Carolina wrens often have an instinctive tendency to push northward from their southern homelands. Although in mild years they will find sufficient food to withstand the winter cold, widescale mortality occurs in these northern areas when the ground is blanketed with snow for long periods, almost wiping out the species. In due course, however, their numbers build up again, until the cycle is repeated at some future stage.

Identification
Chestnut brown upperparts, with black barring on wings and tail, and white bands running across the wings. Distinctive white eye stripes, edged with black above and chestnut below. Black and white speckling on sides of face. Throat white, underparts buff. Sexes alike.

Distribution The range of this species extends throughout eastern USA, notably occuring in North Carolina and South Carolina.
Size 5½ in (14cm).
Habitat Shrubbery.
Nest Cup of vegetation.
Eggs 4–8, whitish with brown spotting.
Food Invertebrates feature prominently in the diet, with some seeds.

CANYON WREN

Catherpes mexicanus

Distribution Range extends from western parts of the USA south as far as southern Mexico.
Size 6in (15cm).
Habitat Rocky areas, canyons, cliffs, and old stone buildings.
Nest Open cup of vegetation.
Eggs 4–7, white, lightly speckled with reddish brown.
Food Invertebrates.

As with other wrens it is the powerful, musical song of this species that attracts attention. However, it can be difficult to see the songster, partly because of its small size and relatively dull coloration, and especially if it is partly concealed among a loose outcrop of rocks. Slightly larger than the house wren, this species has a conspicuous white throat. Unlike the house wren, it is shy and secretive by nature. Canyon wrens generally inhabit rocky terrain but will sometimes adopt old stone buildings as refuges. Their long, narrow bills let them seize invertebrates from small crevices without difficulty, their tails often bobbing up and down as they seek their quarry. Canyon wrens prefer areas around steep slopes or cliffs, whereas rock wrens *(Salpinctes obsoletus)* tend to inhabit flatter areas of countryside. For breeding, these wrens choose a site in a stone wall or a similarly inaccessible place, such as a chimney. The nest is fashioned from a jumble of vegetation on a suitable ledge.

Identification

Black-and-white speckled top to the head, with a white throat and breast. Black barring on the wings and tail, with speckling on the back and underparts. Characteristic rufous underparts, with the red extending across the back, wings, and tail. Long, relatively straight, blackish bill. Sexes are alike. Young birds lack the white speckling of the adults.

WINTER WREN

Troglodytes troglodytes

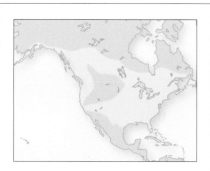

Distribution Occurs in a broad band across North America around the 50-degree line of latitude. Range also extends farther south into the Rocky Mountains, the Midwest, and mountainous parts of the east coast.
Size 4in (10cm).
Habitat Coniferous and mixed woodland, overgrown backyards.
Nest Ball-shaped mass of vegetation with a side entrance, also nest boxes.
Eggs 5–6, white with reddish brown markings.
Food Mainly invertebrates.

This wren's tiny size, drab coloration, and skulking, mouselike habits can make it difficult to see, but its song is remarkably loud for its size and will usually betray its presence. Winter wrens may be found in tangled woodlands and backyards where there is plenty of cover, such as ivy-clad walls, where they hunt for food, scurrying under the vegetation in search of spiders and similar prey. During winter, when their small size could make them vulnerable to hypothermia, these wrens huddle together in roosts overnight to keep warm. In spring, the hen chooses one of several nests that the male has constructed, lining it with feathers to form a soft base for her eggs. These birds will also use nest boxes. Wrens can be surprisingly common, although not always conspicuous. However, populations are often severely affected by prolonged spells of severe weather.

Identification

Reddish brown back and wings with barring visible. Lighter brown underparts and a narrow eye stripe. Short tail, often held vertically, which is grayish on its underside. Bill is long and relatively narrow. Sexes are alike.

THRUSHES AND BLACKBIRDS

One of the most welcome signs of spring in temperate regions is the dawn chorus, indicating the onset of the breeding period and the return of migrant songbirds. At this hour of day, the songs of birds can be clearly heard in backyards and parks, and early morning is an excellent time to watch birds, too.

AMERICAN ROBIN

Turdus migratorius

The return of the American robin to its northern haunts is a long-awaited sign of spring. Adult cock birds usually arrive first, followed by the hens. Last to arrive are the young of the previous year, making their first flight back to the area where they hatched. American robins are alert hunters, hopping across lawns and pausing at intervals, their head tilted slightly to one side as if listening. It is actually their keen eyesight that lets them see earthworms and other invertebrates in the grass. Berries feature in their diet, and they also take seed mix, millet, cracked corn, and fruit from bird tables. The nest is well built, with mud serving as cement to hold plant matter together, and carefully sited in dense vegetation to avoid the attention of predators.

Identification

The cock has a blackish head, with white around the eyes and streaking under the throat. Back and wings are grayish brown, with brick red underparts and white under the vent. Hens have browner heads and orangish underparts. The young birds have dark speckling on their pale underparts.

Distribution All of North America, apart from the central far north, down as far as Mexico. Overwinters in the south of its range, including northern Guatemala, and is also seen in some Caribbean islands, such as Cuba.
Size 10in (25cm).
Habitat Woodlands, parks, and suburban areas.
Nest Cup of vegetation and mud.
Eggs 3–6, bright blue.
Food Invertebrates, and also fruit.

RED-WINGED BLACKBIRD

Agelaius phoeniceus

Unrelated to the European blackbird, the red-winged blackbird is a member of the icterid family. It frequents marshland areas when nesting, but may be seen in a much wider range of habitats, including backyards, during winter. In North America, red-winged blackbirds move southward for the winter period, typically traveling distances of about 440 miles (700km). Populations in Central America tend to be sedentary throughout the year. There is a marked variation in the appearance of these birds through their wide range, and it is also not uncommon for individuals to display pied markings. Both sexes sing, particularly at the start of the nesting period, and some of their call notes are different, so it is possible to tell the sexes apart.

Identification

Only mature males in breeding plumage display the characteristic glossy black feathering and red shoulder patches with a paler buff border. Females have dark streaks down their bodies, with more solid brownish coloration on the head, sides of the face, and over the wings.

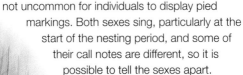

Distribution Occurs over much of North America, breeding as far north as Alaska, and south into Central America.
Size 9½in (24cm).
Habitat Marshland and relatively open country.
Nest Cup shape.
Eggs 3, pale greenish blue with dark spots.
Food Seeds and invertebrates.

RUFOUS-BACKED ROBIN

Rufous-backed thrush *Turdus rufopalliatus*

Distribution Range is restricted to western Mexico, but is also sometimes observed in southwestern USA, particularly during winter.
Size 10in (25cm).
Habitat Trees and shrubbery.
Nest Cup shape.
Eggs 2–3, whitish with reddish brown markings.
Food Invertebrates, berries, and fruit.

These relatively large robins are likely to be found in Mexico at lower altitudes than migrating American robins *(T. migratorius)*. Their song is relatively similar, however, being comprised of attractive liquid call notes uttered in a relatively slow style. There is evidence to show that these members of the thrush family regularly move northward, crossing the border into the United States, where they have been observed feeding on fruit-bearing trees and shrubs in backyards. Records of sightings exist not only in Texas and Arizona, but also in locations farther north in California during the winter period. Rufous-backed robins are common throughout their normal range in western Mexico, although those reported around Oaxaca City may well be the descendants of captive individuals, rather than naturally occurring birds. The same may apply to those seen in the Distrito Federal, another part of their range where the species has not been sighted until recently. Outside the breeding season, rufous-backed robins are often seen in larger groups rather than as pairs.

Identification

This largish robin has a grayish head, with a white throat streaked with black. Back and wing coverts reddish brown. Wings and rump gray with reddish brown underparts, becoming white on the lower abdomen. Sexes alike. Underparts of young birds have conspicuous black spots.

VARIED THRUSH

Ixoreus naevius

Distribution This species occurs in western North America, ranging from Alaska southward as far as northern parts of California.
Size 10in (25cm).
Habitat Coniferous forests in summer, also seen in more open woodlands during winter.
Nest Bulky and cup-shaped.
Eggs 3–5, pale blue with dark spots.
Food Mainly invertebrates, and also some berries.

Varied thrushes are common in the coniferous woodlands of the Northwest, where they sometimes appear in backyards. This migratory member of the thrush family is fairly hard to observe in its habitat, dark woods and areas near water. Varied thrushes are not shy birds, however, and have a powerful song with buzzing tones, which is most often uttered in the rain. They sing most at the start of the breeding period in March, from the upper branches of conifer trees. Varied thrushes normally feed close to the ground, foraging for invertebrates as well as eating berries. They normally nest about 15 feet (4.5m) off the ground. The bulky nest often includes moss. After the breeding period the thrushes leave Alaska, with many overwintering in British Columbia, while others head farther south, where they are sometimes seen in backyards near open woodland.

Identification

Bluish gray upperparts, with a broad black stripe on the sides of the head and a prominent black band across the chest. Bright orange areas above the eyes and on the throat, upper chest, and lower underparts, the latter being mottled with gray. Orange bars also on the wings. Hens browner, with duller orange and an indistinct breastband. Young birds much duller, with brownish mottling on the throat and chest.

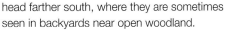

THRASHERS, PIPITS, AND STARLINGS

The present-day distribution of some birds is the direct result of past human interference. In North America, European species, such as the starling, have now become established across virtually the entire continent. Mimics, such as the catbird, may even pick up the songs of these feathered invaders.

BROWN THRASHER

Toxostoma rufum

Identification

Reddish brown upperparts, with streaking across the wings creating a scalloped appearance. Long chestnut tail feathers. Underparts marked with black streaks arranged in vertical lines running down onto the flanks; plumage is whitish in the vicinity of the throat, becoming fawn on the lower parts of the abdomen. Long, slightly down-curved black bill. Sexes are alike.

Thrashers are a native American group of birds. They are common yet inconspicuous, being shy by nature, hiding away in woodland or backyards with dense vegetation. They venture down to the ground to flick over leaf litter and snatch up any invertebrates disturbed. At the outset of the breeding season it is difficult to overlook the courtship of the brown thrasher, because the cock takes up a prominent position to sing to his would-be mate. He perches with his head up and bill open, but any hint of danger will stop his song. The hen responds by offering a piece of vegetation, which probably marks the start of nest building. Pairs work together to construct a bulky nest of plant matter, including grass and twigs. Incubation and fledging each take about 13 days, which allows two broods of chicks to be reared during a single breeding season.

Distribution This species is widely distributed in eastern parts of North America, ranging down as far as Florida and the Gulf coast. It has even been recorded in Newfoundland.
Size 11½in (29cm).
Habitat Woodland, hedges, also dense shrubbery.
Nest Cup shape.
Eggs 2–5, whitish to pale blue with brown speckles.
Food Invertebrates and berries.

CATBIRD

Dumetella carolinensis

The song of these relatives of the mockingbird incorporates a sound like a cat's meowing, which is the reason for their common name. This plaintive song is commonly heard in suburban backyards. Catbirds also possess a harsher alarm call in their vocal repertoire. They can often be heard singing after dark, especially on moonlit nights. Catbirds are shy by nature, and their coloration also helps them to blend into the background. Their chestnut underparts are most conspicuous during the cock's courting display, when he chases the hen in the early stages of courtship. When on the move, the catbird flicks its long tail repeatedly. Insects are a vital part of the diet of these birds, especially when they are rearing chicks, when invertebrates provide valuable protein. Catbirds may catch their insect prey above water, and these birds may be observed hunting in backyards close to ponds and streams.

Identification

Smaller than the American robin, this species is slate gray in color, with a distinctive black cap. It also has chestnut underparts, which may not be clearly visible. The sexes are alike.

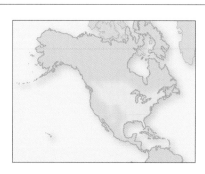

Distribution Range extends from southern Canada south and eastward across the USA, as far down as Florida. Southerly winter range extends as far down as Panama and Cuba.
Size 9in (23cm).
Habitat Scrubland, hedges, and backyards.
Nest Loosely constructed cup of vegetation.
Eggs 4–6, glossy blue-green.
Food Fruit and insects.

AMERICAN PIPIT

Anthus rubescens

Distribution Arctic North America and western USA, in parts of northern New Hampshire, California, and New Mexico. Winters throughout southern USA, and up to British Columbia in the west and New England in the east.
Size 6½ in (17cm).
Habitat Tundra, grassland, and fields.
Nest Cup shape.
Eggs 4–5, gray with dark spots and streaks.
Food Seeds and invertebrates.

American pipits leave their northern breeding grounds in early September, and head south for the winter. At this time, they may appear on farms and golf courses, sometimes in large flocks. Active birds by nature, they tend to walk rather than hop across the ground, bobbing their tails up and down regularly. Their range does not extend to the northeastern United States, probably because until recently this area was heavily forested. The males establish their territories once they reach their breeding grounds in the Arctic tundra.

The nest site is carefully chosen to reduce the risk of the eggs becoming chilled. It may be partly buried, or sheltered by a rock, often apparently orientated to catch the warm rays of the sun. It is not uncommon for hens to reuse a nest built previously. The hen sits alone, and the eggs hatch after about 14 days. The chicks fledge after a similar period, and are reared on invertebrates.

Identification

Grayish upperparts, with an indistinct whitish stripe passing through each eye, becoming more brownish gray over the back. Wings blackish. Streaking on the reddish buff underparts, varying according to race. Rump brown, with the tail being black above. Has darker, more brownish upperparts outside the breeding period, and is more heavily streaked overall. Sexes are alike.

COMMON STARLING

European starling *Sturnus vulgaris*

Distribution Introduced and now present widely throughout North America except the far north, just ranging south into Mexico. Naturally occurs throughout Europe, extending into Asia, and North Africa.
Size 8½ in (22cm).
Habitat Near houses and buildings.
Nest Tree hole or birdhouse.
Eggs 2–9, white to pale blue or green.
Food Invertebrates, berries, and also bird-feeder fare.

The common European starling is a New World invader, introduced in 1890 when a small flock of 60 starlings brought from England was set free in New York's Central Park. A further 40 were released there the following year, making the millions of starlings now present in the whole of North America direct descendants of this initial group of 100 birds. This release came about as part of an unfulfilled plan to introduce all the birds described in the works of British playwright William Shakespeare to North America. Small groups of starlings are often to be seen feeding in backyards, although occasionally much larger groups comprised of hundreds of birds may visit an area. In flight, European starlings are adept at avoiding predators, such as hawks, by weaving back and forth in close formation, to confuse a would-be attacker. Their belligerent nature means that these starlings sometimes commandeer backyard bird tables and even nest holes from native species.

Identification

Glossy, with purplish black plumage on the head and a greenish hue on parts of the body overlaid with spots, particularly the neck and back. Dark brown wings and tail. Hens are similar, but spotting is larger and the base of the tail is pinkish instead of blue, as in breeding males. The young birds are duller, being brownish, and lack iridescence.

WARBLERS AND WOOD WARBLERS

Woodland areas are rich in invertebrate life, so it is not surprising that many warblers seek their food there. Some have a highly specialized style of feeding, while others are opportunistic, which has helped them spread widely. Northern populations head south in fall in order to maintain their supply of insects.

BLACK-AND-WHITE WARBLER

Mniotilta varia

With its bold patterning and a call likened to a noisy wheelbarrow, this warbler is relatively conspicuous. These birds arrive back in their breeding grounds during April, although they may head north before then, appearing in backyards and parks. These are also known as black-and-white creepers, due to their habit of foraging on tree trunks, probing for insects in the bark. They are agile, being able to move both up and down the trunk. In their breeding territories, they prefer deciduous woodland, where cover is available, because they breed on the ground. The pair construct a well-disguised nest, usually close to a tree. They start to head south again from July onward. Like other wood warblers, these birds often forage in mixed flocks, especially in winter.

Identification
Breeding males have black feathering on cheeks and throat, with lower throat becoming white in winter. White stripe above the eyes, black-and-white streaking on flanks. Lower underparts white. Hens have whitish cheeks, with buff suffusion on flanks, more apparent in young.

Distribution Range extends from Canada (southern Mackenzie through central Manitoba to Newfoundland) to much of southern USA east of the Rockies. Overwinters along the Gulf coast and down through Central America into northern South America.
Size 5in (13cm).
Habitat Woodland, backyards, parks.
Nest Cup shape.
Eggs 4–5, white with purple spots.
Food Invertebrates.

WORM-EATING WARBLER

Helmitheros vermivorus

These warblers may appear in backyards near dry woodlands, but are difficult to observe because they frequent dense undergrowth, with their small size and coloration helping them to blend into their environment. Although their distribution is centered on the eastern United States, they have also been recorded in more westerly areas, even in California. They seek their food close to the ground, often on their own, but can sometimes be found in company of other warblers. This species is so called not because they favor earthworms but because they seek out the larvae of various moths, which resemble worms. Pairs return to their breeding grounds during April, and the males sing as they establish their breeding territories, often perching on a high branch, although even here they can be hard to observe. The nest is built on the ground, and is comprised mainly of dry leaves, with moss and feathers used to create a softer lining.

Identification
In this species, a black stripe extends up the sides of the crown down over the neck, with another black stripe passing through the eyes. Rest of upperparts are buff-colored. Back and wings brownish olive. Narrow, light-colored bill with pink legs and feet. Sexes are alike.

Distribution Breeds in the eastern USA, from southeast Iowa to New York and eastern parts of North Carolina, down as far as the central Gulf coast. Overwinters from southeastern parts of Mexico down into South America.
Size 5½in (14cm).
Habitat Dry woodland.
Nest Cup shape.
Eggs 4–5, white with brown spots.
Food Invertebrates.

YELLOW WARBLER

Dendroica petechia

Yellow warblers are one of the most widespread warblers in the Americas. They regularly visit bird tables to take sunflower seeds, peanut hearts, suet, and raisins. They are popular with people seeking a natural form of pest control in their backyard, because they comb the ground for invertebrates. When breeding, their nests are sometimes parasitized by cowbirds. As winter approaches, these warblers head south to southern Mexico, Peru, and Brazil. The small resident population of yellow warblers *(D. p. gundlachi)* in Florida are of Caribbean origin, which helps to explain the green plumage on their crown. Farther south, the so-called mangrove warblers of Mexican coasts are a variety of yellow warbler. There is also wide diversity in the plumage of young birds, which can vary from pale yellow with greener upperparts to a browner shade, or gray with white underparts in the case of young Florida birds.

Identification

Coloration varies, especially in young birds. Yellowish, with red streaking on the underparts, and greener upperparts. Adults from northern areas are greener than those found farther south, while birds from Mexico often have chestnut brown on the head.

Distribution Range extends from northern Alaska east and south across much of northern North America. Ranges down into Central America and through the Caribbean, with a tiny localized population in Florida.
Size 5in (13cm).
Habitat Orchards, backyards, and open woodland.
Nest Cup of plant material in a tree fork.
Eggs 4–5, bluish white with darker speckling.
Food Mainly invertebrates.

AMERICAN REDSTART

Setophaga ruticilla

Distribution Southeastern Alaska to Newfoundland, south to California in the west and South Carolina in the east. Overwinters in the extreme south of the USA and via Mexico to northern South America.
Size 6in (15cm).
Habitat Deciduous woodland.
Nest Cup shape.
Eggs 3–5, white to bluish, with brownish spots.
Food Invertebrates and berries.

Belonging to the wood warbler rather than the thrush family, American redstarts are naturally very lively and active, almost constantly on the move seeking food, fanning open their tails and lowering their wings. Invertebrates may be hawked in flight or grabbed off bark. In parts of Latin America, where they overwinter, they are known locally as "candelita," because their jaunty nature and the coloration of cock birds combine to resemble the movements of a candle flame. One of the most widespread warblers in North America, they may be seen in backyards with wild areas or near second-growth woodlands. Male American redstarts will sing loudly even before they gain adult plumage, which is not attained until they are over a year old. The song is most evident in spring at the start of the breeding season. The nest is built at a variable height in a suitable bush or tree, up to 75 feet (23m) above the ground. The hen incubates alone, with the eggs hatching after approximately 12 days. The young birds are reared almost entirely on invertebrates, and fledge about three weeks later.

Identification

Cock birds are very colorful, with orange patches on the wings and tail contrasting with the white plumage on the underparts and black elsewhere. Hens are a dull shade of olive-brown, with yellow rather than orange markings. Young resemble hens, with yellow patches on wings and tail.

CARDINALS, TANAGERS, AND RELATIVES

Many of these colorful birds are a common sight within their range, thanks to their adaptable nature. Many undertake seasonal movements to warmer climates in search of more favorable feeding opportunities over the winter period. Their return is keenly anticipated as an indicator of the arrival of spring.

VIRGINIAN CARDINAL

Northern cardinal *Cardinalis cardinalis*

One of the most colorful backyard birds, the range of these cardinals continues to increase both in northern and western areas, especially since the first breeding record from Canada, dating to 1901. This expansion probably results from bird-table offerings. The stout, conical bill of these birds is adapted to crushing seeds, although Virginian cardinals will also hunt invertebrates, particularly when they have chicks in the nest.

Identification
Cock mainly red, with a pointed crest. Black mask surrounds the bill extending back to the eyes and onto throat. Wings, back, and tail a slightly duller shade. Hen mainly brown, with a reddish suffusion over the wings and tail. The bill of adults is bright red, whereas that of young birds is blackish, distinguishing them from adult hens.

Distribution Southern Ontario, Canada, south through the USA to the Gulf of Mexico, and southward to Belize.
Size 9in (23cm).
Habitat Edges of woodland, parks, and backyards.
Nest Cup shape, made of vegetation.
Eggs 3-4, whitish or grayish white, with darker spots and blotches.
Food Seeds and invertebrates.

SCARLET TANAGER

Piranga olivacea

These tanagers undertake long flights each year to and from their breeding grounds. Individuals sometimes venture farther afield, and are observed in more northerly and westerly areas than usual, even reaching Alaska on rare occasions. A pair of scarlet tanagers rears only one brood during the summer before returning south. These birds catch invertebrates in the undergrowth and also in flight. More unusually, scarlet tanagers rub live ants onto their plumage. This behavior, known as anting, results in formic acid being released by the ants among the feathers, which in turn drives out parasites, such as lice, from the plumage. The bright coloration of these birds is linked in part to their diet.

Identification
This species is mainly yellowish olive, with the underparts being more yellowish than the upperparts. The cock is distinguishable from the hen by having black instead of brownish wings and tail. In breeding plumage, the cock bird has characteristic vivid scarlet plumage. Young cock birds in their first year have more orange rather than scarlet plumage.

Distribution Migrates north to southeastern Canada and eastern USA, overwintering in Central and South America, east of the Andes to Peru and Bolivia.
Size 7in (17cm).
Habitat Light forest and woodland.
Nest Cup shape, made of stems and roots.
Eggs 2–5, whitish to greenish blue with dark markings.
Food Mainly invertebrates.

BLUE-GRAY TANAGER

Thraupis episcopus

Distribution From Central America, reaching northwest Peru and east of the Andes to northern parts of Bolivia.
Size 6in (16cm).
Habitat Forests, open countryside, parks, suburban areas.
Nest Made of plant matter.
Eggs 2–3, creamy to grayish green and spotted.
Food Fruit and invertebrates.

Blue-gray tanagers are a common sight in many parts of their Central and South American range. They have also been introduced in Miami, Florida. They are rarely observed on the ground, preferring instead to feed in the trees, sometimes even catching insects in flight. Bold by nature, they will become regular visitors to bird feeders in suburban areas if fruit or sunflower seeds are left out for them. Pairs of blue-gray tanagers build their well-disguised nest in a tree up to 30 feet (10m) off the ground. The hen sits alone, with the chicks hatching after a period of incubation lasting 14 days. Both members of the pair contribute food for the growing brood, with insects featuring prominently in their diet. The young leave the nest at just two weeks of age, and soon afterward the adult pair will begin nesting again, although the breeding season varies according to locality. These tanagers are most likely to be encountered at altitudes below 5,000 feet (1,500m), but they may sometimes range up to 6,500 feet (2,000m).

Identification

In cock birds, the head and body varies from pale blue through to bluish gray, and is lighter on the head and darker across the back. Wings and tail invariably a darker shade of blue. Shoulder area is white in individuals occurring east of the Andes, blue in those farther west. Hens may have slightly olive underparts. Young birds are generally duller.

PAINTED BUNTING

Passerina ciris

Distribution Widely distributed across the southern USA and Mexico, with populations moving south in the winter as far as Panama. This species is also present on Cuba.
Size 5½in (14cm).
Habitat Lightly wooded areas, brush, thickets, overgrown backyards.
Nest Woven nest.
Eggs 3–5, pale blue with darker spots.
Food Mainly seeds, some invertebrates.

The painted bunting is popularly regarded as the most colorful of all North America's songbirds. With its vivid plumage, this species was once prized as a cage bird. It is common in parts of the South, and will visit bird tables to take seeds and sunflower hearts. Despite the male's gaudy colors, however, these relatively shy birds are not easily seen, often remaining concealed in vegetation, where their presence is more likely to be revealed by the cock's song. They have a warbling call as well as a short, harsh, warning note that is uttered at any hint of danger. The nest, too, is well hidden, and is constructed from a variety of vegetation. The hen builds the nest on her own and collects a variety of plant matter for this purpose, ranging from strips of bark and dead leaves to grass stems and rootlets. She chooses a well-concealed nest site, often in the fork of a tree. A pair of painted buntings may rear two or even three broods in succession, with insects forming much of the diet at this time.

Identification

Males are very colorful and unmistakable, with bluish violet plumage on the head and a rose red throat and underparts. The wings and back are green, with darker tail and flight feathers. Hens are drab in comparison, with green upperparts, becoming more yellowish on the underside of the body, and no bars on the wings, unlike many other finches.

VISITORS FROM OPEN COUNTRY

Areas of open country have increased in the recent past, with vast amounts of land being cleared for agriculture. Natural habitats have also made way for towns, while highways have cut across country. However, many birds have adapted well to these changes, and thrive in this altered environment.

DICKCISSEL

Spiza americana

These finches take their unusual name from the sound of their song, which at times is repeated almost continuously from a suitable perch. Dickcissels are frequently seen in agricultural areas, often in hay fields where they can forage easily on the seeds that form the basis of their diet. When breeding, they choose a nest site close to the ground, and at ground level may hide the nest among clover or alfalfa. These finches undertake seasonal movements. On migration, they sometimes form huge flocks consisting of thousands of individuals, with the birds flying in tight formation. Many spend the winter in the Venezuelan llanos, although they may also congregate in agricultural areas at this time, mostly in rice fields. While on migration, they may appear at bird tables to take seeds of various kinds.

Identification

This species has a gray head with a yellow stripe above each eye leading back from the short, conical bill. Whitish area on the throat, with black beneath. Chest is yellowish, with white lower underparts. Back and wings are brownish with darker striations. Hens are duller, having gray underparts and lacking the prominent black area under the throat.

Distribution Eastern North America, breeding from the vicinity of the Great Lakes and Montana down to Texas and the Gulf coast. Overwinters in parts of Central and northern South America.
Size 7in (18cm).
Habitat Treeless areas, farmland.
Nest Cup shape.
Eggs 4–5, pale blue.
Food Mainly seeds.

LE CONTE'S THRASHER

Toxostoma lecontei

Thrashers are members of the mockingbird family, and as such are talented songsters, even capable of mimicking the songs of other birds. The powerful, melodious song of these particular thrashers is most likely to be heard either at dusk or dawn, when the birds are most active. At this time of day, it is easier for them to catch the invertebrates that form their diet. This species' coloration provides effective camouflage in the dry, sandy terrain of its habitat, and its habits also make it inconspicuous. If disturbed, these mockingbirds slip away undetected through the scrub, running with their long tail held upright. During the hottest time of day, they hide away in the shade. Their bulky nests consist mainly of twigs and are sited near the ground, hidden in a cactus or shrub. This thrasher is not common in any part of its range, but occasionally appears at bird tables in settlements in arid country.

Identification

Distinguished from other related species by its very pale coloration, having a grayish brown body and darker tail, with tawny undertail coverts. Dark, strongly down-curved bill, with slight streaking on the throat. Sexes are alike.

Distribution Southwestern USA (in California, Arizona, Nevada, and Utah) and adjacent parts of Mexico, as well as Baja California and Sonora.
Size 11in (28cm).
Habitat Arid, open country.
Nest Made of twigs.
Eggs 2–4, light bluish green with brown speckling.
Food Invertebrates.

BOBOLINK

Dolichonyx oryzivorus

The bobolink's unusual name originates from the sound of the male's song, which is audible through the breeding period. Like many birds found in open country, these icterids often sing in flight. They gather in hay fields and sometimes appear at bird tables on farms. In South America, they are known as ricebirds, due to the way they have adapted to feeding on this crop. Though found in open country in North America, bobolinks are more likely to be observed in reedy areas of marshland during their winter migration. Remarkably, despite flying such long distances, these birds travel back to the same familiar breeding grounds every spring, with the mature males arriving first. Studies of their unique song patterns have revealed not only local dialects but also that the males use different call notes to communicate with each other and to attract females. Although the majority pair individually with a female, some males have more than one partner.

Identification

Cock in breeding condition is primarily black, with pale buff on the hind neck. Prominent white wing bar, with the lower back and rump also white. Hens have a dark crown with a streak down the center, and a dark streak behind each eye. Their underparts are yellowish, with streaking on the flanks. Young birds have spotting on the throat and upper breast, with no streaking on their underparts.

Distribution Breeds from British Columbia to Newfoundland south to northern California, Colorado, and Pennsylvania. Winters in southern South America, reaching Argentina and southern Brazil. Precise range unclear.
Size 7in (18cm).
Habitat Prairies and open areas, marshes during migration.
Nest Cup shape.
Eggs 4–7, gray with reddish brown spotting.
Food Seeds and invertebrates.

WESTERN MEADOWLARK

Sturnella neglecta

Male western meadowlarks are very vocal, especially at the start of the nesting season when they are laying claim to their territories. They will choose a conspicuous site, such as a fence post on farmland, and produce a series of flutelike notes to attract females and warn away rival males. They look very similar to eastern meadowlarks but can be distinguished by their songs. In areas where their distribution overlaps with eastern meadowlarks, the eastern males are perceived as a threat and chased off, because hybridization between these two forms is not unknown. Meadowlarks are polygamous in their breeding habits, with a single male mating with several females. Each female constructs a fairly elaborate, dome-shape nest, which takes about a week, before starting to lay. The male plays no part in nest building, but will help to provide food for the young. Western meadowlarks become more social in winter, when they may be observed in small flocks.

Identification

Brown crown extends back over the top of the head, with a brown stripe running behind the eyes. Pale brown cheeks; back and wings are brown with darker barring. A black band runs across the chest, with the lores, throat, and central underparts yellow. Flanks are whitish with darker spotting. Sexes are alike. Young birds are paler with barring instead of a band across the chest.

Distribution This species breeds from British Columbia and Manitoba southward via Ohio and Missouri to parts of Texas and into northern Mexico. Northern populations move slightly southward in winter.
Size 10in (25cm).
Habitat Grassy meadows, plains, and prairies.
Nest Domed cup.
Eggs 3–7, white with darker markings.
Food Invertebrates.

TOWHEES AND MIGRATING SPARROWS

Brown predominates in the coloration of these adaptable birds, but there can actually be a huge variety of appearance through what is often a wide range. Despite their fairly small size, a number of towhees and sparrows undertake extensive migrations to and from their breeding grounds in spring and fall.

CALIFORNIA TOWHEE

Pipilo crissalis

The taxonomy of the towhees can be confusing. In the past, the Californian towhee and the closely related canyon towhee, which occurs farther west, were grouped together under the name brown towhee, although it is now clear that they are, in fact, distinct species. Even so, eight distinctive races of California towhee are recognized through its relatively small range. Pairs, which bond for life in many cases, are most likely to be observed in backyards during the breeding season, because this is when the cock bird sings loudly from a prominent perch. Even after egg laying, he continues this behavior, laying claim to their territory; any intruders will be driven away aggressively. Their nest, made of various plant materials, is hidden low in vegetation and the hen incubates alone. Once the chicks have hatched, these towhees become largely insectivorous, frequently foraging on the ground, using their feet to scratch around in the hope of discovering invertebrates hiding under leaves or other vegetation.

Identification
This towhee is predominantly brown, with the crown being a warmer shade than the brown of the body. The throat is buff, marked with dark spots that are largest across the upper chest. Undertail coverts are cinnamon brown. Sexes are alike. Young birds are duller with more extensive speckling on their underparts.

Distribution Range extends along coastal western North America, from Oregon down to Baja California, and eastward as far as the Cascades and Sierra Nevada Mountains.
Size 9in (23cm).
Habitat Chaparral, parks, and backyards.
Nest Cup shape.
Eggs 3–4, bluish green with dark markings.
Food Seeds and invertebrates.

CHIPPING SPARROW

Spizella passerina

These sparrows are not easy to observe in backyards, partly because their coloration provides camouflage, but also because they hide among vegetation. Even when singing, the cock chooses a fairly secluded location. The sound is a distinctive, monotonous "chip"-like call, which explains the species' common name. These sparrows forage mainly on the ground, although they may visit bird feeders to take seeds, especially during winter when snow blankets the ground. Each fall, chipping sparrows desert most of their North American range, migrating to southern states and farther south in late September. They return to their breeding grounds in the far north the following May. The well-hidden nest is constructed from vegetation, with incubation and fledging each lasting about 12 days. This rapid breeding cycle means that in favorable conditions, they may rear two broods.

Identification
Breeding adults have a chestnut crown with white stripes beneath, and a black stripe running through the eyes. Grayish neck and underparts, with whitish throat. Wings are black and brown with whitish markings. Dark notched tail. Head coloration is brownish with darker speckling outside the nesting season.

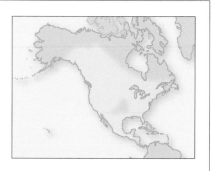

Distribution Most of North America south of Hudson Bay, except for central-southern USA. Winters along the southern Mexican border and through Central America as far south as northern Nicaragua.
Size 5½in (14cm).
Habitat Parks and wooded backyards.
Nest Cup shape.
Eggs 3–5, light blue with darker markings.
Food Seeds and invertebrates.

LARK SPARROW

Chondestes grammacus

Distribution Range extends across the far south of Canada, and western and central parts of the USA. Winters farther south along the Mexican border and the Gulf coast to Florida.
Size 6½ in (17cm).
Habitat Roadsides, farms, grasslands, open country.
Nest Cup shape.
Eggs 3–5, white with dark spots.
Food Seeds and invertebrates, especially grasshoppers.

Lark sparrows have a very musical song, incorporating trills and buzzes. In common with larks, they are terrestrial birds, foraging on the ground not just for seeds but also insects, especially grasshoppers, during summer, which are used to rear their chicks. They breed on the ground or in a low bush, frequently in scrubland, where the nest can be hidden from predators, and sometimes in loose colonies. Northern populations fly south during late July and August, returning again the following spring. During the winter period, they can often be seen in flocks, including in fields and by roadsides. They sometimes visit rural bird feeders in search of seeds. The range of the lark sparrow has declined over recent years. This may be due to changes in habitat. Their distribution formerly extended up the East Coast to Maryland and New York, while today they are relatively scarce east of the Mississippi.

Identification
This sparrow has a black stripe extending up from the bill, with a central white area dividing the chestnut coloration on the head. White bordered with black encircles the chestnut cheek patches. Underparts are whitish with a very distinctive dark central breast spot. Upperparts are grayish brown with black markings. The wings and tail are dark brown, with white edging evident. The sexes are alike.

SAVANNAH SPARROW

Passerculus sandwichensis

These widely distributed birds are as adept at running as they are flying. It is not unusual for them to escape danger by dropping down into vegetation and scurrying away. Savannah sparrows can be found in a wide range of habitats, from the tundra of the far north to the grassy sand dunes of Mexico. They breed on the ground, with spiders usually featuring in the diet of the young. In fall, large numbers migrate southward, appearing in parks and backyards in both cities and rural areas. Various distinctive races of these sparrows are recognized; some have very limited distributions. The so-called Ipswich sparrow *(P. s. princeps),* breeds on tiny Sable Island, Nova Scotia. It winters more widely along the East Coast, including around Ipswich, Massachusetts. Another localized and distinctive form, *P. s. rostratus* from the western side of the United States, has a much broader bill and a different song pattern from other savannah sparrows.

Identification
Varies through its range, with birds from the West Coast darker than those found farther east or in Alaska. Streaked appearance, with dark markings running over the head and flanks. Brownish gray to blackish upperparts. Underparts grayish white. Often a yellow or whitish streak above or through the eyes, with a paler stripe on center of crown. Sexes alike.

Distribution Breeds from Alaska east across Canada, extending south across much of the USA (except for part of the southwest) and into northern Mexico. This species has a remarkable migration, flying thousands of miles north to breed and then south again for the winter.
Size 5½ in (14cm).
Habitat Fields and open terrain.
Nest Cup shape.
Eggs 4–6, blue-green with dark speckling.
Food Seeds and invertebrates.

SPARROWS AND GRACKLES

Some sparrows are widespread, being prolific breeders. The house sparrow has spread to many parts of the Americas since being introduced from Europe in 1850. The colors of sparrows and grackles are subdued, but grackles can display a striking iridescent sheen when sunlight catches their plumage.

HOUSE SPARROW

Passer domesticus

A common visitor to bird feeders and city parks, house sparrows have adapted to living close to people. They were originally brought to New York from Europe in 1850, and by 1910 had spread west to California. There are now noticeable differences within the North American population: northern individuals are larger, while those from southwestern arid areas are paler. House sparrows form loose flocks, with larger numbers gathering where food is plentiful. They spend much time on the ground, hopping along while watching for predators, such as cats. It is not uncommon for them to build nests during winter to serve as communal roosts. The bills of the cock birds turn black at the start of the nesting season in spring. Several males often court a single female in what is known as a "sparrows' wedding."

Identification

Rufous brown at the back of the head, with gray above. A black stripe runs across the eyes and a broad black bib extends down over the chest. Ear coverts and underparts are grayish, with a whiter area under the tail. Hens are browner overall with a pale stripe prominent behind each eye.

Distribution Southern Canada, southward across the USA, and into Central and much of South America.
Size 6in (15cm).
Habitat Urban and more rural areas.
Nest Under roofs and in tree hollows.
Eggs 3–6, whitish with darker markings.
Food Seeds and invertebrates.

DARK-EYED JUNCO

Junco hyemalis

These sparrows display variable coloration through their wide range, but the fact that they breed together freely and produce fertile offspring means that they rank as one species, not four. Rather tame, they are widely seen in woodlands, and also backyards, particularly in winter when they take seeds, millet, and peanuts from feeders. Dark-eyed juncos are mainly terrestrial in their habits, living in loose flocks that may forage widely. They are prolific when nesting, with incubation lasting just 12 days and the young fledging after a similar period. The nest is well-disguised and sited close to the ground, so that if the young are disturbed they can escape a predator by running away on their surprisingly large feet. Hens produce up to three rounds of chicks over the summer. The young feed largely on invertebrates.

Distribution Breeds from Alaska to Newfoundland, extending south to Mexico and Georgia in the east. Winters along the Gulf coast and into Mexico.
Size 6¼in (16cm).
Habitat Woodland, backyards.
Nest Cup of vegetation.
Eggs 3–6, pale green to blue, with brown spots.
Food Seeds, berries, invertebrates.

Identification

Variable appearance. Eastern North American birds mainly slaty gray, with brownish gray hens. In the west, the Oregon junco (J. h. thurberi) has a black head and orange-red flanks and back, with paler brown hens. Other variants include the pink-sided J. h. mearnsi of the central Rockies, and the white-winged J. h. aikeni, gray with white wing bars and white underparts. All have dark eyes. Sexes are alike. Young birds have streaked patterning.

COMMON GRACKLE

Quiscalus quiscula

Distribution Central and eastern North America, from British Colombia to southeastern USA. Occasionally sighted in Pacific states and Alaska during spring.
Size 12½ in (32cm).
Habitat Open country, from marshland to suburban areas and parks.
Nest Large cup-shape structure.
Eggs 3–7, pale green to pale rust.
Food Very varied, including seeds, invertebrates, fish, and small birds.

These familar birds thrive alongside humans, and particularly relish cracked corn on bird tables. Opportunistic feeders, they will raid trash cans for scraps. The song of the common grackle is highly distinctive, making it easy to recognize individual birds. While singing, they perform a so-called "rough out" display, in which they fluff up their plumage. This may be accompanied by dancing on the perch and flashing their yellow eyes. Males sometimes react more to other males than females. In flight, the tail feathers are splayed to create a wedge shape. As fall approaches the grackles leave northern and western haunts; they only reside all year in southern areas. These can be long-lived birds, surviving to 22 years.

Identification
Variable in color, with a powerful pointed bill and long tail. The bronze form of northern and western areas has bronze feathering with a blue head, in contrast to the more purplish suffusion that characterizes the purple grackle from the Appalachian region. The southerly Florida race has a more olive green body with a purplish head. Hens are smaller than the males and display less iridescence, especially on their underparts.

GREAT-TAILED GRACKLE

Quiscalus mexicanus

Distribution From Oregon south and east through Mexico (except Baja California) and into South America, eastward to Venezuela and as far south as northern Peru.
Size 15–18in (38–46cm).
Habitat Open areas, including farmland and suburbs.
Nest Cup shape, made of twigs lined with grass.
Eggs 3–4, blue with brownish black markings.
Food Varied, including seeds, invertebrates, small vertebrates.

The great-tailed grackle is rapidly extending its North American range in a northwesterly direction, nesting for example in Montana for the first time in 1996. This trend is probably due to these birds' bold, adaptable nature, especially since they thrive in areas where relatively few trees remain. They are common in backyards in the southwest, and will take many different foods including seeds, sunflowers, suet, and wheat from bird tables. Great-tailed grackles forage on the ground and will feed in large groups, particularly after nesting when pairs split up to form single-sex flocks. At the start of the breeding season, males set up a territory in which several hens nest and lay, although under this system the cock does not help to incubate or rear the chicks. Perhaps not surprisingly, populations tend to have a high proportion of females, which mirrors the breeding pattern.

Identification
In this species, the cock birds are glossy black, with a purplish suffusion on the head, back, and underparts. They have keel-shape tail feathers and yellow eyes. Hens are smaller and mainly brown. The young birds resemble the hens, but with striped underparts.

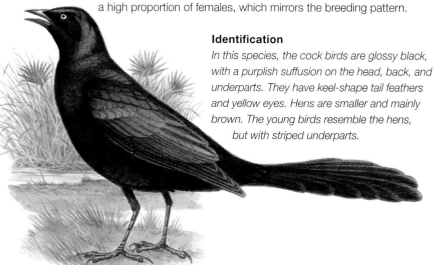

COWBIRDS AND ORIOLES

Like European cuckoos, cowbirds are mainly noted for their unusual breeding habits, relying on other birds to raise their young. Orioles are small, colorful birds, often graced with an attractive song. A glimpse of yellowish orange and black plumage and a pointed bill is indicative of an oriole sighting.

BROWN-HEADED COWBIRD

Molothrus ater

Cowbirds are so called because they traditionally followed herds of bison across the plains, hunting insects attracted to the animals. Bison no longer roam the prairies, but brown-headed cowbirds have expanded their range. This is partly due to the abundance of small birds that will rear the cowbirds' chicks. At nesting time, female cowbirds seek out the nests of species such as vireos. They watch until the nest is complete, then deposit their own eggs before the host has laid. The young cowbirds hatch before their unlucky nestmates, and monopolize the food supply.

Identification
Cock has brown head and metallic, green-black body. Hen has gray-brown upperparts, with paler areas around eyes and throat. Underparts have dark streaks. Young resemble hens but with whitish scalloping on upperparts and more streaking below.

Left: *A young cowbird is fed by its foster parent. It grows so fast it may fledge at just nine days old.*

Distribution Occurs across much of North America, except the far north, and south as far as Mexico.
Size $7\frac{1}{2}$ in (19cm).
Habitat Woodland, open farmland, and suburban backyards.
Nest Parasitizes those of other birds.
Eggs 10–12, white with dark speckling.
Food Feeds on invertebrates, seeds, and berries.

NORTHERN ORIOLE

Icterus galbula

These orioles and particularly their young vary in appearance, which makes them hard to identify. To add to the confusion, this species used to be called the Baltimore oriole, and was considered distinct from the Bullock's oriole found in the west. New studies suggest they are the same species, now known as the northern oriole. The orange eyebrows and cheeks of the cock distinguish the western form from the eastern. The forestation of the Great Plains enabled these birds to meet and hybridize, to create what is in some respects a new species. These orioles may be seen in backyards with mature trees. Large flocks migrate south in September, and return again in April.

Identification
Breeding adult male has a black head, with black extending over the back and wings. Narrow white bar above the flight feathers, which are edged with white. Rest of the body orange, vivid on the chest but paler on underparts. Rump orange, with black upper tail feathers, orange below. Narrow, pointed grayish bill, blacker on upper surface. Hens have brown instead of black on head and upperparts. Young have olive-brown upperparts, and dull underparts with variable orange coloring.

Distribution British Columbia in Canada eastward to Nova Scotia and across virtually all of the USA, except Florida and parts of the Gulf coast. Overwinters in Central America down to northern South America.
Size $8\frac{1}{4}$ in (22cm).
Habitat Deciduous woodland.
Nest Pendulous woven structure.
Eggs 4–6, grayish with darker markings.
Food Invertebrates and fruit.

Distribution South-central Canada, down across central and eastern USA to Florida and Mexico. Occasionally seen in westerly US states. May overwinter in South America.
Size 7in (18cm).
Habitat Open woodland close to water, moving into grassland and marshes, also backyards with mature trees.
Nest Hanging cup of grass.
Eggs 3–7, bluish white with darker blotches.
Food Fruit, insects, nectar.

ORCHARD ORIOLE

Icterus spurius

Each year these small orioles fly long distances to and from their northern breeding grounds, often not being sighted in the far north of their range until the end of May. Some head north through Florida, while the majority fly directly across the Gulf of Mexico. Having reached their breeding grounds they will nest in backyards with large trees, especially oaks. Oriole pairs tend to be solitary, although they may sometimes associate with eastern kingbirds *(Tyrannus tyrannus),* which defend their nest sites vigorously. Even so, the number of orchard orioles is declining, partly, it is feared, because of nest parasitism by bronzed and brown-headed cowbirds *(Molothrus),* where the young cowbirds hatch first from eggs laid in the host nest and then eject the oriole eggs or chicks. In some areas, over one-quarter of orchard oriole nests host the young of these species, which greatly reduces the rate of survival of their natural offspring. In their wintering quarters, hundreds of orchard orioles may congregate together, feeding on the nectar of flowering trees and shrubs.

Identification

Mature male has a black head, back, and chest, with the remainder of the body being a distinctive shade of chestnut. Hens in contrast have olive upperparts and are yellowish beneath. Young males are similar to females but with a black bib.

SPOT-BREASTED ORIOLE

Icterus pectoralis

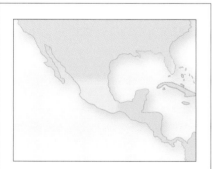

Distribution Native to central Mexico. Separate introduced population in Florida, ranging from Brevard County southward to Dade County.
Size 9½in (24cm).
Habitat Open woodland, also orchards, parks. Favors suburban backyards in Florida.
Nest Hanging basket of grass and other vegetation, measuring up to 20in (50cm) long.
Eggs 3, bluish white with dark markings.
Food Fruits, invertebrates, and nectar.

The melodic, whistling song of these orioles is heard repeatedly, and though both sexes sing, the call notes of cock birds are more complex. Spot-breasted orioles may be seen in the company of other oriole species, seeking food both on the ground and from flowers. The hanging nest of tightly woven grass is secured at the tip of a branch, usually anchored around a convenient fork, making it difficult for potential predators to reach. Mimosa trees are especially favored because their spiky thorns offer added protection, although the nests may still be parasitized by cowbirds. This beautiful bird is native to Central America but has also been introduced to Florida, probably following the escape of cage birds. The population in Florida, which was first recorded breeding in 1949 in the vicinity of Miami, has not spread very far in the intervening decades, occurring today in a radius of some 40 miles (64km) around the city, where these birds frequent suburban backyards. There are even suggestions that they have recently declined here. Spot-breasted orioles have also been introduced to Cocos Island, Costa Rica.

Identification

Mainly orangish yellow, often most fiery on the head, offset against black lores and throat. Wings black with white barring. Tail also black. Distinctive black spotted pattern on the sides of the breast. Sexes alike. Young birds are olive green over the back and lack spotted markings.

FINCHES

Members of this group have benefited from changes to the environment. Along with a greater availability of food, urban areas provide a multitude of nesting sites as people seek to attract these birds into their backyards. Pairs may establish breeding territories, but these birds form flocks for much of the year.

HOUSE FINCH

Carpodacus mexicanus

Two separate populations of these finches occur in North America: one native to the west and the other in the east. The eastern population is descended from birds released on Long Island, near New York City, during the 1940s. There they bred successfully, but it was not until the 1960s that they began to spread more widely and become established. They appear to have benefited significantly from bird feeders, although they also forage for berries and other items in backyards. Males have an attractive song, not unlike that of a canary. Nesting pairs are very adaptable and often breed in loose colonies, utilizing nesting baskets secured under the eaves of houses. They frequently raise two or more broods of chicks in rapid succession. During fall, house finches often associate together in large flocks, and in more rural areas may be seen feeding in the fields. In spring, flocks can cause damage in orchards by pecking the buds and flowers.

Identification
Cock has a brown cap on the head and brown ear coverts. Remainder of the head and breast are red, sometimes more orange, depending on race. Streaked white underparts, browner on the flanks. Back is streaked, with dark wing feathers typically edged with white. Hens are much duller, being streaked over their entire head and underparts.

Distribution Range extends from southwestern Canada through western parts of the USA to Texas and into Mexico. Separate population occurs in eastern USA south of the Great Lakes. Also found on Hawaii.
Size 6in (15cm).
Habitat Open areas including cities, suburban backyards.
Nest Cup shape.
Eggs 4–5, pale blue with black spots.
Food Seeds and invertebrates.

PURPLE FINCH

Carpodacus purpureus

Purple finches are bold and conspicuous in backyard settings, often visiting feeders, with oil-rich seeds, such as sunflower, being favored foods. These birds are territorial by nature, especially during the breeding season. Males sing loudly from branches and also undertake display flights to attract a partner. The nest is built on the branch of a conifer, often at a considerable height from the ground. Although some individuals remain on their breeding grounds throughout the year, others move south, where they may be sighted in small flocks. The availability of pine seeds influences their distribution during winter in particular, since in years when the crop fails these finches move to new areas in search of other food. Although their breeding range is continuous, the population splits into distinct western and eastern groups for the duration of the winter.

Identification
Cocks are rose red over much of their body, with color especially pronounced on the head and rump. The back is red with brown streaking, while lower underparts are whitish in the center. Hens are brownish, with light stripes encircling the eyes and a white area under the throat. Pale underparts are heavily streaked with brown.

Distribution Canada south of Hudson Bay, most common in the east. Extends to southern California. Winters in the west and through much of eastern USA down along the Gulf coast, and occasionally into northern Mexico.
Size 6in (15cm).
Habitat Suburban backyards, parks, and woodland.
Nest Cup shape.
Eggs 5–6, pale bluish with dark markings.
Food Seeds and invertebrates.

AMERICAN GOLDFINCH

Carduelis tristis

Distribution Range extends from Canada southward through much of USA to northern Mexico.
Size 5½ in (14cm).
Habitat Wooded or lightly wooded areas, backyards with mature trees.
Nest Cup shape.
Eggs 2–7, pale blue.
Food Seeds, other plant matter, and invertebrates.

These attractive songbirds are common throughout their range. Familiar backyard visitors, they take sunflower hearts, peanut hearts, and thistle supplied on bird tables. Goldfinches in northern areas move south to warmer areas for the winter. They are often seen in larger flocks at this time, frequently in the company of related birds, such as redpolls (*Acanthis* species) and pine siskins. Their diet varies through the year, being influenced by the availability of food. Shoots and buds of trees, such as spruce and willow, are eaten when other foods are in short supply. Seeds are a principal food, consumed through much of the year, and goldfinches delay their breeding until midsummer when weed seeds are available. Invertebrates also provide protein for rearing chicks in the nest.

Identification
Cock has bright yellow plumage, with a black forehead and black wings and tail, and white bars on the wings. Duller in winter plumage, being a more olive shade with a less distinct black cap. Hens can be identified by their olive-yellow upperparts and more yellowish underparts, becoming brownish during winter, especially on the upperparts. The white wing barring is still apparent, enabling hens to be distinguished easily from juvenile birds.

PINE SISKIN

Carduelis pinus

Distribution Breeds from southern Alaska across Canada south of Hudson Bay to Newfoundland, and in the USA south to California and around the Great Lakes. Occurs widely through the USA during winter, extending south to parts of Florida, Texas, and New Mexico.
Size 5in (13cm).
Habitat Coniferous and mixed woodland, pastures.
Nest Shallow cup shape of twigs, bark, and moss.
Eggs 3–4, pale green with dark speckles.
Food Seeds of hemlock, alder, birch, and cedar, also some insects.

This small, streaked finch is a bird of northern woodlands. A sociable species, it is often seen in flocks, including mixed flocks with American goldfinches, which it somewhat resembles in form and movement. However, this siskin is less brightly colored and darker than its relative, with yellow only on the wings and base of the tail, and a longer bill. Pine siskins feed mainly on the seeds of hemlocks, alders, birches, and cedars in northern forests. In years when seed supplies fail in these forests, flocks of these small birds are seen wandering as far south as Florida, in areas where they are absent in other years. Relatively tame by nature, they may visit backyards at this time to peck at seeds and thistle on bird tables. Their liking for salt can also cause them to alight by the sides of highways, where they harvest salt deposited to melt snow. In summer, they also eat insects, particularly aphids. The flight pattern is undulating, with the flock alternately bunching and spreading. Calls include a rising buzzing sound and a song similar to that of the goldfinch, but hoarser. Pine siskins nest colonially, constructing shallow cups of twigs, bark, and moss lined with feathers in conifer trees. In backyards, they may be encouraged to nest in standard enclosed nest boxes with a small, circular entrance hole.

Identification
This species of finch has dark, streaky patterning over the entire body, with solid black areas and variable patches of yellow on the wings and at the base of the tail. The narrow, pointed bill is darker above. The tail is deeply notched. The sexes are alike.

GROSBEAKS AND REDPOLLS

Predominantly woodland birds, some grosbeaks are associated with conifer forests, and others with deciduous woodlands, while the blue grosbeak has adapted to more open habitats. The hoary redpoll is another bird of open country. These small birds feed on various foods, including seeds and invertebrates.

EVENING GROSBEAK

Coccothraustes vespertinus

These large, thick-set finches have a powerful bill. When first described in the 1820s, it was believed that they emerged from cover only at dusk. This is incorrect, but they became known as evening grosbeaks. Their range has expanded since then. Up until the 19th century, these finches were restricted to northern Canada, but suddenly, perhaps because of persistent food shortages, evening grosbeaks started traveling and ultimately breeding in northeastern parts of the United States. They continued to spread, partly thanks to bird-table offerings, reaching Maryland by the 1960s, and Florida and the Gulf coast a decade later.

Pairs build their nest at the end of a branch, up to 70 feet (21m) off the ground, choosing a site where it will be hidden. The hen sits alone, with the chicks hatching after about two weeks. They fledge after a similar interval.

Distribution Southern Canada through western parts of the USA to northern Mexico. Extends eastward to Newfoundland and south to southeastern parts of the USA.
Size 8in (20cm).
Habitat Coniferous woodlands, also parks and backyards.
Nest Cup shape.
Eggs 2–5, bluish green.
Food Seeds, berries, and invertebrates. Favor sunflower seeds on bird tables.

Identification

Cocks have a yellow forehead and eyebrows. The rest of the head and upper chest are greenish, with yellow underparts. There is a white area on the wings, with black flight feathers and tail. Hens and young are mainly gray, with a pale throat and underparts.

PINE GROSBEAK

Pinicola enucleator

Identification

Cock is mainly reddish, with gray on the sides of the body and along the wings. Wings darker, with variable white edging and gray wing bars. Black forked tail. Hens are gray overall, with a yellowish head, rump, and flanks, and a grayish area under the throat. Yellow color can be more russet in some cases.

As their name suggests, pine grosbeaks are closely linked with coniferous forests, although they move into deciduous woodlands and also backyards in fall. Living in flocks, these finches prefer to feed off the ground, resorting to nibbling buds when seeds and fruit are scarce and snow covers the ground. In some areas, such as the western United States, they are regular bird-feeder visitors. Their winter range is influenced by availability of food, with flocks sometimes moving south of their normal range when berries, such as mountain ash, fail. Pine grosbeaks are not active by nature. They are also tame, so are fairly easy to observe. The nest is built in a tree, often close to the ground, with the young fledging after three weeks.

Distribution Circumpolar, being present right across northern parts of North America, and in western USA. Overwinters in central parts.
Size 9in (23cm).
Habitat Woodland, orchards, and backyards.
Nest Bulky, cup shape.
Eggs 2–5, pale bluish green with dark blotches.
Food Seeds, berries, invertebrates; sunflower seeds and fruit on bird tables.

BLUE GROSBEAK

Guiraca caerulea

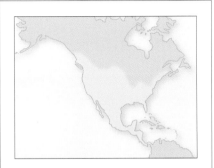

Distribution Occurs widely across the USA, from California in the west through to New Jersey on the east coast, and south to Costa Rica. Northern populations overwinter in Central America, ranging from Mexico south as far as Panama.
Size 7½ in (19cm).
Habitat Brush, often near water.
Nest Cup shape.
Eggs 3–4, pale blue.
Food Seeds and invertebrates.

Despite the cock bird's distinctive plumage, the blue grosbeak is not as conspicuous as its coloration would suggest. Indeed, in poor light its feathering can appear so dark that, at a distance, it is sometimes confused with the male brown-headed cowbird *(Molothrus ater)*. It is also easily confused with the male indigo bunting *(Passerina cyanea),* which also has blue plumage and a stout, conical beak. The grosbeak's melodious song is most commonly heard early in the day, although the birds may start singing again at dusk. The song consists largely of short notes interspersed with longer trills. Cock birds usually return from their winter haunts a few days ahead of hens, frequently spending this time searching for food in groups on the ground before splitting up to nest. Pairs are likely to rear two broods of chicks over summer before migrating south again. In fall, these birds gather in flocks to comb fields for seeds and insects, and they may also appear at bird tables at this time.

Identification

Adult male is a dull shade of blue, with a large, grayish bill. The wings are darker, with two distinctive wing bars close to the shoulder. Hens are predominantly brownish, lighter on the underparts, and also display two buff-colored wing bars. They have some bluish feathering on the rump. Young cock birds display more widespread blue feathering among their plumage.

HOARY REDPOLL

Arctic redpoll *Carduelis hornemanni*

Distribution Breeds along the Arctic coast of North America. In winter, found over much of Canada and northern parts of the USA.
Size 5½ in (14cm).
Habitat Tundra in summer, open country and by roads in winter.
Nest Cup of vegetation.
Eggs 5–6, pale blue with light brown spots.
Food Seeds and invertebrates. Will also take fruit from bird tables.

Similar in appearance to the common redpoll *(C. flammea),* this species can be identified by its slightly paler coloring, plain rump, and undertail coverts. Although both redpolls occur together in some parts of their range, they do not interbreed. The distribution of the hoary redpoll extends farther north, with these birds flying as far as the treeless tundra to breed. Here, they are forced to nest on the ground, creating a warm, cup shape of plant matter lined with feathers, often concealed among rocks or under a shrub. Occurring so far north, it is perhaps not surprising that this redpoll has a circumpolar distribution, being also found in the far north of Europe and Asia. The chicks are reared largely on a diet of insects, which are readily available in the Arctic through the summer months, while for the remainder of the year these finches subsist primarily on seeds. In fall, they fly south to wander much of Canada and the United States. Here, they are often observed in pairs or family groups, although occasionally they are spotted in larger flocks of up to 100 individuals, which may also contain common redpolls. They may be seen foraging for weed seeds by roads in winter and may take seeds and fruit from bird tables.

Identification

This small finch has a red patch on the crown. Pale, frosty gray-streaked upperparts and a prominent white wing bar, with wings otherwise appearing black. A black area surrounds the base of the stocky bill. Breeding males have pinkish chests. Hens similar but with some streaking present on the flanks.

TEMPLATES

The templates provided here will enable you to complete some of the more complex projects illustrated in this book. They should be used in conjunction with the instructions and cutting lists for lumber given earlier. Each template provides specific dimensions for the project. All the dimensions are listed in both standard and metric measurements. You should decide which system you are going to use and then follow it, not mixing the two. You might like to make paper templates from these plans and arrange them on your lumber before cutting. It's always a good idea to double-check your measurements before cutting.

Left: *This hanging nest box with a small, round entrance hole will suit acrobatic wrens, chickadees, and titmice. It is best hung from a branch.*

Above: *A nest box with a small entrance hole will suit bluebirds, wrens, and titmice. A taller box would suit woodpeckers.*

Above: *Open-front boxes will attract nesting wrens. Species such as robins and bluebirds may use the box as a roost.*

Above: *Birdhouses, such as this one, can look highly ornamental in the backyard and be finished according to personal taste.*

PALLADIAN BIRD TABLE, page 118

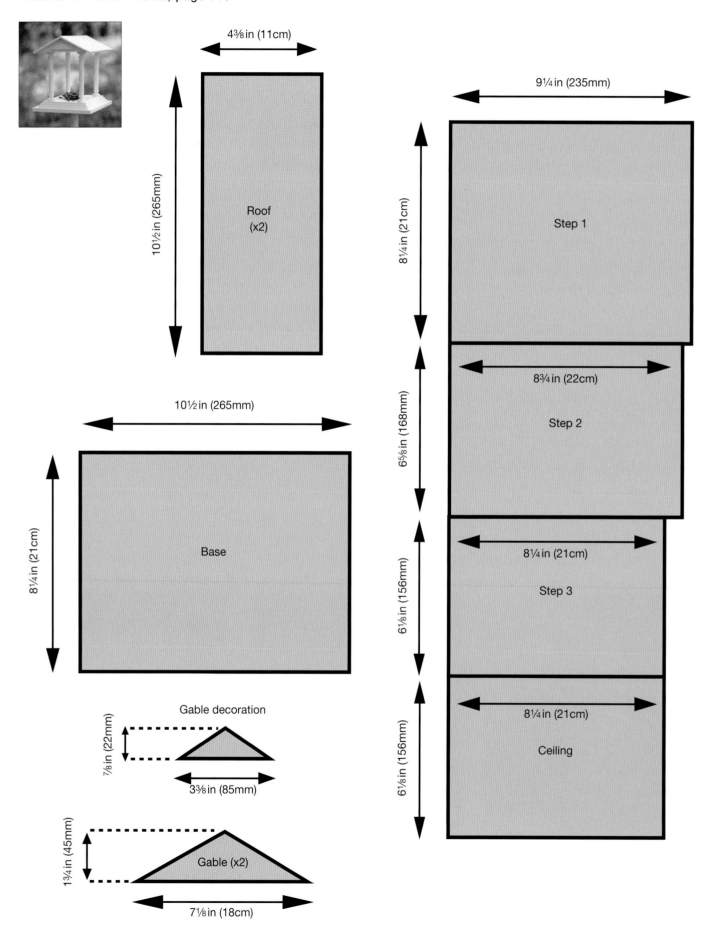

Roof (x2) — $4\frac{3}{8}$ in (11cm) × $10\frac{1}{2}$ in (265mm)

Base — $10\frac{1}{2}$ in (265mm) × $8\frac{1}{4}$ in (21cm)

Gable decoration — $\frac{7}{8}$ in (22mm) × $3\frac{3}{8}$ in (85mm)

Gable (x2) — $1\frac{3}{4}$ in (45mm) × $7\frac{1}{8}$ in (18cm)

Step 1 — $9\frac{1}{4}$ in (235mm) × $8\frac{1}{4}$ in (21cm)

Step 2 — $8\frac{3}{4}$ in (22cm) × $6\frac{5}{8}$ in (168mm)

Step 3 — $8\frac{1}{4}$ in (21cm) × $6\frac{1}{8}$ in (156mm)

Ceiling — $8\frac{1}{4}$ in (21cm) × $6\frac{1}{8}$ in (156mm)

SHORESIDE BIRD TABLE, page 120

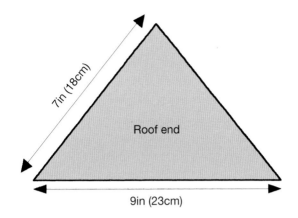

Roof end

7in (18cm)

9in (23cm)

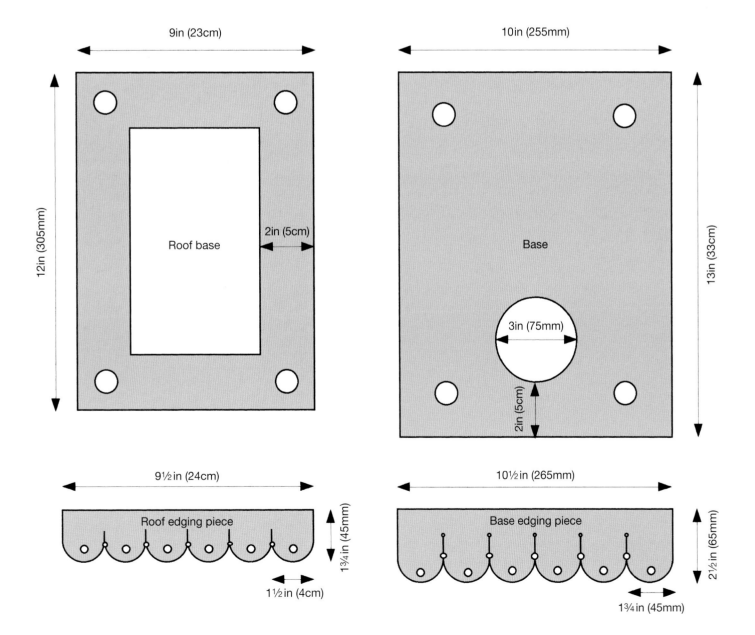

9in (23cm)

Roof base

12in (305mm)

2in (5cm)

10in (255mm)

Base

13in (33cm)

3in (75mm)

2in (5cm)

9½in (24cm)

Roof edging piece

1¾in (45mm)

1½in (4cm)

10½in (265mm)

Base edging piece

2½in (65mm)

1¾in (45mm)

BAMBOO BIRD TABLE, page 122

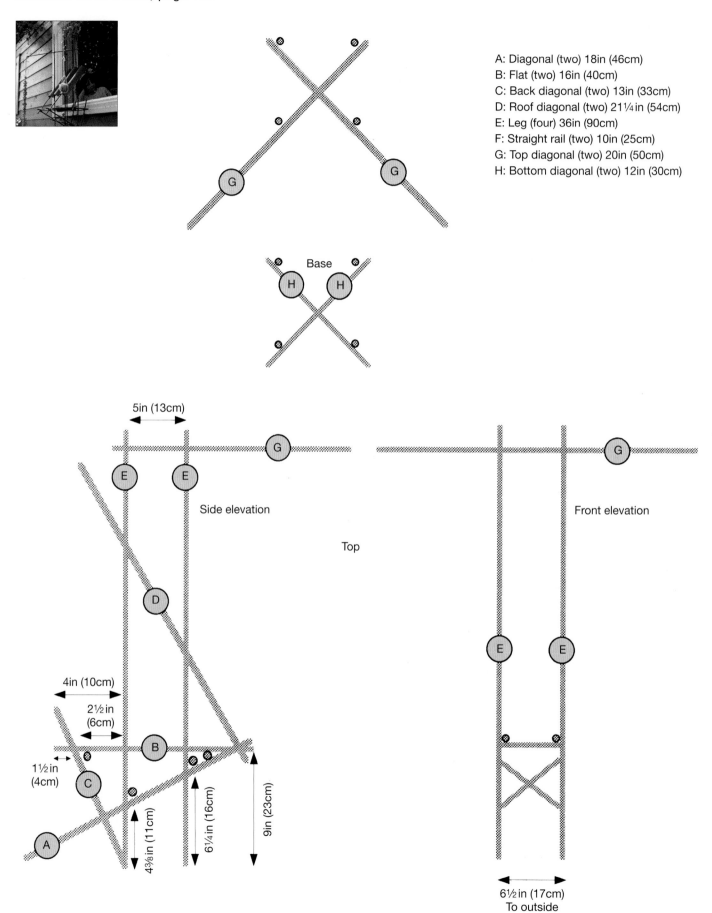

A: Diagonal (two) 18in (46cm)
B: Flat (two) 16in (40cm)
C: Back diagonal (two) 13in (33cm)
D: Roof diagonal (two) 21¼in (54cm)
E: Leg (four) 36in (90cm)
F: Straight rail (two) 10in (25cm)
G: Top diagonal (two) 20in (50cm)
H: Bottom diagonal (two) 12in (30cm)

Base

5in (13cm)

Side elevation

Front elevation

Top

4in (10cm)

2½in (6cm)

1½in (4cm)

4⅜in (11cm)

6¼in (16cm)

9in (23cm)

6½in (17cm)
To outside

ENCLOSED NEST BOX, page 138

ROOST AND WREN BOX, page 140

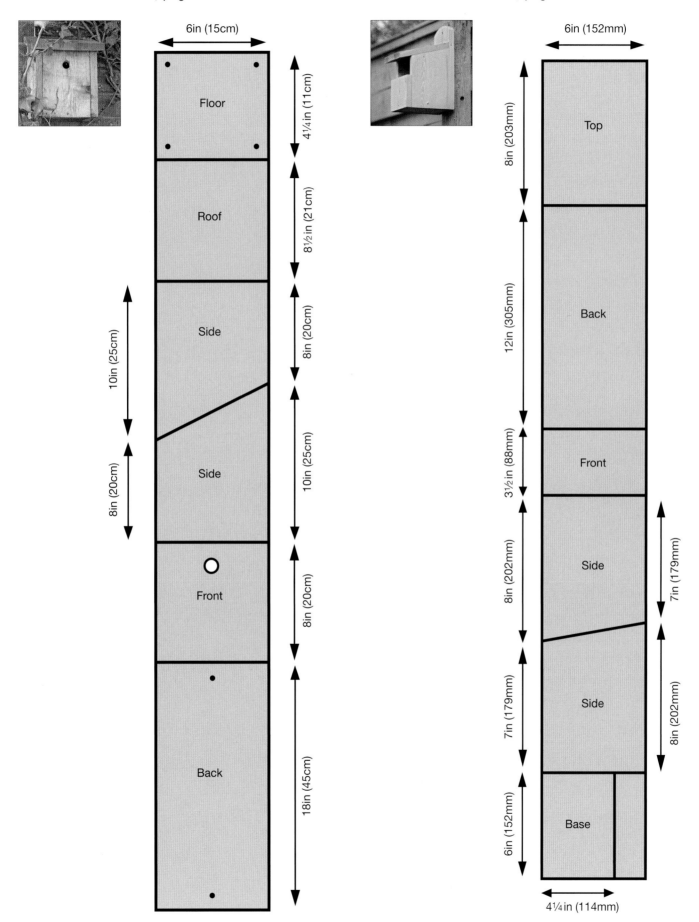

ENCLOSED NEST BOX:
- 6in (15cm)
- Floor — 4¼in (11cm)
- Roof — 8½in (21cm)
- Side — 8in (20cm), 10in (25cm)
- Side — 10in (25cm), 8in (20cm)
- Front
- Back — 18in (45cm)

ROOST AND WREN BOX:
- 6in (152mm)
- Top — 8in (203mm)
- Back — 12in (305mm)
- Front — 3½in (88mm)
- Side — 8in (202mm), 7in (179mm)
- Side — 7in (179mm), 8in (202mm)
- Base — 6in (152mm)
- 4¼in (114mm)

LAVENDER HIDEAWAY, page 146

POST BOX, page 158

FOLK-ART TITMOUSE BOX, page 148

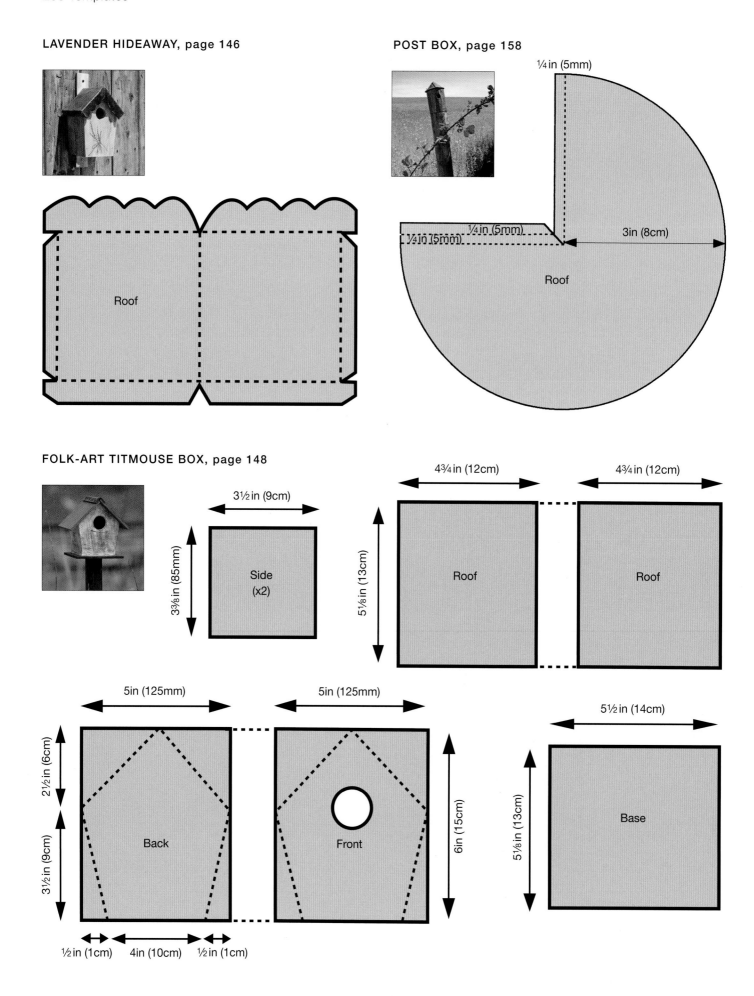

ROCK-A-BYE BIRDIE BOX, page 150

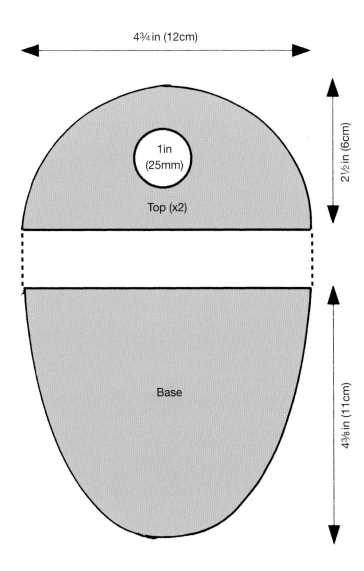

4¾in (12cm)

2½in (6cm)

1in
(25mm)

Top (x2)

Base

4⅜in (11cm)

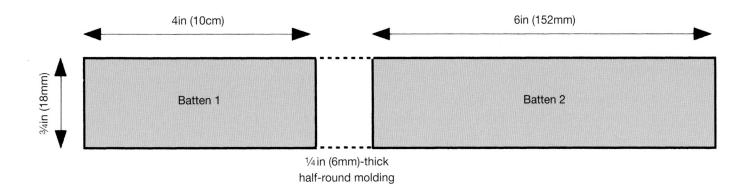

4in (10cm)

6in (152mm)

¾in (18mm)

Batten 1

Batten 2

¼in (6mm)-thick
half-round molding

SLATE-ROOF COTTAGE, page 152

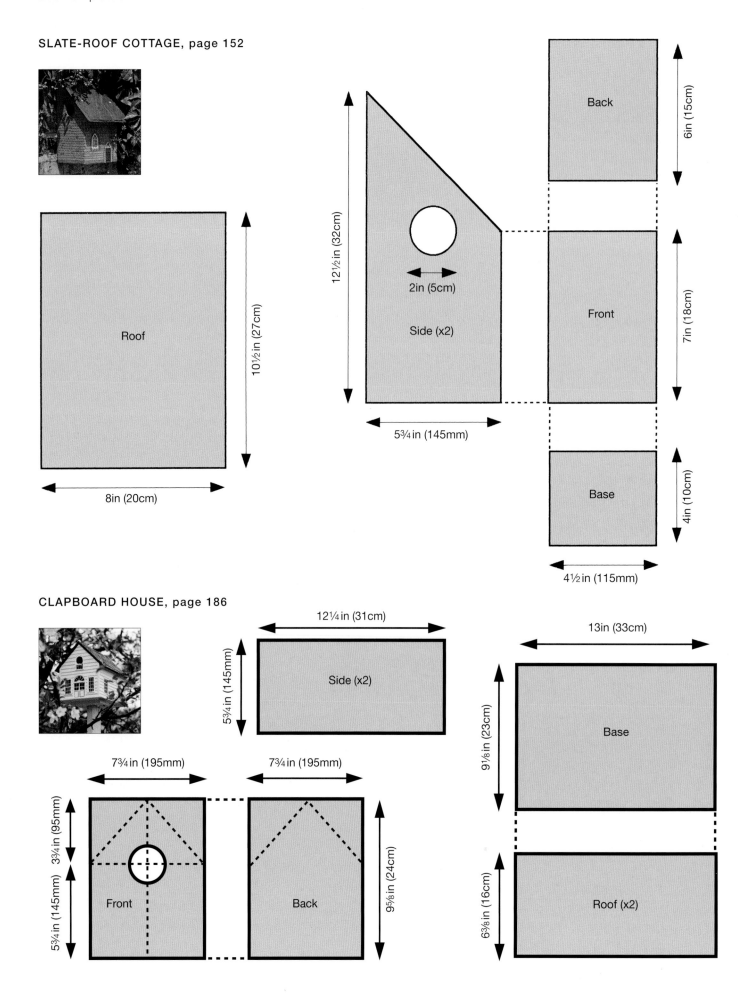

Roof
10½in (27cm)
8in (20cm)

Side (x2)
12½in (32cm)
2in (5cm)
5¾in (145mm)

Back
6in (15cm)

Front
7in (18cm)

Base
4in (10cm)
4½in (115mm)

CLAPBOARD HOUSE, page 186

Side (x2)
12¼in (31cm)
5¾in (145mm)

Front
7¾in (195mm)
3¾in (95mm)
5¾in (145mm)

Back
7¾in (195mm)
9⅝in (24cm)

Base
13in (33cm)
9⅛in (23cm)

Roof (x2)
6⅜in (16cm)

RIDGE TILE RETREAT, page 154

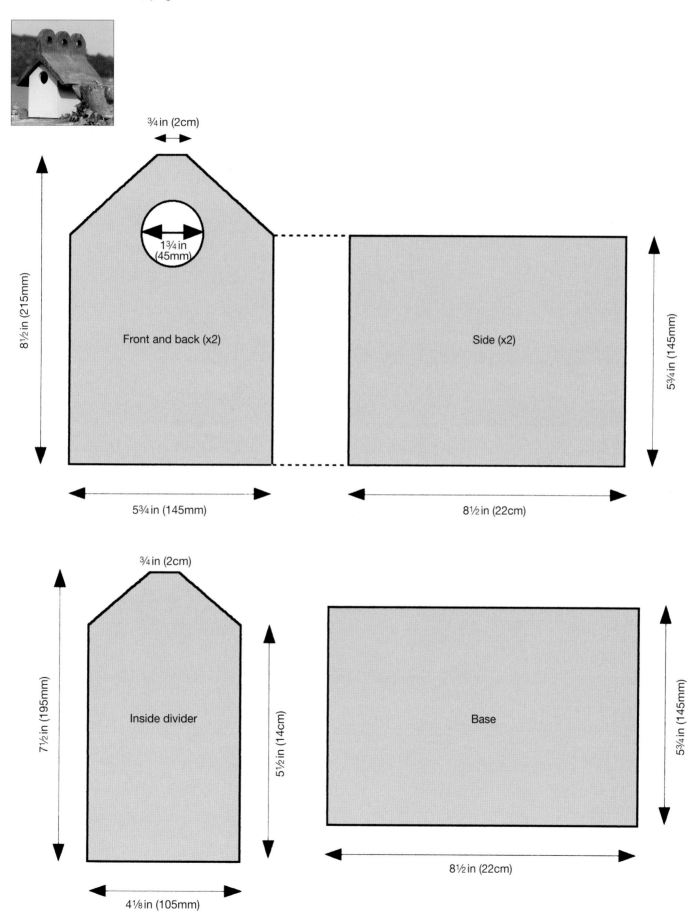

¾ in (2cm)

1¾ in (45mm)

8½ in (215mm)

Front and back (x2)

5¾ in (145mm)

Side (x2)

5¾ in (145mm)

8½ in (22cm)

¾ in (2cm)

7½ in (195mm)

Inside divider

5½ in (14cm)

4⅛ in (105mm)

Base

5¾ in (145mm)

8½ in (22cm)

SWIFT NURSERY, page 156

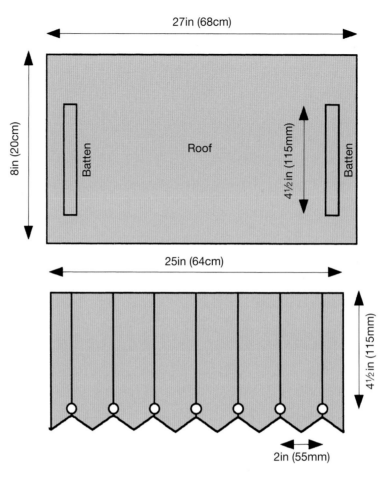

27in (68cm)

8in (20cm)

Batten

Roof

4½in (115mm)

Batten

25in (64cm)

4½in (115mm)

2in (55mm)

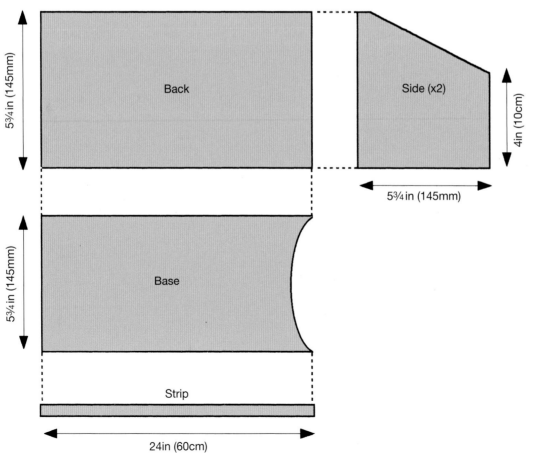

5¾in (145mm)

Back

Side (x2)

4in (10cm)

5¾in (145mm)

5¾in (145mm)

Base

Strip

24in (60cm)

SEASHORE NEST BOX, page 162

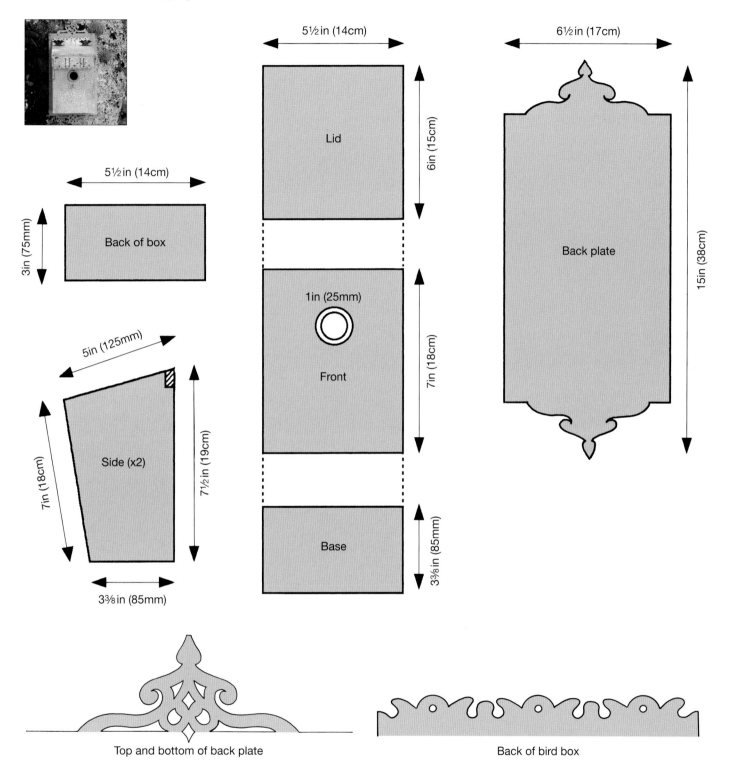

Back of box — 5½in (14cm) × 3in (75mm)

Side (x2) — 5in (125mm), 7in (18cm), 7½in (19cm), 3⅜in (85mm)

Lid — 5½in (14cm) × 6in (15cm)

Front — 1in (25mm), 7in (18cm)

Base — 3⅜in (85mm)

Back plate — 6½in (17cm) × 15in (38cm)

Top and bottom of back plate

Back of bird box

Front edge of lid

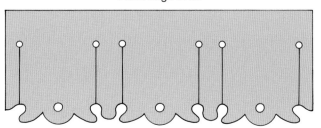

DUCK HOUSE, page 164

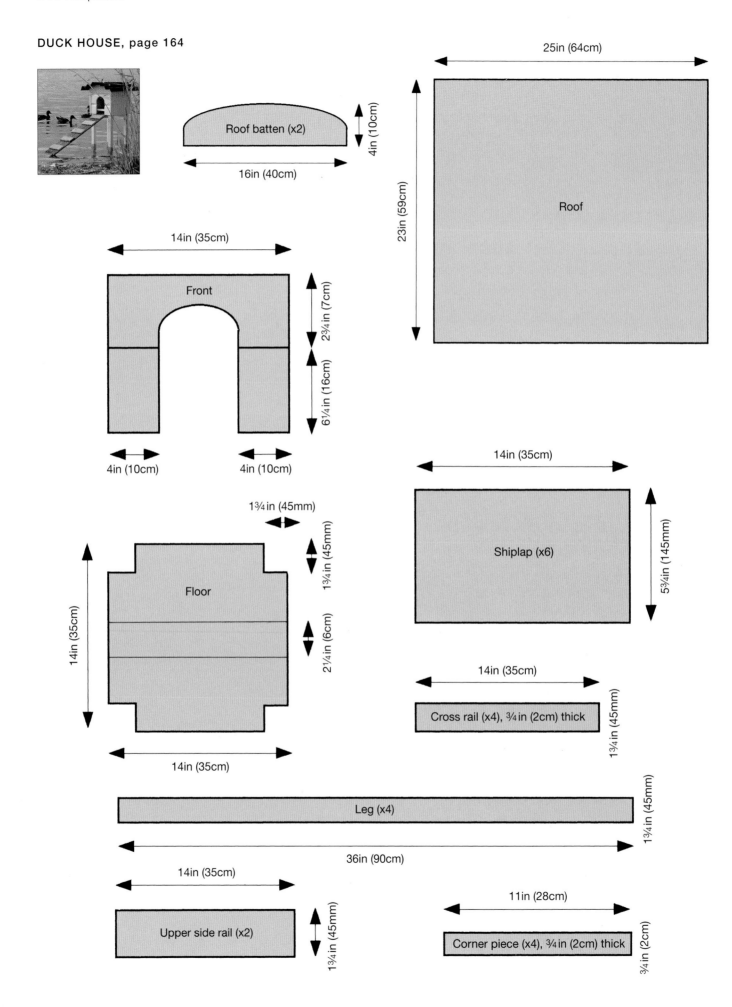

Roof batten (x2) — 4in (10cm), 16in (40cm)

Roof — 25in (64cm), 23in (59cm)

Front — 14in (35cm), $2\frac{3}{4}$in (7cm), $6\frac{1}{4}$in (16cm), 4in (10cm), 4in (10cm)

Floor — 14in (35cm), 14in (35cm), $1\frac{3}{4}$in (45mm), $1\frac{3}{4}$in (45mm), $2\frac{1}{4}$in (6cm)

Shiplap (x6) — 14in (35cm), $5\frac{3}{4}$in (145mm)

Cross rail (x4), $\frac{3}{4}$in (2cm) thick — 14in (35cm), $1\frac{3}{4}$in (45mm)

Leg (x4) — 36in (90cm), $1\frac{3}{4}$in (45mm)

Upper side rail (x2) — 14in (35cm), $1\frac{3}{4}$in (45mm)

Corner piece (x4), $\frac{3}{4}$in (2cm) thick — 11in (28cm), $\frac{3}{4}$in (2cm)

RUSTIC CABIN, page 168

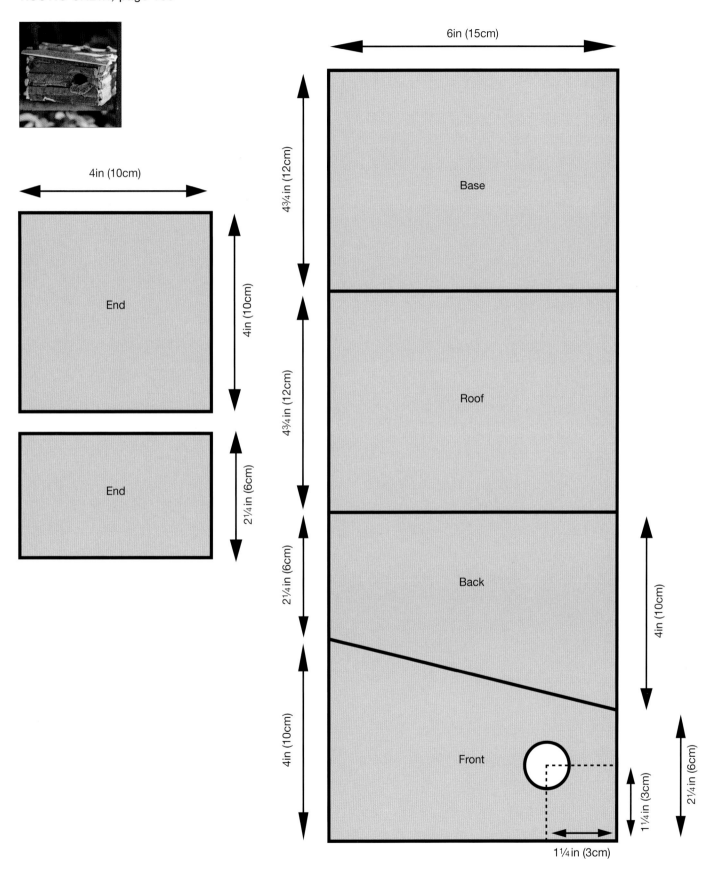

THATCHED BIRDHOUSE, page 172

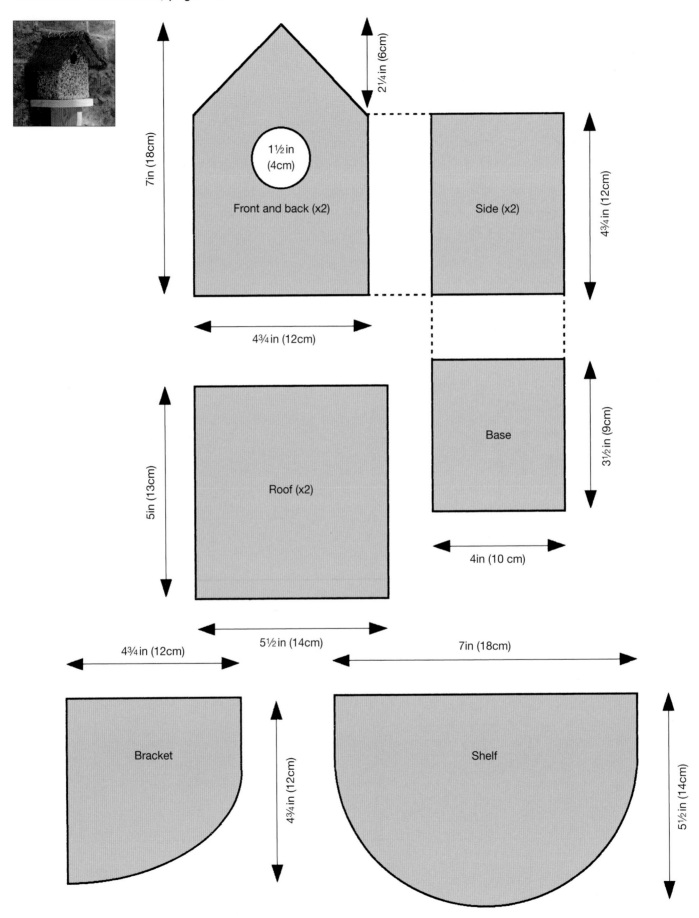

1½ in (4cm)

Front and back (x2)

7in (18cm)

4¾ in (12cm)

2¼ in (6cm)

Side (x2)

4¾ in (12cm)

Base

3½ in (9cm)

4in (10 cm)

Roof (x2)

5in (13cm)

5½ in (14cm)

4¾ in (12cm)

7in (18cm)

Bracket

4¾ in (12cm)

Shelf

5½ in (14cm)

DOVECOTE, page 184

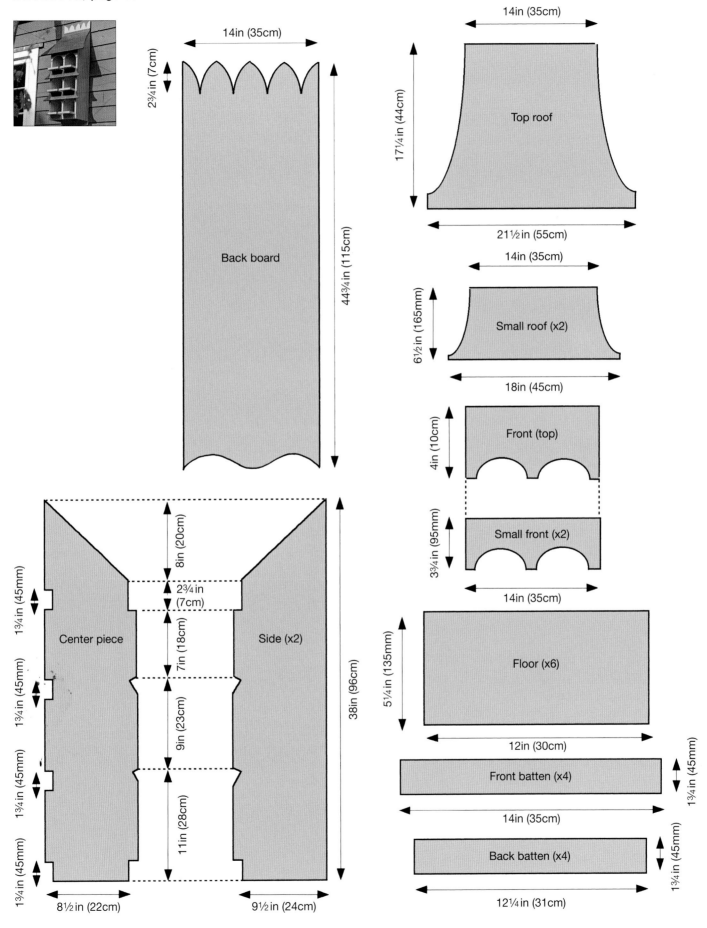

NEST BOX SIZES

The dimensions given here will enable you to modify basic nest box designs to suit a wide range of bird species. You may need to alter the dimensions slightly according to the thickness of your lumber. Inner surfaces can be left rough, but you should drill a few small holes in the floor of the box for drainage.

ENCLOSED NEST BOXES

This style of nest box has a small, round entrance hole positioned high on the front face. Enclosed nest boxes are suitable for birds that usually nest in tree holes, such as chickadees, titmice, nuthatches, wrens, bluebirds, martins, finches, flycatchers, and some swallows. Larger bird species, such as starlings, woodpeckers, flickers, owls, American kestrels, and Carolina wood ducks will nest in a larger box of this type, with a bigger entrance hole.

	Floor size	Depth of box	Height of entrance above floor	Diameter of entrance hole	Siting height above ground
Chickadee	4 x 4in (10 x 10cm)	8–10in (20–25cm)	6–8in (15–20cm)	1¼in (3cm)	6–15ft (1.8–4.5m)
Titmouse	4 x 4in (10 x 10cm)	8–10in (20–25cm)	6–8in (15–20cm)	1¼in (3cm)	6–15ft (1.8–4.5m)
Nuthatch	4 x 4in (10 x 10cm)	8–10in (20–25cm)	6–8in (15–20cm)	1¼in (3cm)	12–20ft (3.6–6m)
Wrens					
House wren	4 x 4in (10 x 10cm)	6–8in (15–20cm)	4–6in (10–15cm)	1–1¼in (2.5–3cm)	6–10ft (1.8–3m)
Bewick's and					
Carolina wren	4 x 4in (10 x 10cm)	6–8in (15–20cm)	4–6in (10–15cm)	1¼in (3cm)	6–10ft (1.8–3m)
Winter wren	4 x 4in (10 x 10cm)	6–8in (15–20cm)	4–6in (10–15cm)	1¼in (3cm)	6–10ft (1.8–3m)
Bluebird	5 x 5in (13 x 13cm)	8in (20cm)	6in (15cm)	1½in (4cm)	5–10ft (1.5–3m)
Violet-green swallow					
and tree swallow	5 x 5in (13 x 13cm)	6–8in (15–20cm)	1–5in (2.5–13cm)	1½in (4cm)	10–15ft (3–4.5m)
Purple martin	6 x 6in (15 x 15cm)	6in (15cm)	1in (2.5cm)	2¼in (6cm)	15–20ft (4.5–6m)
House finch	6 x 6in (15 x 15cm)	6in (15cm)	4in (10cm)	2in (5cm)	8–12ft (2.4–3.6m)
Crested flycatcher	6 x 6in (15 x 15cm)	8–10in (20–25cm)	6–8in (15–20cm)	2in (5cm)	8–20ft (2.4–6m)
Starling	6 x 6in (15 x 15cm)	16–18in (40–46cm)	14–16in (36–40cm)	2in (5cm)	10–25ft (3–7.6m)
Woodpeckers					
Downy	4 x 4in (10 x 10cm)	8–10in (20–25cm)	6–8in (15–20cm)	1¼in (3cm)	6–20ft (1.8–6m)
Golden-fronted	6 x 6in (15 x 15cm)	12–15in (30–38cm)	9–12in (22–30cm)	2in (5cm)	12–20ft (3.6–6m)
Red-headed	6 x 6in (15 x 15cm)	12–15in (30–38cm)	9–12in (22–30cm)	2in (5cm)	12–20ft (3.6–6m)
Hairy	6 x 6in (15 x 15cm)	12–15in (30–38cm)	9–12in (22–30cm)	1½in (4cm)	12–20ft (3.6–6m)
Flicker	7 x 7in (18 x 18cm)	16–18in (40–46cm)	14–16in (36–40cm)	2½in (6cm)	6–20ft (1.8–6m)
Owls					
Saw–whet	6 x 6in (15 x 15cm)	10–12in (25–30cm)	8–10in (20–25cm)	2½in (6cm)	12–20ft (3.6–6m)
Screech	8 x 8in (20 x 20cm)	12–15in (30–38cm)	9–12in (22–30cm)	3in (7.5cm)	10–30ft (3–9m)
Barn	10 x 18in (25 x 46cm)	15–18in (38–46cm)	4in (10cm)	6in (15cm)	12–18ft (3.6–5.5m)
American kestrel	8 x 8in (20 x 20cm)	12–15in (30–38cm)	9–12in (22–30cm)	3in (7.5cm)	10–30ft (3–9m)
Carolina wood duck	10 x 18in (25 x 46cm)	10–24in (25–60cm)	12–16in (30–40cm)	14in (36cm)	10–20ft (3–6m)

NESTING SHELVES

Not all birds like nest boxes with small entrance holes. Nesting shelves—also known as roosting boxes—have an entirely open front, and may used for resting and sleeping as well as nesting. They are suitable for song sparrows, American robins, barn swallows, and phoebes. Other species, such as blue jays and cardinals, may also roost or nest in this type of box.

	Floor size	Depth of box	Siting height above ground
Song sparrow	6 x 6in (15 x 15cm)	6in (15cm)	1–3ft (30–90cm)
American robin	6 x 6in (15 x 15cm)	8in (20cm)	6–15ft (1.8–4.5m)
Barn swallow	6 x 6in (15 x 15cm)	6in (15cm)	8–12ft (2.4–3.6m)
Phoebe	6 x 6in (15 x 15cm)	6in (15cm)	8–12ft (2.4–3.6m)

USEFUL CONTACTS

NORTH AMERICA
Organizations
American Bird Conservancy
http://www.abcbirds.org/

American Birding Association
http://www.americanbirding.org/

American Ornithologists' Union
http://www.aou.org/

Audubon Society state contacts
http://www.audubon.org/chapter/
(Append state abbreviation at the end of
this URL, for example, for Alaska, type
http://www.audubon.org/chapter/ak)

Bird Studies Canada
http://www.bsc-eoc.org/

Bird Watcher's Digest magazine
http://www.birdwatchersdigest.com

Birding in Canada
http://www.web-nat.com/bic/

Birdnet.com
http://www.nmnh.si.edu/BIRDNET/

Birdzilla.com
http://www.birdzilla.com/

Canadian Nature Federation
http://www.cnf.ca/

Canadian Peregrine Foundation
http://www.peregrine-foundation.ca/

Canadian Wildlife Service
http://www.cws-scf.ec.gc.ca

Cooper Ornithological Association
http://www.cooper.org/

Cornell Lab of Ornithology
http://birds.cornell.edu

National Audubon Society
http://www.audubon.org/

National Parks, Forests, Wilderness areas
http://gorp.away.com/gorp/resource/

National Wildlife Federation
http://www.nwf.org/

North American Bird Sounds
http://www.naturesongs.com/birds.html

North American Rare Bird Alert
http://www.narba.org/

Sierra Club
http://www.sierraclub.org/

US Fish & Wildlife Service
http://www.fws.gov/

Advice on gardening for birds
Birds-n-garden
http://www.birds-n-garden.com/
birdgarden.html

Cornell Lab of Ornithology
http://www.birds.cornell.edu/AllAboutBirds/
attracting/landscaping/

Council on the Environment of
New York City
http://www.cenyc.org/files/citylot/
Birds_in_Urban_Gardens.pdf

National Wildlife Federation
http://www.nwf.org/backyard/

NSiS: Florida Native Plants
http://www.nsis.org/garden/
garden-native-birds.html

Bird boxes and food supplies
The Backyard Bird Company
http://www.backyardbird.com/

The Bird Feeders Society
http://www.thebirdfeederssociety.com/

Birds-n-garden
http://www.birds-n-garden.com/

Duncraft
http://www.duncraft.com/

Krismer's Plant Farm bird feed chart
http://www.krismers.com/
Bird_Feeding_Chart.pdf

National Bird-Feeding Society
http://www.birdfeeding.org/

Wild Bird Habitat Store
http://www.wildbirdhabitatstore.com/

CENTRAL AND SOUTH AMERICA
Organizations
Caribbean Species Listings
http://camacdonald.com/birding/
Comparisons-Caribbean.htm

Central American Species Listings
http://camacdonald.com/birding/
Comparisons-CentralAm.htm

Neotropical Bird Club
http://www.neotropicalbirdclub.org

South American Species Listings
http://camacdonald.com/birding/
Comparisons-SouthAmerica.htm

INTERNATIONAL ORGANIZATIONS
African Bird Club
http://www.africanbirdclub.org

BirdLife International
http://www.birdlife.org/

European Ornithologists' Union
http://www.eou.at

International Ornithological Committee
http://www.i-o-c.org/IOComm/

Neotropical Bird Club
http://www.neotropicalbirdclub.org/

Pacific Seabird Group
http://www.pacificseabirdgroup.org/

Surfbirds.com
http://www.surfbirds.com/

250

INDEX

Epilobium spp. 91
Eremophila alpestris 23, 200
escallonia 70
Eschscholzia californica 67
Eupatorium dubium 83
evening primrose *61*

Fagus sylvatica 60
fairy moss 82
Falciformes 16
Falco
    mexicanus 18, 192
    peregrinus 18, 32
    sparverius 18, *50*, 192
    tinnunculus 15
falcon
    peregrine (duck hawk) 18, 32,
      33, 50
    prairie 18, 192
falcons 14, 50, 102, 192
false acacia 92
false indigo 71
fat balls 55, *55*, 116
fat cakes 52, 53
fat treat 58, *58*
feathers 12–13, *12*, *13*, 26
    care of 48
    function of 12–13
    iridescence 13, *13*
    molting 13
    social significance of
      plumage 13
feeders *see* bird feeders
feeding birds 48–9, 52–3
    bird tables 52–3, *53*
    ground stations *52*, 53
    hanging feeders 53, *53*
    see also food
feet and toes 10, *10*
fernbush 71
fertilizers 64, 66, 75
festive treats 59, *59*
Festuca ovina 67
fieldscopes 40–1, *41*
finch
    Darwin's finches 11, *11*

goldfinch *4*, *6*, *11*, *26*, *53*, *60*,
    86, *86*
grosbeak *see* grosbeak
house *62*, 86, 105, *110*, 138,
    152, *152*, 228, 248
purple *35*, 86, 228
woodpecker *11*
finches 15, 18, 19, 22–6, 32, 34,
    36, 45, 48–9, *52*, 53, 58,
    64, 65, 86, 87, 88, 90, 92,
    94, *94*, *95*, 106, 110, *110*,
    114, 118, 120, 122, 124,
    126, 128, 132, 134, 136,
    220, 228–9
firethorn *45*, 61, *61*, 93
    see also pyracantha
flag
    blue 83, *83*
    sweet 83
fledging 17, 25
fledglings 6, 34, *48*, 60
flicker, northern *180*
flickers 36, *85*, 248
flight 14–15
    the airfoil principle 15, *15*
    flight patterns 14, 15
    lightening the load 14
    take-off sequence *14–15*
    weight and flight 14
    wing shape and beat 14
floating pennywort 82
flock behavior 27, 30
flood meadows 65
flower eaters 19
flycatcher
    crested 142, 160, 248
    great crested *142*
    tyrant *142*
flycatchers 18, 84, 85, *95*
food
    adapting to the seasons 19
    for aquatic birds 38
    common bird foods 55, *55*
    digestive system 18, *18*
    fat products 54, *54*
    fat treat 58, *58*
    festive treats 59, *59*
    finding 18–19, *18*, *19*
    flower and fruit eaters 19
    live 54, *54*
    meat eaters 18, *18*
    nut and seed eaters 19, *19*
    omnivores 19, *19*
    plant eaters 19
    predators and scavengers
      18–19
    ritualized feeding *21*
    seeds and grains 54

sweet treat 56–7, *56*
unsalted peanuts 54, *54*
see also feeding birds;
    feeding habits
forest floor 72
forget-me-not 83
    field *61*
formic acid 27, 218
fountains 47, 103
foxglove 95, *95*
Fragaria vesca 61
Fringillidae 15, 25
frogs *63*, 81, *82*
fruit, dried and fresh 49, *49*, 55,
    55, 88
fruit suet treats 55, *55*
fruit-eating birds *11*, 19
    attracting 88–9, *88*, *89*
fuchsia, California 91
Fulica americana 190

Galapagos Islands 11, *11*
Gallinago spp. 17
Gallinula chloropus 38, 190
game birds 16, 21, 25, 31
gannet 24
garlic, wild *62*
geese 15, 28, 38
gift basket (bird food) 59, *59*
girdling 75
gizzard 18
global warming 31
golden currant 71
golden rod *61*, 87
goldeneye *39*
goldfinch
    American *4*, *11*, *26*, *60*, *110*,
      122, 229
    lesser *94*
goldfinches *6*, *53*, 86, *86*, 108, 112
gooseberry *61*, 71, *71*, 89, *89*, 91
goshawk *37*
grackle
    common *16*, *35*, 225
    great-tailed 225
grackles 34, 53, *65*, 225
grains 54, 55
grape, wild 89
grape vine 94, *94*
grass
    planting wildflowers into
      existing 67
    types of 64–5, 67, *67*
grasshoppers 64
grit (for digestion) 18, 55
grosbeak
    blue 231
    evening 230

pine 34, 230
    rose-breasted *9*
grosbeaks 19, 36, *70*, 108, *110*,
    230–1
ground feeders *63*
ground stations *52*, 53
group living 30–1, *31*
grouse, sage 21
Gruidae 28
guelder rose *61*, 93
Guiraca caerulea 231
gull
    black-headed *33*
    herring *39*
gulls 49, 90

Haliaeetus leucocephalus 11
hatching 25
hawk
    duck *see* falcon, peregrine
    goshawk *37*
    Harris's *14–15*
    pigeon 50
    sparrow *see* kestrel, American
hawks 30, 50
hawthorns 45, 68–71, *68*, 93, *93*
hay meadows 65, 67, 86
hazelnuts 55
hearing 17, *17*
Hedera helix 91
hedges 44, 45, 50, *63*, 68–9
    dead 69
    formal *68*, 69
    hedges for birds 68–9, *68*, *69*
    informal 69
    mixed 69
    planting a wildlife hedge 70–1,
      70, *71*
    single-species 69
    threats to traditional 68, 89
    types of 69
    and wildlife 68–9
Helianthus annuus 60, *61*, 87
Helmitheros vermivorus 216
herbaceous plants: planting
    guide for birds 94–5, *94*, *95*

Troglodytes
  aedon 210
  troglodytes 170, 211
Turdidae 34, *34, 93*
Turdus
  merula 27
  migratorius 19, 23, 34,
    212, 213
  rufopalliatus 213
Typhaceae 83
Tyrannidae *142*
Tyrannus tyrannus 227
Tyto alba 30, 193

understory 72
urbanization 85

Vallisneria americana 83
Viburnum 77, 77
  dentatum 77, 93
  lentago 93
  opulus 61, 88, 93
  prunifolium 77, 93

tinus 93
vireo 25, 88, 93
Virginia creeper 94, *94*
Virginian cardinal *9, 118*
vitamin D3 27
Vitis
  californica 89
  vinifera 94
vulture 16, 17

wading birds 10, *10, 11*, 25
warbler
  black-and-white 216
  blue-winged *20*
  wood 36
  worm-eating 216
  yellow *4, 25, 36, 37*, 217
warblers 34, 49, 84, 93, *93*, 94,
  128, 136, 216–17
watching birds 40–1
  drawing birds for reference *40*
  fieldscopes 40–1
  getting a good view 40, *40*
  making notes 41, *41*
water, providing 47, *47*, 48, *49*,
  53, *53*, 102
water celery 83, *83*
water feature *78*, 80
water fern 83
water hyacinth 82, 83
water lettuce 82
water lilies *63*, 79, *79, 82*, 83, *83*
water meadows 67
water soldiers *79*
waterfowl *15*, 21, 25

Waterton, Charles 44
waterweed 83, *83*
wax myrtle 89
waxwing 28, 36, 56, 88, *91, 92*
  cedar 89, *89*
waxworms 54
weed killers 64, 66, 87
wet meadows 65
wetlands, plants for 79
wheat rust 68
White, Gilbert and Thomas 44
whitebeam 92
wigeon 38, *39*
wild area for birds 62, *63*
  maintenance 62
wild servicetree 92
wildflower meadows *63*, 64
  planting 66–7
willow 85, *85*, 128–31, 178–9
wings 11
wood duck, Carolina *38*, 248
woodbine 94
  see also honeysuckle
woodcock, American 16
woodcocks 16, *16*
wooded areas for birds 72–3,
  72, 73
woodland birds 36, *36, 37*
  coniferous woodlands 36, 73
  creating woodland edges
    76–7, *76, 77*
  deciduous woodlands 36, *36*
  tips for observing 36
woodpecker
  downy *35, 61*, 195, 248

gila 194
golden-fronted 248
hairy 248
pileated *11, 37*, 75, *77, 189*
red-bellied *19, 22*, 194
red-headed *4*, 195, 248
woodpeckers 10, 13, 18, 19, 22,
  22, 34, 36, 44, 48, 50, 58,
  73, 84, *85*, 88, 104, 105,
  106, *106*, 124, 142, 174,
  180, 194–5, 248
worms 18, 48, 89
wren
  Bewick's 248
  cactus *31*, 209
  canyon 211
  Carolina *150*, 210, 248
  house 210, 248
  rock 209, 211
  winter *37, 140, 170*, 211, 248
wrens *20*, 23, 26, *27*, 49, 84, *84*,
  104, 105, 138, 140, 146,
  148, 150, 158, 160, 168,
  170, 174, 178, 180, 208,
  209–11, *233*, 248

yarrow 85, *85*, 95, *95*
  common *61*
yew 60, *61*

Zenaida
  asiatica 196
  macroura 184, 196
zinnia 45
Zonotrichia leucophrys 20

ACKNOWLEDGMENTS

The publisher would like to thank the following for allowing their photographs to be reproduced in the book (l = left, r = right, t = top, m = middle, b = bottom):
AllCanadaPhotos/Photoshot: 27br.
Ardea: 13b.
Amy Christian: 90l.
Bruce Coleman/Photoshot: 156tl (Laura Riley).
Felicity Forster: 5r, 44b, 47tl, 97l, 97r, 103bl.
iStockphoto: 1, 2, 3l, 3m, 3r, 4l, 5l, 6, 7, 8, 9l, 9m, 9r, 11 (all photos), 12r, 13tl, 13tr, 14tl, 14tr, 16r, 17bl, 17br, 18l, 19t, 19bl, 19br, 20t, 20bl, 20br, 21t, 21b, 22t, 22b, 23tl, 24t, 25t, 25b, 26tl, 26tr, 26b, 27t, 27bl, 28t, 28b, 29b, 30t, 30b, 31t, 31m, 31b, 32t, 32m, 32b, 34l, 34r, 36l, 36r, 38tl, 38tr, 38b, 43m, 46, 47tr, 48t, 48b, 49tr, 50t, 50b, 51tr, 51b, 53tl, 56ml, 60bl, 61tl, 61tr, 62tl, 62br, 64t, 64bl, 65tl,

65bl, 66t, 68bl, 69t, 70t, 71b 3rd from l, 72tr, 73b, 74t, 77tl, 78tl, 80t, 83b 3rd from l, 84t, 85t, 85br, 86l, 86r, 87br, 88l, 88r, 89bm, 89br, 90r, 91br, 92bl, 94tl, 94br, 102tr, 102b 2nd from l, 103t, 104tl, 104tr, 105b, 106br, 110tl, 112tl, 114tl, 120tl, 122tl, 124tl, 128tl, 134bl, 136tl, 140tl, 142tl, 150tl, 152tl, 154br, 158tl, 160tl, 162tl, 164t, 164m, 168bl, 170tl, 172tl, 174tl, 176tl, 178bl, 180tl, 182tl, 184tl, 186tl, 189l, 189m, 189r, 249, 251t, 252t, 255b.
NHPA/Photoshot: 25m (John Shaw), 67tr (David Woodfall), 83bl (Photo Researchers), 83b 2nd from l (Stephen Dalton).
Nigel Partridge: 51tl.
Photolibrary Group: 12l, 23br.

Illustrations were provided by the following:
Peter Barrett: 11 (finches), 33, 35, 37, 39, 190t, 190b, 191t, 191b, 192t, 192b, 193t,

193b, 194t, 194b, 195t, 195b, 196t, 196b, 197t, 197b, 198t, 198b, 199t, 200t, 200b, 201t, 201b, 202t, 202b, 203t, 203b, 204t, 204b, 205t, 206t, 206b, 207t, 207b, 208t, 208b, 209t, 209b, 210t, 210b, 211t, 212t, 212b, 213t, 213b, 214t, 214b, 215t, 215b, 216t, 216b, 217t, 217b, 218t, 218b, 219t, 219b, 220t, 220b, 221t, 221b, 222t, 222b, 223t, 223b, 224t, 224b, 225t, 225b, 226t, 226b, 227t, 227b, 228t, 228b, 229t, 230t, 230b, 231t, 231b.
Anthony Duke: 190–231 (distribution maps).
Lucinda Ganderton: 234–247 (templates).
Stuart Jackson-Carter: 199b, 205b, 229b.
Martin Knowelden: 10, 14–15b, 15tr, 16l, 17t, 18r, 23m, 24b, 29t, 40.
Liz Pepperell: 61b, 63t, 79b.
Tim Thackeray: 211b.